CONTENTS

**THE UNIVERSITY
OF BIRMINGHAM**

URBAN PROBLEMS AND PLANNING IN THE DEVELOPED WORLD

Edited by Michael Pacione

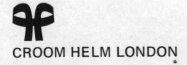

CROOM HELM LONDON

©1981 Michael Pacione
Croom Helm Ltd, 2-10 St John's Road, London SW11

British Library Cataloguing in Publication Data

Urban problems and planning in the developed world.
   1. City planning
   I. Pacione, Michael
   711'.4   HT166
   ISBN 0-7099-0191-7

Printed and bound in Great Britain
Redwood Burn Limited
Trowbridge and Esher

TABLES

Tables

FIGURES

Figures

TO CHRISTINE

PREFACE

Growing concern for the future of cities and for the well-being of city dwellers, stimulated by trends in world urbanisation, the increasing number and size of cities, and the deterioration of many urban environments, has led in recent years to much emphasis being placed upon the applied or problem-solving approach to the study of the city. The importance of this viewpoint has been widely recognised. The consequent scale and pace of developments in applied urban geography and related fields have inevitably diminished the relevance and usefulness of many standard urban texts. Much of the material that is available on urban problems and planning is now outdated or is restricted in its geographical coverage. These deficiencies were highlighted during the preparation of a series of undergraduate lectures on urban geography and planning. It soon became evident that lecturers, students and others interested in urban problems and planning in the modern world must be prepared to expend considerable time and energy scouring less accessible reports and numerous academic journals across several disciplines in order to obtain satisfactory detailed information. This book together with the companion volume on *Problems and Planning in Third World Cities* attempts to offset some of these deficiencies by providing a collection of discussions on the problems and planning activities in a number of cities selected to reflect the differing economic, cultural and political regimes of the modern world.

Michael Pacione
Milton of Campsie

INTRODUCTION

The problems of cities and the efforts directed towards their alleviation command global attention because of the increasing proportion of the world's population being affected by such issues. Urbanisation and its consequences are world-wide phenomena and the increasing size and scale of urban settlements are characteristics of the contemporary era. Four out of every ten of the world's population now live in an urban setting and the expectation is that by the year 2000 AD half of the world's inhabitants will be urban dwellers.

In North America 54 per cent of the population was urban in 1925; 50 years later this proportion had increased to 77 per cent (Table I.1). Even more dramatic increases in urbanisation have been experienced in the USSR where the urban population rose from 18 per cent in 1925 to 61 per cent in 1975, and in Latin America where the corresponding figures were 25 per cent and 60 per cent. The rate of world urbanisation in general has shown no slackening since 1800 and in all regions the trend is towards increased urbanisation and city growth.

Table I.1: Percentage of Total Population in Urban Localities in the World and Eight Major Areas, 1925-2025

Major area	1925	1950	1975	2000	2025
World total	21	28	39	50	63
Northern America	54	64	77	86	93
Europe	48	55	67	79	88
USSR	18	39	61	76	87
East Asia	10	15	30	46	63
Latin America	25	41	60	74	85
Africa	8	13	24	37	54
South Asia	9	15	23	35	51
Oceania	54	65	71	77	87

Source: United Nations (1974)

Table I.2: Urban Population in the World and Eight Major Areas, 1925-2025 (millions)

Major area	1925	1950	1975	2000	2025
World total	405	701	1,548	3,191	5,713
Northern America	68	106	181	256	308
Europe	162	215	318	425	510
USSR	30	71	154	245	318
East Asia	58	99	299	638	1,044
Latin America	25	67	196	464	819
Africa	12	28	96	312	803
South Asia	45	108	288	825	1,873
Oceania	5	8	15	26	38

Source: United Nations (1974)

The pronounced rate of growth in the world's total urban population over the period 1925-75 is clearly shown in Table I.2. While the growth rate between 1925 and 1950 was 73 per cent, this figure more than doubled over the next 25 years. In some areas the growth of urban population was even more spectacular. In Oceania the number of city dwellers trebled over the half-century from 1925 to 1975; in the USSR and East Asia it grew fivefold, in South Asia sixfold, and in Latin America and Africa nearly eightfold. United Nations estimates for the next 50 years call for most of these trends to continue. The distribution of the world's population is also changing. Whereas in 1925 two-fifths was in Europe, by 1975 this proportion had fallen by half. Meanwhile, East and South Asia which together had about one-quarter of the urban population in 1925 had increased their joint share to 38 per cent by 1975. A continuation of present trends would mean that these two areas together will contain about one-half of the world's urban population by 2025. By the same date the urban populations of both Africa and Latin America will also exceed those of Europe. These trends in urbanisation and city growth are reflected in the distribution and different growth rates of metropolitan areas (Table I.3) and 'million cities' (Table I.4). In both cases while the number and relative importance of such cities remains greatest in the developed realm the fastest rates of growth are occurring in the developing world.

The major trends in world urbanisation and city growth seem clear but there are difficulties in predicting future levels of urban population; this is illustrated by the classic S-shaped urbanisation curve (Figure I.1).

Table I.3: Number of Metropolitan Areas* and Average Annual Growth Rate, by World Region

World region	No. of metropolitan areas	Average annual growth rate of metropolitan areas (%)	% of regional population in metropolitan areas
World	1387	2.4	—
North America	169	2.4	51.0
Europe	308	1.5	27.0
USSR	220	2.3	27.0
Latin America	125	3.8	30.0
Africa	59	4.5	13.5
East Asia)	481	(3.4)	14.0
)		( )	
South Asia)		(2.6)	
Oceania	12	2.4	50.0

*Defined as a single functional unit with a population of at least 100,000.
Source: R.M. Northam, *Urban Geography*, 2nd edn (New York, 1979)

Table I.4: Million-Cities, 1950-85

Region	Number of cities			Million-city population as a percentage of total population		
	1950	1970	1985	1950	1970	1985
World total	75	162	273	7	12	16
More developed realm	51	83	126	15	20	27
Less developed realm	24	79	147	3	8	13
Europe	28	36	45	15	19	22
North America	14	27	39	23	32	38
USSR	2	10	28	4	9	17
Oceania	2	2	4	24	27	37
East Asia	13	36	54	5	11	17
South Asia	8	27	53	2	6	10
Latin America	6	16	31	9	19	28
Africa	2	8	19	2	5	9

Source: United Nations Population Division (1972)

Figure I.1: The Urbanisation Curve

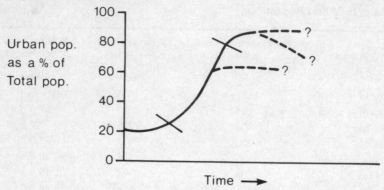

Urban pop.
as a % of
Total pop.

Time ⟶

Different countries reach different points on the curve at different times. Britain was the first country to experience large scale urbanisation, and England and Wales reached the upper portion of the curve shortly after 1900, whereas the USA did not reach the same point until approximately 1950. The initial stage of the urbanisation process is characterised by a 'traditional' economic structure (Rostow 1960). The emphasis is on the agrarian sector of the economy, characteristically accompanied by a dispersed population with a relatively small proportion resident in cities. During the acceleration stage there is a pronounced redistribution of the population such that from less than 25 per cent the urban component rises to around 70 per cent of the total. This is a phase of concentration of people and economic activity during which the secondary and tertiary sectors of the economy assume increased importance. As the urbanisation curve approaches 100 per cent it will tend to flatten, as has occurred in England and Wales since 1900. In this terminal stage the urban population is typically in excess of 70 per cent with the remainder being rural farm and non-farm inhabitants.

Speculation on the future form of the urbanisation curve must include the possible flattening of the upper portion at a lower level, or even a reversal of the curve. In the former case reduced migration to urban centres, perhaps as a result of government action in some countries, might produce a condition of equilibrium at a lower level and so lead to an earlier beginning to the terminal stage. In the latter case the 'flight to the city' might be replaced by a 'flight to the countryside' in which outmigration from the city would more than offset inmigration and natural increase. The appearance of either of these alternatives would be contrary to past human behaviour. There is however clear evidence of a counter-urbanisation stage emerging in parts of the developed world

(Alexandersson and Falk 1974; Falk 1978), and some countries, such as the USSR, China, Poland and Nigeria, have employed or are considering the use of legal constraints to curtail the growth of cities. In the USA counter-urbanisation has replaced urbanisation as the dominant force shaping the settlement pattern (Berry 1976). In Britain and parts of Western Europe the dominant trend is accelerating decentralisation (Hall *et al.* 1973) and in Australia and Canada metropolitan growth rates are beginning to decline (Bourne and Logan 1976). In the developing world most states are moving into the middle section of the curve although a distinct minority are still in the initial stage of urbanisation (McGee 1971; Breese 1972; Ford Foundation 1972; Abu-Lughod and Hay 1977).

Study of the magnitude of the urbanisation process should not be confused with an analysis of its underlying dynamics. The urbanisation process denotes a complex interplay of social, economic, political, technological, geographical and cultural factors. Acknowledgement of the utility of the urbanisation curve as a normative model does not carry with it acceptance of the similar-path or convergence theory of development. As Berry (1973) points out we must disavow the view that urbanisation is a universal process, a consequence of modernisation that involves the same sequence of events in different countries and that produces progressive convergence of forms. Neither can we accept the view that there may be several culturally specific processes but that they are producing convergent results because of underlying technological imperatives of modernisation and industrialisation. Not only are we dealing with several fundamentally different processes that have arisen out of differences in culture and time but these processes are producing different results in different world regions, transcending any superficial similarities.

Clearly therefore in examining urban problems and planning in the modern world some disaggregation of the global view is essential. In applying the conventional distinction between the developed world (the focus of this volume) and the developing world (the concern of a companion volume on *Problems and Planning in Third World Cities*) we are acutely aware of the problems of defining development, and of the great variations within these broad realms, as well as within individual countries, and within cities. Nevertheless, the distinction is a useful and valid classificatory base. Within each of these broad areas individual cities were selected as representatives of the main socio-political and geographic regions. In the context of the study of urban problems and planning the USA, UK, Australia, Japan, USSR, Poland, Spain and

South Africa are regarded as developed countries, and Singapore, Iran, Mexico, Colombia, China, Tunisia, Nigeria and India as part of the developing world. Some basic characteristics of the nations from which cities have been selected for inclusion in this volume are presented in Table I.5.

Rodwin (1970) has remarked on how prior to World War II almost no one wanted the central government to determine how cities should grow and yet today, only a generation later, national governments throughout the world are adopting or being implored to adopt urban growth strategies. These comments highlight the fact that large-scale urban planning is essentially a post-war phenomenon, and that the planning method and political process are inextricably linked. As Webber (1969) puts it, planning is inside the political system. The selection of cities aimed to provide representatives of the range of socio-political ideologies that directly determine the nature of the planning response to urban problems. Subsidiary aims were to provide a reasonable geographic coverage of the modern world and to include important cities previously neglected or which merit attention as a result of changing world circumstances.

This book together with its companion volume is a direct response to the increasing importance that is attached to the problems of cities by governments, international organisations and independent researchers. The book does not set out to provide an account of urbanisation, or a history of planning in the different countries. This book is concerned with the major product of the urbanisation process—the city. The method of analysis favoured is the in-depth case study.

Contents Overview

The New York Metropolitan Region (NYMR) is one of the major capital markets and financial centres of the USA, but it is also a region with serious and deepening structural problems. Unemployment is acute. Real personal income per capita was stagnant throughout the 1970s. The population is diminishing and ageing. Racial tensions are fuelled by discriminatory housing practices. Accelerating depreciation is affecting the vital urban infrastructures of sewerage systems, utilities and roads, and the environment is subject to increasing deterioration through the impact of pollution and neglect, with serious health implications. Foot-loose commercial enterprises are leaving for the suburbs and New York City is perennially threatened with financial bankruptcy. This complex

Table I.5: National Characteristics: Selected Urban, Economic and Demographic Indices

Country	Per Capita GNP ($)		Population (millions)		Urban population as % of total population			Proportion of urban population in largest city		Proportion of urban population in cities of >500,000		Number of cities of >500,000		
	1977	1978	1977	1978	1960	1975	1980	1975	1980	1975	1980	1960	1975	1980
USA	5941	9590	220	222	61	70	73	13	12	75	77	40	57	67
Australia	5025	7990	14	14	81	87	89	25	24	68	68	4	5	5
Japan	3562	7280	113	115	62	75	78	21	22	41	41	5	9	9
UK	3072	5030	56	56	86	90	91	21	20	56	52	15	16	18
USSR	2030	3700	259	261	49	61	65	5	4	22	33	25	38	50
Poland	2090	3670	35	35	48	54	57	16	15	45	43	5	7	8
Spain	1605	3470	36	37	57	71	74	16	16	43	44	5	6	6
South Africa	1125	1480	27	28	47	48	50	13	13	51	53	4	6	7

Sources: World Bank (1979, 1980); International Bank for Reconstruction and Development (1976)

of issues has led some authors to characterise the large American city as ungovernable (Yates 1977). The geographical pattern of public finance in the NYMR is closely related to these problems and, in Chapter 1, George Carey highlights the relationships between public fiscal policy, individual and corporate behaviour, and the city's problems. He suggests that to find solutions will require large scale investment of public funds and, more critically, an effective regional-scale planning organisation to implement priority strategies. He is forced to conclude that, given the present mood of the nation towards parsimony in government, towards budget cutting, and towards local autonomy rather than regional planning, it does not seem likely that a major regional planning effort intended to address all of the economic, technical and social needs of the city will be forthcoming.

Australia, like North America, is essentially a conservative capitalist society with no great tradition of planning intervention in the urban development process. During the 1970s, however, the country came to accept greater government involvement. The Melbourne metropolitan area comprises 56 separate territorial authorities and some attempt to integrate the vast urban complex and provide a liveable environment has been found necessary. Peter Newton and Ron Johnston describe the political background and planning framework for Melbourne and assess the strategies employed to combat the city's problems. They examine the consequences of the low-density sprawling form of development typical of Australian cities; its effects on transportation, intra-urban travel time, and the costs of providing basic urban services; the role of the central business district; the quality of the physical environment; and the possible effects of oil prices, the changing structure of employment opportunities and demographic trends on future patterns of development. The question of whether location in a particular low income sector of a city actually increases the extent of inequality for residents is tested with particular reference to the availability of educational and health care services. They conclude with the suggestion that in the face of mounting problems governments, at least in times of economic hardship, may try to disengage themselves from planning activities.

Japan has experienced a rate and scale of urbanisation probably unparalleled in the developed world, to such an extent that over half the Japanese people live in cities with over 100,000 inhabitants. Within the urban system Tokyo enjoys an unchallenged pre-eminence. As in other industrialised countries, however, economic success has generated its wake of societal problems such as housing shortages, traffic congestion, and deterioration of the physical and biotic environment. The desire to find solutions to these and other problems has prompted the gradual emergence in Japan of what is essentially an ameliorative problem-solving mode of planning (Berry 1973). In Chapter 3 Michael Witherick discusses the efforts of Japanese planners in the post-war era to cope with the problems created by the seemingly relentless growth of population and employment in Tokyo. He identifies the fundamental commitment to free enterprise capitalism and a consequent lack of conviction in decentralisation policies as major factors behind the intense form of urbanism and the related problems. He suggests now that the post-war economic recovery and Japan's status in the international community have been successfully consolidated, motivation and sacrifice of a patriotic complexion may be beginning to give way to individual aspirations which focus on different priorities such as access to decent housing, environmental quality, leisure time and the whole ethos of the good life, and that the need for a more progressive and comprehensive form of planning is being recognised.

Public policy and the planning of metropolitan areas in South Africa display an ambivalence marked by less constraint in the economic and spatial systems as a whole and to the White sub-system in particular, and to severe constraint as they apply to the life and work of Blacks, especially Africans. This ambivalence is manifested in contrasting planning styles which, as a reflection of social process, give rise to spatial forms that provide sharp contrasts not only within South African metropolitan areas but between these areas and metropolitan regions in the rest of the world. The Johannesburg metropolitan area faces most of the challenges associated with the present metropolitan age, such as urban sprawl, congestion in and pressure on city centre space, and the increased costs imposed by greater separation of homes and workplaces, but in addition has to contend with three major problems. These refer to difficulties arising from the rapid transformation of the economy from one heavily dependent on gold mining to one based on industry and tertiary activities; the need to plan a new physical structure to meet the requirements of this changed economic base and to incorporate vast areas of abandoned mining land into the metropolitan landscape; and the social challenge of a multi-racial urban society with its roots in the policy of apartheid. In analysing these problems Denis Fair and John Muller point out that the overriding goal of planning in the Johannesburg metropolitan area is the need to sustain a high level of economic growth in the interest of national development and to promote those physical and social structures which will help do so. They

conclude, however, that the relentless pressures of an expanding urban
economic system can no longer be met by the rigidities of *apartheid
planning* and its emphasis on a race-class system maintained through
the coercive organisation of a minority elite.

Chapter 5 examines urban problems and planning in a city representative of the redistributive welfare states of Western Europe in which the
free enterprise system is modified by government action aimed at
reducing social and spatial inequalities. Public involvement in urban
development is explicit and the direction of urban growth is deliberately
led by the state through the building of new housing and by the
enforcement of development controls and planning regulations. Over
the last decade the regeneration of older urban areas has become a
central issue in British planning policy, and of all British cities Glasgow
is the most easily called to mind when an example of severe urban
deprivation and the problems associated with it is sought. The city is
faced with a host of problems including serious population decline
which the authorities are now desperately trying to reverse, traffic congestion, environmental degradation and a range of social problems, but
the two critical problem areas identified for priority attention relate
to the high rates of unemployment due largely to the post-war decline
of the traditional heavy industrial economic base, and the large number
of sub-tolerable houses both in the older inner city tenement areas and
in some of the post-war peripheral council estates. Michael Pacione
describes the factors underlying these problems and presents a critical
assessment of the strategies employed to resolve them. He concludes
that while substantial progress has been made since World War II it will
have been a major achievement if analysis of the 1981 Census statistics
indicates the city's place at the top of the national deprivation league to
be in danger.

Barcelona is one of the fastest growing urban agglomerations in
Southern Europe. The modern expansion of the city and its planning
experience reflect the political climate of Franco's Spain (1939-75).
Most of the city's growth pains stem directly from the government's
preoccupation with maximising national economic growth and its
failure to diminish the inequalities between countryside and town. John
Naylon points to Barcelona as an example of what can happen when
urban growth is left to the uncontrolled play of market forces, with
private entrepreneurs amassing profits without regard to social effects.
In this and other senses it occupies an intermediate position between
the great cities of the fully-fledged industrialised countries and those
of the Third World. He suggests that the true lesson of Barcelona's

experience has been the irrelevance of sophisticated projects when local authorities are not democratically representative and when they lack the funds and the human resources to translate theory into practice, and concludes that the key issue to be resolved for an improved planning future in post-Franco Spain is the conflict between public and private interest. The decentralisation of financial as well as administrative control to the regions in 1979 and the new democratic climate raise hopes for a more effective urban planning to tackle the enormous social difficulties confronting Barcelona.

At the opposite end of the ideological spectrum from the free-market capitalist system is the centrally planned or command economy prevalent in the socialist states of Eastern Europe and the USSR, where the political system is dominated by a single party. A basic contention of the socialist system is that control by the state of all the means of production, including land, and the centralised allocation of resources would permit the planned and harmonious development of society along desired lines, and would enable society to avoid the errors and contradictions of capitalism. In the case of urban planning however many of these goals have proved difficult to realise. For example, despite restrictions on the movement of population Leningrad with a current population of 4.4 million exceeds the level forecast for 1990 by the 1966 General Plan for the city. The root of the problem lies in the fact that planning in practice is concerned with priorities, and in the socialist bloc the prime objective has been economic progress. The repercussions of this include preference for industrial development to the detriment of environmental considerations, lack of investment in town planning, and the setting aside of long term ideals in the face of the short term needs of industrial production.

In Chapter 7 Keith Grime and Grzegorz Węcławowicz examine Warsaw, a city which literally has had to be rebuilt from the rubble of World War II. For the past 35 years Warsaw has been developed as part of a centrally planned society. Despite almost total control over social and economic development the city suffers many problems which are remarkably similar to those of cities in the Western world. Housing is a major problem area and the authors examine the role of socialised, co-operative and private housing in the city's attempts to attain the goal of providing an individual apartment for every family, an objective reminiscent of the early post-war aims in many of Britain's older cities. In conclusion, they argue that the major reason for the limited success in resolving Warsaw's problems lies not in plan preparation, which is often imaginative and innovative, but in plan implementation in the face of scarce resources and an increasing list of priorities.

In Chapter 8 Denis Shaw explains the structure of Soviet urban planning and discusses the problems which face Leningrad, the country's second city. These include population growth, urban sprawl, lengthening journeys to work, transportation, housing, and levels of service provision. He suggests that the major lesson which Soviet planners have learned in the past two decades is that the centralised planning system needs modification to cope with the problems which have arisen in the cities, and concludes that steps towards a more comprehensive local planning framework which would embrace both physical and economic planning are underway.

Many of the key problems identified independently in these studies are common to several cities despite often wide differences in socio-political ideologies. Furthermore, similar solutions have been attempted in many instances. Nevertheless it must be accepted that no one country and no one city has developed techniques, models, plans or policies which can serve as a guide to all. The disparities in political, administrative, economic, social and cultural conditions preclude the formation or adoption of rules capable of universal application. Provided these qualifications are borne in mind, however, there are valuable lessons of experience to be learned from the study of selected cities which *mutatis mutandis* may be applied elsewhere.

References

Abu-Lughod, J. and R. Hay (1977) *Third World Urbanisation*, London
Alexandersson, G. and T. Falk (1974) 'Changes in the urban pattern of Sweden 1966-1970: the beginning of a return to small urban places?', *Geoforum, 8,* 87-92
Alain, S.M. and Pokshishensky, V. (1977) *Urbanisation in Developing Countries*, Hyderabad
Berry, B.J.L. (1973) *The Human Consequences of Urbanisation*, London
——(ed.) (1976) *Urbanisation and Counterurbanisation*, London
Bourne, L.S. and M.I. Logan (1976) 'Changing urbanization patterns at the margin: the examples of Australia and Canada', in Berry (1976) *ibid.*, pp. 111-43
Breese, G. (1972) *The City in Newly Developing Countries*, New Jersey
Falk, T. (1978) 'Urban development in Sweden 1966-1975: population dispersal in progress', in N.M. Hansen (ed.) *Human Settlement Systems: International Perspectives on Structure Change and Public Policy*
Ford Foundation, (1972) *International Urbanization Survey: Findings and Recommendations*, New York
Hall, P., H. Gracey, R. Drewett and R. Thomas (1973) *The Containment of Urban England Volume I: Urban and Metropolitan Growth Processes*, London

Hall, P. (1977) *The World Cities*, London
International Bank For Reconstruction and Development, (1976) *World Tables*, Baltimore
McGee, T.G. (1971) *The Urbanization Process in the Third World*, London
Northam, R.M. (1979) *Urban Geography*, 2nd edn, New York
Rodwin, L. (1970) *Nations and Cities*, Boston
Rostow, W.W. (1960) *The Stages of Economic Growth*, Cambridge
United Nations Population Division, (1972) 'The World's Million Cities', *ESA/P/WP 45*
United Nations, (1974) *Concise Report On The World Population Situation in 1970-75 and its Long Range Implications*, New York
Webber, M.M. (1969) 'Planning in an environment of change', *Tn Plan Rev., 39(4)*
World Bank, (1979, 1980) *World Development Report*, Washington DC
Yates, D. (1977) *The Ungovernable City*, New York

1 THE NEW YORK METROPOLITAN REGION

George W. Carey

The intensely developed metropolitan region which surrounds the city of New York is the western terminus of a set of sea and air links connected to the major port cities of the world, particularly in Western Europe and Puerto Rico. Most of the passengers, goods, and information which move across that network make use of the modern transportation and communication facilities which are concentrated in the New York Metropolitan Region (NYMR). Looking from the Port of New York westward towards the continent, transportation channels of all kinds – pipe-lines, power lines, highways, railroads and waterways – converge from inland upon that busy location. Goods shipped by firms as distant as Western Ontario often utilise the region for marine trans-shipment despite the intent of such projects as the St Lawrence Seaway which made Toronto an oceanic seaport, and thus a potential competitor.

The Port of New York-New Jersey lies at the core of the conurbation to which Gottman (1961) gave the name *megalopolis* and close to the heart of its major geographical function: that of a hinge between North America and the rest of the world. A 1979 study illustrates that, as of 1976, one in every four jobs within New York City lay in industries serving the national and international markets (Port Authority of New York and New Jersey 1979).

Lying behind the 'hinge' function, and energising it, the highly developed financial sector is found to be concentrated in the region. The prestigious Regional Plan Association (RPA) puts it succinctly:

> The Region's most important function in the nation is that of a capital market. Multinational investment, banking and credit, securities and trusts, and insurance are activities in which the region is most specialized. More than a quarter of the nation's output from them originates in the region, and the activities, in turn, are responsible for 10 percent of the Gross Regional Product. The Region also houses one fifth of the national headquarters of the 3,500 major corporations (of the United States). The headquarters exercise control over 40 percent of the nation's corporate profits. (RPA 1979)

Furthermore in 1975, the last year for which hard data are available, no less than 43.3 per cent of the profits earned abroad by firms in the United States was concentrated in businesses located in the region, forming 2.6 per cent of the Gross Regional Product.

Yet this is a region with serious and deepening structural problems. Unemployment is more acute here than in most other major metropolitan regions of the United States. The population of the region is diminishing and ageing. The region as a whole, during the brief period 1972-75, lost more than 300,000 jobs—nearly 6 per cent of the total regional employment. Although the major national capital market is located in New York City, business investment declined by 38 per cent in the region over the same period. Real personal income per capita has been stagnant in the region during the 1970s, at a time when some gains have been recorded in the nation. The regional environment is subject to increasing deterioration through the impact of pollution and neglect, with serious health implications. And very serious indeed has been the accelerating depreciation of the poorly maintained yet vital infrastructure of the region—sewerage systems, utilities, roads, railroads, bridges and tunnels, for example. Not only New York City but also other regional cities like Newark and Yonkers are perennially threatened with financial bankruptcy.

How can a region which is of such national and world significance be allowed to decline in this way? What factors lie at the root of the pattern? What geographical variations lie within it? What public policies have been adopted in order to arrest the perilous trend? This chapter will attempt to suggest some answers to these questions.

The New York Metropolitan Region Defined

It is instructive to note at the outset that the region's estimated population of 19.6 million people in 1975 lived on a land area of 12,788 square miles—a little smaller than the Netherlands, but with a substantially greater population. Thus, its density of 1,532 persons per square mile places it well above that European country of comparable size which is widely cited as an example of dense settlement and intense urbanisation.

Figure 1.1 presents the major political divisions contained in the region. Three states, New York, Connecticut and New Jersey, lie partially within its boundaries. In fact, as of 1975, no less than 68.8 per cent of their total population resided there. The major subdivisions of each state are counties, and the region is currently defined as the 31 counties

Figure 1.1: The Political Framework of the New York Metropolitan Region (NYMR)

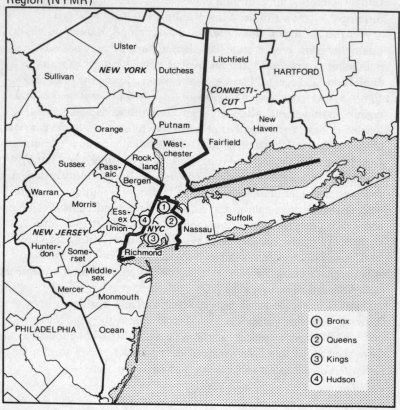

surrounding the Port of New York which constitute a largely closed system of residence and employment. Thus, the regional boundary, as depicted in Figure 1.1, encloses an area which

> is essentially a closed commuter shed, with less than 1 percent of its job opportunities held by nonresidents. The latest detailed data, from the 1970 Census journey-to-work inquiry, showed that 7,603.3 thousand of the Region's 7,696.4 thousand resident workers lived and worked in the 31-county area. (RPA 1979)

Thus, the 31-county NYMR is essentially an integrated urban socio-economic region. Nevertheless there is no corresponding political region whose jurisdiction remotely corresponds to it. Unlike many other

comparable urban areas such as Greater London, Toronto Metro and
the Paris Region, to name but three, there is no metropolitan regional
governmental body with comprehensive planning or administrative
powers able to deal with questions of governance of the region as a
whole. The RPA is a private, nonprofit voluntary organisation established
in 1922 which continues to produce invaluable studies and plans for the
region. Yet these, although of great influence, have no official status.
They are the closest equivalents to regional plans which are available. It
is therefore obvious that another key problem in the region involves the
creation of an official framework for comprehensive planning, with
ancillary mechanisms for implementing such plans.

At the centre of this region lies the city of New York. Manhattan
Island (for all practical purposes identical with New York County) is
the focus of the five counties comprising the political city, the other
three counties being Kings (often called Brooklyn after the old city
which formed its nucleus, now long annexed to the city), Queens,
Bronx and Richmond (which is largely equivalent to Staten Island).

Of these five counties, all but Richmond (Staten Island) are so
densely developed in terms of jobs and housing that they are considered
part of the region's *core*. Only Richmond still retains a lower density
suburban aspect over much of its landscape, owing to the fact that, until
the Verrazano-Narrows Bridge connecting it with Kings (Brooklyn) was
completed in 1964, access to the rest of the city was limited to a ferry
crossing.

On the other hand, tunnel connections across the Hudson to New
Jersey were completed long ago. The Hudson Tubes, a passenger subway
connection to Manhattan, was created in 1908, while the Pennsylvania
Railroad's main line tunnel was finished in 1910. Two vehicular tunnels,
the Holland (1927) and the Lincoln (1937), along with the George
Washington Bridge (1931) were completed in one busy decade. Thus,
on the west bank of the Hudson towns like Hoboken, Weehawken and
Bayonne, responding to the stimulus of an easy connection to Manhattan,
merged with Jersey City to form the densely inhabited city region which
occupies eastern Hudson County, New Jersey. The growth of Newark,
in south-eastern Essex County, New Jersey, has spilled over into Hudson
County from the west in a similar fashion, and so the NYMR core region
is reckoned as New York (Manhattan), Kings (Brooklyn), Queens and
Bronx Counties, all in the state and city of New York, and Hudson
County plus the Newark portion of Essex County in New Jersey.

Around this bi-state urban core is an *inner ring* of old suburban
counties which are densely developed: Bergen, Essex (excluding Newark),

and Union in New Jersey; Richmond (Staten Island) in both the city
and state of New York; Nassau and the southern portion of Westchester
including the cities of Yonkers and White Plains in the state of New
York but outside the political jurisdiction of New York City.

The *intermediate ring* of suburbs is largely of post-World War II
vintage. There are six in New Jersey, ranging from Mercer to Passaic. The
state of New York counts three in this zone: Rockland, northern
Westchester and western Suffolk. Southern Fairfield and New Haven
Counties in Connecticut round it out. The remaining *outer ring* counties,
although tied within the regional commuting system, are substantially
less developed than those of the intermediate ring and the inner region,
and still include appreciable areas of farmland.

It is worth observing that a number of semi-autonomous cities lie
within the NYMR, outside of New York City, Jersey City and Newark.
They are presented in Table 1.1. Trenton, the capital of the state of
New Jersey, lies in the intermediate ring of the NYMR in Mercer
County. Hartford, the capital of Connecticut, is but one county away
from the outer ring. The sphere of economic influence of the NYMR
thus extends to the state houses of New Jersey and Connecticut.

When, to the mosaic of the 31 independent county governments
which vary widely in efficiency of organisation, taxing, administrative
and legislative powers, are added the overlapping independent patterns
of the numerous city and municipal governments in the NYMR; when
to this confusion we add a mixture of state and federal governmental
jurisdictions with their powers and prerogatives; when we consider
that there are also independent special purpose governmental agencies
in the region, such as the Tri-State Regional Planning Commission (with
federal responsibilities in the areas of transportation and environmental
policy planning), the bi-state Port Authority of New York and New
Jersey (with port development responsibilities) and the tri-borough
Bridge and Tunnel Authority (with major transportation responsibilities
in New York City); finally, when we realise that there exists a patchwork
of small-scale special districts, each with separate taxing powers in the
region—fire districts, water and sewerage districts and school districts,
for example—whose boundaries and activities have arisen through
historical accident and are coordinated poorly or not at all with those
jurisdictions of larger scale, we are then not surprised that Robert
Wood's celebrated volume detailing these complexities of government
in the NYMR as it existed in 1961 was entitled *1400 Governments* (RPA
1959-61).

The present author, in a discussion with a planner in Amsterdam, was

Table 1.1: The Populations of Old Core Cities (except New York City) located within the New York Metropolitan Region, 1970

City	County	State	1970 Population
Atlantic City	Ocean	New Jersey	47,859
Bayonne	Hudson	.. ..	72,743
Clifton	Passaic	.. ..	82,437
East Orange	Essex	.. ..	75,471
Elizabeth	Union	.. ..	112,654
Jersey City	Hudson	.. ..	260,545
Newark	Essex	.. ..	382,288
New Brunswick	Middlesex	.. ..	41,885
Passaic	Passaic	.. ..	55,124
Paterson	..	.. ..	144,824
Trenton	Mercer	.. ..	104,638
Union City	Hudson	.. ..	58,537
Hempstead	Nassau	New York	39,411
Mount Vernon	Westchester	.. ..	72,788
New Rochelle	.. ..	.. ..	75,385
Poughkeepsie	Dutchess	.. ..	32,029
White Plains	Westchester	.. ..	50,346
Yonkers	.. ..	.. ..	204,297
Bridgeport	Fairfield	Connecticut	156,542
New Haven	New Haven	.. ..	137,707
Norwalk	Fairfield	.. ..	79,111
Stamford	..	.. ..	108,798
Waterbury	New Haven	.. ..	108,033

Source: US Census of Population, 1970

told that the average resident of that city was only confronted with two direct taxes (in addition to the indirect value-added tax): the national income tax, whose structure is uniform throughout the Netherlands, and a dog licensing tax—and that only if he were a dog owner! The reader in such a city is therefore ill-equipped to understand the dilemma facing an individual or firm in the NYMR when confronted with the need to factor projected taxes into the planning of his affairs.

A New Jersey resident, for instance, working in New York City (there were more than 200,000 such in 1975) must deal separately with the problem of how much he owes in income tax to the city of New York, the state of New York, the state of New Jersey and the federal government.

Moreover, he must pay a tax on his real estate to county or municipal government and to his school district if he is a homeowner. Furthermore, sales and excise taxes are often levied on the goods which he purchases. In this jurisdictional chaos, moreover, the rates of all of these, excepting only the federal tax, are far from equal and the burdens far from equitably distributed within the NYMR. In order to try to influence tax policy, he must engage in politics with his representatives at the local district, municipal, county, state and federal levels!

The chaotic disarray of this mode of governance tends to render neighbouring governments hostile and competitive. The situation is not unlike that of a region subdivided among numerous antagonistic nations whose politics become a politics of ephemeral power coalitions for short term gains, and without an effective overarching planning and co-ordinating mechanism, as in the case of a well known model proposed by Holden (1964).

Patterns of Economic Activity in the NYMR

Table 1.2: Patterns of Economic Activity in NYMR, 1975

	As a share of GNP in 1975	As a share of growth in GNP 1972 to 1975	As a share of GRP in 1975
Rest of world	43.3%	43.3%	2.6%
Apparel	30.7	11.2	2.0
Banks & credit	28.0	21.1	3.3
Securities & trusts	26.6	4.1	1.1
Printing	24.0	12.9	2.5
Misc. manufacturing	22.5	5.6	0.8
Insurance	21.8	19.5	2.9
Chemicals	21.3	24.8	3.5
Business services	17.3	10.5	5.6
Wholesale trade	15.6	11.6	10.2
Instruments	14.7	3.2	0.9
Communication	14.2	12.1	3.3
Nondurable manufacturing	13.8	10.5	12.8
Leather	13.3	6.3	0.2
Nonprofit type services	13.3	11.3	6.5
Transportation	12.0	9.8	4.0

	As a share of GNP in 1975	As a share of growth in GNP 1972 to 1975	As a share of GRP in 1975
Private gross product	11.7	8.1	90.0
Personal services	11.6	6.2	3.0
Rubber	10.9	7.4	0.6
Utilities	10.7	11.2	2.4
Real estate	10.6	5.4	10.1
Electrical machinery	10.5	10.7	1.8
Paper	10.2	12.1	0.8
Textiles	9.8	4.2	0.6
Retail trade	9.8	6.6	8.5
Furniture	9.4	73.6	0.3
Nonelectrical machinery	9.2	9.4	2.2
Fabricated metals	9.1	2.9	1.4
Construction	8.7	7.1	3.4
Food	8.0	6.7	1.9
Durable manufacturing	7.9	6.5	9.6
Stone	6.8	9.5	0.5
Petroleum refining	5.9	4.7	0.6
Transportation equipment	4.4	92.6	1.0
Primary metals	4.1	1.7	0.7
Tobacco	2.4	4.5	0.1
Lumber	2.2	0.4	0.1
Agr., for., & fish.	1.1	0.4	0.4
Mining	1.1	0.7	0.2

Source: RPA, 1979.

Table 1.2 presents a listing of major economic activities carried on in the NYMR. Column 1 compares the activity within the NYMR with the Gross National Product (GNP) of the United States for the year 1975. Thus the Regional Product of apparel in 1975 was 30.7 per cent of the corresponding GNP entry for the whole United States. The activities listed are in declining shares of the US GNP. Thus, those at the top of the list are specialised in the NYMR. The row labelled *private gross product* tells us that the NYMR as a whole produced 11.7 per cent of the 1975 US GNP. It divides the specialised NYMR activities (above this line) from the nonspecialised ones (below).

The category 'rest of world' heads the list. It

> is the region's number one specialization—the multinational invest-
> ment function which brings returns from domestic ownership abroad.
> The Region's share of GNP in this category is 43 percent. The next
> most prominent specializations are in the financial sector . . . . Com-
> bined, they account for 25 percent of financial output in the nation.
> (RPA 1979)

Column 2 shows that from 1972 to 1975 the multinational investment
function of the region captured a 43.3 per cent share of the national
growth in that category. In column 3 we see that its share of the Gross
Regional Product (GRP) in 1975 was 2.6 per cent. In general, the
private sector of the GRP captured 8.1 per cent of national growth
during 1972-5, a disappointing figure which reflected a slower overall
NYMR growth rate than national, causing the region to lose some ground.
In 1972 the private sector of the NYMR accounted for 12.8 per cent
of the US GNP, while, as we have seen, the 1975 share was but 11.7
per cent.

The pattern of the table is fairly consistent, with but few exceptions.
Those activities which are already specialised in the region tended to
manifest stronger growth than those which are not. The slippage of
securities and trusts should be regarded as episodically related to the
acute recession and urban financial crisis of New York City in 1975.
It is probably not a long term trend. The losses in *leather, instruments*
and *miscellaneous manufacturing* are real, however, and represent
economic activity leaving the region. In terms of their share of the
GRP (column 3), regardless of their specialisation in the NYMR, their
importance is slight.

Of the industries in the lower portion of the table, which are not
regionally concentrated, the apparently large gains made by *transportation equipment* and *furniture* must be read with caution. These
industries are very small within the NYMR, and thus a small absolute
gain is amplified into a large percentage gain. Also, 1975 was a year in
which those industries slipped nationally, compounding the effect.

The slippages in *retail trade, durable manufacturing, construction*
and *real estate* are not statistical artifacts, however, and have had strong
local and regional impacts. These are sectors which had a substantial
share of the 1975 GRP, and in which thousands of jobs have been lost—
many of them to the lower-skill stratum of the regional labour force.
The growth in *wholesale trade* and *nondurable manufacturing*,

unfortunately, has not compensated for the loss of low skill jobs, while other growing sectors (*chemicals, communication, transportation, utilities* and *electrical machinery*) are capital intensive and require a skilled labour force, or else are the province of the white collar specialist. Subsumed within the category *transportation*, of course, is the extremely important port function of the NYMR, which has moved strongly in the direction of capital intensity since the trend towards general cargo containerisation has developed.

Figure 1.2 presents us with a view of the NYMR from 1970 to 1976 with respect to jobs and unemployment.The small net gain of 167,000 jobs in the region outside of New York City was overwhelmed by the net loss of more than half a million jobs in the City. Thus the NYMR total employment went down from almost 8.6 million wage and salary jobs in 1970 to less than 8.2 million in 1976 — a net regional loss in the order of magnitude of 400,000 jobs, nearly 5 per cent of all jobs.

We notice from Figure 1.2b that the NYMR components manifested greater unemployment rates than the rest of the nation from 1970 to 1976, and that recently the pattern appears to be diverging even more. While this was partly due to the fact that over these years the region's labour force increased by about 3 per cent to 270,000, it is nevertheless also true that regional employment 'declined more and recovered less than the nation's during the 1970 and 1974 downturns in the business cycles. This was unlike previous postwar recessions in which the region's unemployment declined relatively less than the nation's.' (*RPA News* 1977)

The pattern was unequally distributed over the NYMR in its impact. Table 1.3 shows that the counties in the NYMR in 1976 with markedly higher unemployment rates among their residents than the norm for the NYMR outside of New York City (9.3 per cent) are either outer ring counties like Litchfield, Ocean, Warren, Orange, Sullivan and Ulster, or counties containing core cities like New Haven, Essex, Hudson, Passaic (Paterson City), and of course the New York counties. In the case of Ocean County, New Jersey, both factors were present. Although it lies in the outer ring, it contains an older city — Atlantic City — which has been steadily in a state of decline until recently, when the state of New Jersey authorised the development of casino gambling there in an effort to bolster its economy. In general, outer ring unemployment, where it occurs, may be attributed to the fact that job growth has lagged behind population growth. The unemployment rates there are on relatively small base numbers, in contrast to the situation of the old city-dominated counties. There we encounter large declines in absolute

Figure 1.2: Employment and Unemployment in the NYMR, 1970-76

Jobs*in the Region 1970 - 1976

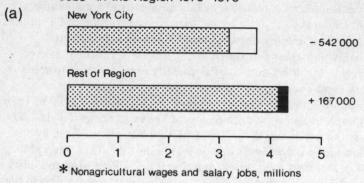

(a)

New York City

– 542 000

Rest of Region

+ 167 000

0   1   2   3   4   5

* Nonagricultural wages and salary jobs, millions

(b)   Unemployment, 1970 - 1976

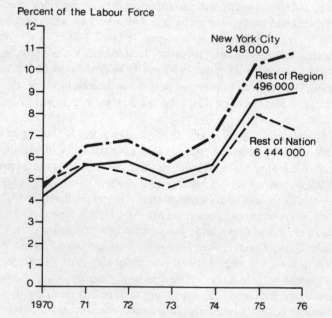

Percent of the Labour Force

New York City
348 000

Rest of Region
496 000

Rest of Nation
6 444 000

1970   71   72   73   74   75   76

numbers in the civilian employment labour force accompanying high unemployment rates, as Table 1.4 shows.

Only in the case of Westchester and New Haven is the absolute number of residents employed in the civilian labour force in 1976 larger

The New York Metropolitan Region

Table 1.3: Civilian Unemployment Rate of Labour Force by Place of Residence, 1970-76

	1970	1971	1972	1973	1974	1975	1976
			Per cent of the Labour Force				
Connecticut	6.0%	8.7%	8.9%	6.6%	6.4%	9.7%	9.2%
Fairfield	5.4	8.2	8.6	6.5	6.4	8.7	8.4
Litchfield	7.5	10.7	9.3	6.5	6.2	11.4	9.4
New Haven	6.4	9.0	9.1	6.7	6.5	10.4	10.0
New Jersey	4.4	5.5	5.6	5.4	6.1	9.9	9.1[a]
Bergen	3.4	4.7	4.5	4.4	4.6	8.0	7.6
Essex	5.3	6.7	7.2	6.2	7.8	12.5	11.0
Hudson	6.0	7.4	7.8	7.8	8.1	12.5	11.6
Hunterdon	3.8	5.5	5.1	4.2	4.3	7.3	6.3
Mercer	4.0	4.3	4.2	4.5	5.2	7.7	6.4
Middlesex	4.5	5.3	5.4	5.3	5.6	9.5	8.8
Monmouth	4.5	4.9	5.3	5.4	5.9	9.0	8.1
Morris	3.2	4.1	4.5	3.8	4.8	7.9	6.9
Ocean	4.0	4.5	5.3	5.5	6.7	10.2	9.5
Passaic	5.6	6.4	6.4	7.3	7.5	12.0	10.5
Somerset	2.7	3.4	3.7	3.2	4.0	6.6	5.7
Sussex	3.5	4.1	4.5	5.0	5.5	8.7	8.2
Union	3.7	4.8	5.2	4.4	5.6	9.0	8.0
Warren	4.0	7.2	5.9	4.2	5.8	12.0	12.5
New York	4.4	6.2	6.4	5.5	6.5	9.5	10.5
NY excl NYC	3.5	5.3	5.2	4.5	5.4	7.7	9.5
Dutchess	2.5	4.3	4.5	2.9	3.5	5.8	6.7
Nassau	3.3	4.9	4.8	3.7	4.7	6.9	8.9
Orange	4.2	5.9	6.1	5.0	8.7	9.5	10.5
Putnam	2.9	4.5	4.4	5.1	5.8	7.6	8.8
Rockland	2.7	4.3	4.2	4.8	5.5	7.2	8.3
Suffolk	4.1	6.2	6.1	4.7	5.9	8.2	11.1
Sullivan	6.2	8.4	8.6	7.1	8.3	9.4	10.1
Ulster	5.0	7.2	7.4	5.5	8.8	11.1	12.4
Westchester	2.9	4.5	4.5	5.2	5.9	7.7	8.9
New York City	4.8	6.7	7.0	6.0	7.2	10.6	11.2
Bronx	4.9	6.7	7.1	6.1	7.2	10.7	11.3
Kings	5.4	7.4	7.8	6.7	7.9	11.7	12.3
New York	5.4	7.5	7.9	6.8	8.0	11.8	12.5
Queens	3.9	5.4	5.7	4.9	5.8	8.7	9.2
Richmond	3.2	4.5	4.7	4.0	4.8	7.2	7.6

	1970	1971	1972	1973	1974	1975	1976
Outside NYC	4.3	5.9	6.0	5.3	5.9	9.0	9.3
Region	4.5%	6.2%	6.4%	5.5%	6.4%	9.6%	10.0%

Note: a. 1976 figures for New Jersey are preliminary.
Source: *RPA News*, no. 101 (1977).

Table 1.4: Civilian Employment Labour Force by Place of Residence (annual average, 000s) 1970-76 for Selected NYMR Counties Dominated by Major Core Cities

County	(City)	1970	1972	1974	1976
New Haven	(New Haven)	314.6	319.2	331.3	318.8
Essex	(Newark)	370.3	380.2	377.0	357.5
Hudson	(Jersey City)	248.0	235.6	231.9	220.1
Passaic	(Paterson)	188.7	188.4	185.5	175.7
Union	(Elizabeth)	232.0	238.1	236.2	223.9
Westchester	(Yonkers, White Plains)	366.3	373.4	367.9	389.8
New York City		3,143.0	2,969.0	2,904.0	2,765.0

Source: *RPA News*, no. 101 (1977).

than that in 1970. These two counties are dominated by their respective cities far less than the others in the list, and so their relatively better performance may be attributed to suburban rather than urban factors.

We shall now turn to a consideration of regional demographic patterns, where it will become clear that the high unemployment rates and slackening resident labour force numbers so frequent in these old-city counties are accompanied (in all but New Haven) by an absolute decline in population. Put another way, had population not emigrated from these counties from 1970 to 1976, the strikingly high unemployment percentages which we noticed in 1976 might very well have been higher.

The Population Geography of the NYMR

Table 1.5 presents the recent growth of the NYMR. The peak population was reached in 1972 (19.9 million), and since then has declined. Since 1970 there has been a net annual outmigration averaging 112,000 through 1975. This is the first time in the 350-year history of the region that a

Table 1.5: Population in the Region by County and by Ring, 1970-76 (000s)

	1970 (Census April 1)	1972	1973	1974	1975	1976P
Connecticut	1,681.8	1,700.4	1,695.4	1,698.4	1,705.6	1,719.6
Fairfield	792.8	793.9	788.6	790.2	799.3	802.7
Litchfield	144.1	145.7	148.8	148.2	146.0	150.6
New Haven	744.9	760.8	758.0	760.0	760.3	766.3
New Jersey	5,802.7	5,928.7	5,938.2	5,870.4	5,864.4	5,855.2
Bergen	897.1	904.0	897.9	880.0	879.1	870.1
Essex	932.5	939.4	936.9	894.4	881.6	872.1
Hudson	607.8	621.9	617.7	584.9	577.6	572.9
Hunterdon	69.7	73.2	74.2	76.9	78.5	79.1
Mercer	304.1	313.3	316.1	319.8	318.0	318.7
Middlesex	583.8	596.4	597.1	594.9	594.0	592.7
Monmouth	461.8	474.9	477.6	486.1	491.4	492.8
Morris	383.5	391.7	393.4	394.1	395.0	394.5
Ocean	208.5	236.4	250.0	282.2	293.8	308.5
Passaic	460.8	468.2	467.8	456.7	452.2	449.0
Somerset	198.4	201.3	201.2	201.2	203.7	205.4
Sussex	77.5	82.5	85.6	95.2	99.0	102.4
Union	543.1	550.0	546.3	524.8	520.5	516.3
Warren	74.0	75.5	76.4	79.2	80.0	80.7
New York	12,270.2	12,289.3	12,159.3	12,071.2	12,020.9	12,031.8
NY excl NYC	4,374.6	4,465.5	4,495.0	4,493.6	4,548.3	4,578.2
Dutchess	222.3	226.3	230.7	232.4	233.4	235.1
Nassau	1,428.8	1,427.8	1,415.6	1,392.7	1,400.9	1,396.6
Orange	221.7	231.3	235.2	239.3	243.8	247.8
Putnam	56.7	61.2	64.1	67.0	69.4	70.7
Rockland	229.9	237.4	243.2	245.2	252.1	254.2
Suffolk	1,127.0	1,179.6	1,205.6	1,225.2	1,255.3	1,278.7
Sullivan	52.6	56.4	58.7	59.8	60.3	60.8
Ulster	141.2	149.1	151.5	152.1	153.7	156.2
Westchester	894.4	896.4	890.4	879.9	879.4	878.1
New York City	7,895.6	7,823.8	7,664.3	7,577.6	7,472.6	7,453.6
Bronx	1,471.7	1,477.4	1,425.5	1,390.5	1,359.4	1,343.0
Kings	2,602.0	2,554.1	2,484.1	2,445.4	2,411.0	2,398.0
New York	1,539.2	1,484.5	1,462.3	1,451.1	1,412.8	1,416.7
Queens	1,987.2	1,997.9	1,976.3	1,969.9	1,965.1	1,967.7
Richmond	295.4	309.9	316.1	320.7	324.3	328.2

	1970	1972	1973	1974	1975	1976ᴾ
Outside NYC	11,859.2	12,094.6	12,128.6	12,062.4	12,118.3	12,153.0
Core	8,589.8	8,514.8	8,337.4	8,181.3	8,065.2	8,032.9
Inner ring	4,802.0	4,836.7	4,813.4	4,721.8	4,708.9	4,684.7
Intermediate ring	4,889.3	5,014.1	5,047.7	5,084.2	5,127.1	5,163.0
Outer ring	1,473.4	1,552.8	1,594.4	1,652.7	1,689.7	1,726.0
Region	19,754.8	19,918.4	19,792.9	19,640.0	19,590.9	19,606.6

ᴾ preliminary
Note: Detail may not add to total due to rounding.
Source: *RPA News*, no. 101 (1977).

major net outmigration and a significant population loss have occurred together over a five-year period. Table 1.5 indicates that only the intermediate and outer rings of the region manifested any net growth over the period. Moreover, every county in the core and inner ring lost population, saving only Richmond in New York City, where there was a late growth surge arising from the building of the Verrazano-Narrows Bridge. Of those intermediate ring counties which may be regarded as dominated by single cities, only one—New Haven—experienced growth. The conclusion reached by the RPA that, 'The Region's development in the seventies has been characterized by stagnation and deconcentration', (*RPA News* no. 101, 1977) is inescapable. Moreover, all of the traditional demographic parameters contributed to the effect: birth rates declined, death rates increased and outmigration accelerated.

While deconcentration of the population as a whole has been the fact, black and Hispanic subpopulations have not appreciably shared in this movement, and remain concentrated within the core and inner ring of the NYMR (Figure 1.3).

The central Brooklyn (Bedford-Stuyvesant), Harlem, south Bronx (Hunt's Point), Essex County (Newark) and south-eastern Queens (Jamaica) regions were by far the largest of such areas. While they comprised only 1.35 per cent of the NYMR's land surface, they housed two thirds of the NYMR's black families (*RPA News* no. 104, 1979).

Three explanations have been advanced to explain this fact. Examples abound in the NYMR of people with ethnic and cultural ties voluntarily clustering into communities of mutual support and benefit: Cubans in Union City, New Jersey, Portuguese and Ukranians in the East Ward of Newark, Greeks in northern Queens, Japanese in Fort Lee, New Jersey, among others. Thus, as one possibility, blacks might be voluntarily clustered. Since black family incomes fall below the regional average, it

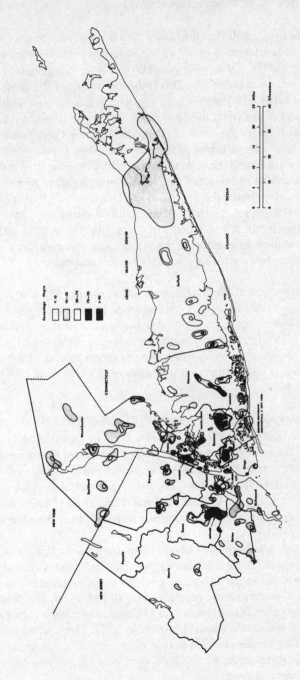

Figure 1.3: The Concentration of the Negro Population

has also been suggested that the basic cause is economic. By this interpretation, they are unable to afford the deconcentrated housing which
they desire. Finally, there is the possibility that the grouping is
involuntary and not economic. This is the hypothesis of the ghetto —
segregation enforced by discriminatory social and economic practices.

A comprehensive study of segregated housing was completed in mid-
1978 by the RPA for the Tri-State Regional Planning Commission, and
supported by the Department of Housing and Urban Development as
well as the Ford Foundation. Among other things it examined these
three explanations and rejected the 'voluntary segregation' hypothesis.
Furthermore, it rejected the economic argument, finding that only 6 per
cent of racial segregation in the NYMR could be statistically linked to
income differentials. It concluded that discriminatory housing attitudes
and practices must be considered the major cause of segregation.

This finding was coupled with another important discovery.

> Fully 60 percent of the Region-wide imbalance in 1970 was due to
> the uneven distribution of black and white families among census
> tracts *within* counties, as opposed to uneven distribution *between*
> counties. This intra-county imbalance is largely unrelated to income.
> In fact, there are instances where the per capita income of suburban
> black areas is higher than that of neighboring white areas. (*RPA News*
> no. 104, 1979).

Thus, any attempt to study segregation in housing in the NYMR at the
county scale of analysis will tend to mask the true extent of the problem,
which only becomes clear at the tract scale of analysis. Furthermore,
since the ghetto areas tend to lie within the urbanised sections of those
counties dominated by old cities, the ghetto population is much more
seriously affected by the unequal regional distribution of unemployment and stagnation, which we have just reviewed, than the general
population.

Since 1970, it is doubtful whether the pattern has changed much.
Despite state and federal fair housing practice legislation, a careful
field-testing of the rental and home buying market revealed ample
evidence that discriminatory practices were still going on. The National
Committee Against Discrimination in Housing conducted a nationwide
field audit of real-estate market practices in 1977. The results for the
New York City sample revealed that in 61 per cent of cases there was a
finding of discrimination, while 33 per cent were inconclusive, leaving
only 6 per cent unimpugned.

The selective outmigration from the NYMR of adult wage earners
and their children, coupled with declining regional birth rates, has had
serious effects on regional public school systems. After an explosive
expansion of school facilities and teaching staffs in the suburbs during
the 1950s and 1960s, the enrolment of numerous core, inner ring and
even intermediate ring school districts has fallen dramatically in the
1970s. Schools which are barely 15 years old, and which are still being
paid for, are now faced with closure in some districts. Younger,
untenured—and less expensive—teachers must be discharged to ease
budgets, while communities must continue to carry the incubus of
building debt for unneeded schools. An ageing population which has
increasing public service needs other than education, and which cannot
easily be served with so much regional public investment tied up in the
premise of a different age structure, is denied adequate attention. With
real regional per capita income, virtually unchanged from 1968 to
1975, at $US7,000 in constant 1975 dollars, compared to a nation-wide
per capita income growth of 6 per cent over the same period, and with
the regional pattern of loss of manufacturing activity seriously affecting
the most heavily urbanised counties, the tax base necessary to support
a requisite public service effort in the NYMR is skimpy and eroding,
while transfers from the state and federal realm are not commensurate
to the task. The geographical pattern of public finance in the NYMR is
closely related to these problems.

The Pattern of Public Finance in the NYMR

If the total revenues accruing from the region to all levels of government are compared to the expenditures of all levels of government
within the region, it will be seen that there was an overall outflow of
revenues from the NYMR, largely owing to federal governmental
practices. Figure 1.4 presents a breakdown of gross revenues (stippled)
and gross expenditures (in white) of government in the NYMR for
1975. Note that about 20 per cent of all federal revenue generated in
the region leaves the region—a sum of $6.3 billion. In contrast, the
pattern of state public finance tends to allocate somewhat more than it
receives to the NYMR not only by means of direct payments, but also
through passed-along federal assistance funds granted to the state. This
closes the gap somewhat. However it is basically up to each and every
local jurisdiction—county, city, municipality and special district—to
tax itself in order to meet its own governmental service burden. The

Figure 1.4: Gross Revenue and Expenditure of Government in the NYMR, 1975

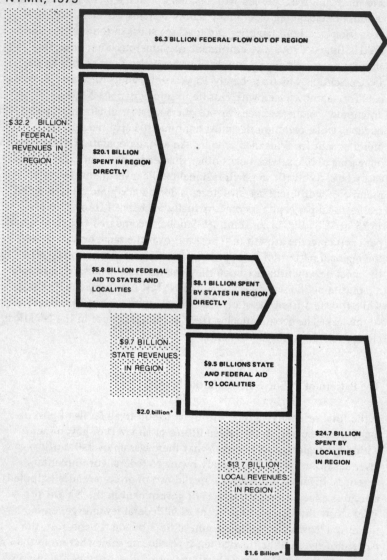

magnitude of the sum thus generated is $13.7 billion — a total tax effort which not only approaches one-half that of the total federal burden, but is largely regressive in nature, since it is obtained through such devices as real property taxation, sales taxes and licensing fees.

Thus, in contrast to many other advanced nations where the taxation system is relatively progressive and concentrated at the national level, and where metropolitan regional budgets largely flow from national social service commitments, each individual local taxing jurisdiction is largely responsible for meeting its own budgetary obligations. Making matters more difficult, state and federal law often require the local jurisdiction to provide a minimum level of service—in education and welfare matters, for example—without always providing a mechanism for allocating the necessary funds. Keeping these considerations in mind, the figures of $1.6 billion at the local revenue level and $2.0 billion at the state level which are shown in Figure 1.4 as equilibrating accounts represent local efforts to balance the regional books through borrowing— largely through the sale of state or municipal bonds on the private bond market.

The consequences of this system of public finance upon the NYMR are serious. Based upon its rigorous regional accounting study, the RPA has recently (1977) ventured the following view of the $6.3 billion 'leakage' of federal funds from the NYMR.

> ... assuming a multiplier of 1.5 for direct federal expenditures and an average annual labor payment of $14,000 per employee, up to $9.5 billion in resources or 700,000 potential jobs may have been lost to the Region through the 'leakage' of federal taxes in 1975. This was about equal to the number of unemployed in the Region that year.

Furthermore, the regional crisis in public finance has a geography of its own within the NYMR. If shares of the federal leakage are allocated by place of taxpayer residence 'New York City lost $1.0 billion of the total $6.3 billion leakage, the New York State subregion another $1.0 billion, the New Jersey subregion $3.1 billion and the Connecticut sub-region $1.2 billion' (RPA 1977).

If the calculation is made by place of work, the share of New York City rises to $3.0 billion, and the shares of the other sub-regions become smaller. The argument has been made that while federal public finance has a genuine redistributive function over the United States as a whole, the NYMR's contribution to that effort, although necessary, ought to be diminishing as income growth elsewhere coupled with regional income stagnation has appreciably narrowed the differential. If, for example, federal expenditures in the NYMR had been kept proportionally equal to the NYMR's share of the national population, the leakage

disbursed to the rest of the country for redistributive purposes would
have been $1.7 billion instead of $6.3 billion.

In any event, the overall impact of the tax system varies widely from
municipality to municipality. In an old core city like Newark, for
example, with a diminishing population, largely black and Hispanic, and
of low average family income, plagued by unemployment and the loss
of jobs—especially in the durable goods manufacturing and retailing
sectors—the service needs are large: education, health, police, welfare,
fire protection and special programmes for the elderly and unemployed.
Yet as factory buildings are left vacant, and burned-out houses are
abandoned while retail institutions move to more profitable suburban
locations, the real-estate tax yield falls off, and money becomes unavailable to fund these essential services. If the rate of real-estate
taxation is raised on those firms which remain, many of them will join
the exodus, exacerbating the problem. If a sales tax is imposed to close
the budgetary gap retailers will move, removing jobs and increasing the
service burden. Since some services are required to be kept at state or
federally mandated levels, those which are vulnerable will be cut back
in order to balance the shrivelling public fisc. These often turn out to be
police, fire protection and municipal hospital services, as in the city of
New York. These measures, in turn, increase the uninhabitability of
the afflicted municipality and escalate the problem. Simply put, the
minimum revenues necessary to sustain local service functions in a city
like Newark or New York are often unavailable within its boundaries,
and the effort to meet these needs will be likely to drive increasing
numbers of businesses and home owners over the boundary to suburban
refuges.

This leads us to ponder the contrasting cases of the declining core
city and the municipality which has succeeded in attracting large,
modern and clean firms to locate within its boundaries. Montvale in the
suburban region of Bergen County, for example, has a number of major
establishments located within its boundaries in attractively landscaped
industrial park settings. These firms, like Mercedes and the Otis Elevator
Company, contribute to the municipal tax base and yet they do not
proportionally increase the service needs of the community since they
do not materially add to the residential population of the town.

Since the residential structure of the town tends towards single
family homes and is appropriately zoned, the lower income workers
must find their apartment residences elsewhere. Thus, a low income
production worker at a factory in Montvale often contributes to the
continued existence of a lucrative tax rateable there, but the service

needs of his family may have to be met by the city of Paterson, Newark, or New York. It is not surprising that the rate of real-estate taxation in Montvale is among the lowest in northern New Jersey. In Newark it is much higher for poorer services.

Elsewhere I have generalised this pattern into a geography of costs and benefits (Carey and Greenberg 1974). In a region like the NYMR, which is economically interconnected yet politically fragmented, the impact of a local facility of the suburban industrial park type may be represented as in Figure 1.5a. The facility, located within the boundaries of a municipality like Montvale, has the effect of concentrating the benefits which it conveys at the local jurisdiction: thus the benefit density curve has a sharp local peak. This represents such beneficent considerations as increased tax revenue at lower tax rates without concomitant costs incurred through municipal service needs, and positive spillover effects on sites neighbouring the industrial park arising from the boost to land value and neighbourhood business activity which results through a local multiplier process.

On the other hand, the cost density curve has a flat peak in the community since many costs arising from the service needs of low-income workers' residential neighbourhoods are spilled over into nearby older cities (like Paterson or Newark). Within the town benefits exceed costs, while outside of the town the reverse is true. Ironically therefore, the lower-income property owner in Newark is confronted with much higher rates of taxation on real estate than the resident of the suburban Montvale, despite the fact that the latter is, on the average, more affluent.

As a number of suburban communities adopt a strategy of seeking to attract these tax rateables which yield high revenues at low service-demand increments to their jurisdictions, the older financially pressed adjacent city has only a very limited ability to compete with its rivals who possess the advantage of low cost developable open space which may be manipulated through zoning ordinances to encourage industrial parks and discourage high-density residential development. Thus the hapless city will tend to have thrust upon it facilities which concentrate costs locally and diffuse benefits widely to the region, as in Figure 1.5b.

Low-income housing developments are one kind of facility which transfers social costs to a city like Newark or New York. Land-intensive transportation facilities which consume much real estate and yield little or nothing to the tax base provide lucrative benefits to the suburban industrial park zone. The costs are borne by the community in which they are located. The massive container-port which is located largely

Figure 1.5: Patterns of Development Costs and Benefits

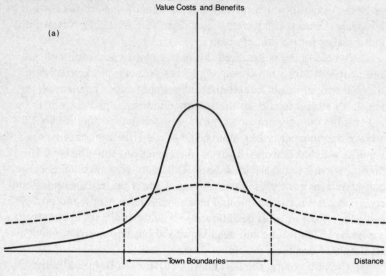

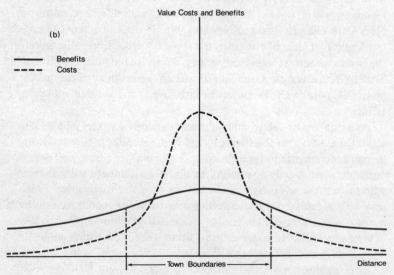

within Newark is a case in point. Along with its twin facility, Newark International Airport, it occupies a vast piece of Newark's real estate, and contributes heavily to the pivotal 'hinge' function of *megalopolis*. Yet, as Hughes (1974) has shown, its contribution to the public fisc in Newark is very small by virtue of the fact that it is operated by a public

institution which does not pay taxes: the Port Authority of New York
and New Jersey (hereafter designated the Port Authority). Great
advantages accrue to Montvale-based firms (like Mercedes, for instance)
and thus to Montvale from the vast general cargo and automobile
import operations at Port Newark, yet the city of Newark has to bear
much of the burden. The peaked cost density curve penalising the jurisdiction in which the facility is located and flat benefit density curve
benefiting the circumambient region symbolise this situation.

In the intricate regional political geography, which as we have
remarked bears a resemblance to that of a competitive small-nation
system, coalitions of suburban beneficiaries with comfortable budgets
can exercise a powerful influence in the state legislature to continue
the established pattern. As every community in a region follows a
similar strategy of concentrating benefits and distributing costs, the
entire region approaches the state in which it finds itself drowning in
accumulated cost spillovers. The ultimate outcome of this 'beggar-thy-
neighbour' system is a special case of the 'tragedy of the commons'
(Hardin 1968). Infrastructure and public service delivery suffer on a
grand scale, and many firms ultimately must face the prospect either
of sinking with a core city or an older inner ring suburb, or swimming
to the enlarged perimeter of benefit concentration—or else out of the
NYMR completely.

The behaviour of all participants in the process, including the workers
in the government service provision bureaucracies and the private
financial institutions which form the structure of the municipal bond
market, contribute to the problem. Municipal employees and their
unions have responded to inflationary pressures and the concentration
of service needs in the core where their numerical strength is greatest,
by aggressive campaigns to increase their salaries and fringe benefits.
Since the municipal service function partly serves the purpose of deflect-
ing and defusing the potential impact of discontent among the poor
(Piven 1972), their leverage has been considerable in just those hard-
pressed jurisdictions where the poor are concentrated—and the budgets
most precarious. Thus, from 1972 to 1975,

New York City labor payments per local government employee rose
by 40.8 percent during the period, 116 times as fast as per capita
income in the City measured in current dollars, and reached $17,220
in 1975, among the highest of any government in the Region. By
contrast, local government payments per employee in the New York
subregion increased by 18.3 percent to $12,590; those in Connecticut

by ·17.9 percent to $9,770, and those in New Jersey by only 5.7 per-
cent to $8,660. (RPA 1977)

In each sub-region the core city counties tended to lead the local trend.
The fiscal restraint observable in suburban areas, where municipal
employees have less leverage, was described in these terms.

> . . . the relative fiscal restraint in suburban municipalities between
> 1972 and 1975 was purchased, in large part, at the expense of
> municipal employees, who appear to have suffered a substantial
> reduction in real wages during the period, especially in New Jersey.
> (RPA 1977)

The pressures of the NYMR's chaotic fiscal geography thus come to a
head at the core city. In order to meet the additional expenditures
incurred by the increase of municipal employee benefits to New York
City, desperate city administrations resorted to shaky fiscal practices.
It has been reliably estimated that if municipal employee salaries had
only kept pace with salary levels in the city as a whole, instead of leading them, the expenditures of New York City in the crisis year of 1975
would have been less by $1 billion. Instead, the inflated needs were met
by municipal borrowing through short term bonds. When the financial
position of the city in a declining economy caused the bond market to
deny further credit, the perennial and celebrated bankruptcy crisis
resulted.

It should be noted that the banking and financial institutions were
not blameless. During the period when the problem was being generated,
they profited greatly from continuous lending and apparently made no
effort to head off the crisis. When the crisis hit, the costs were borne
by retrenchment of services in a plan supported by the federal government. This hit most the poor areas of the city, but the bond holders were
saved from the default which a bankruptcy proceeding would have
implied.

Subsequently, the post-crisis city administrations have been accused
of abetting the devastation of areas like the south Bronx, where literally
acres of strewn rubble and burned-out houses may be viewed, by policies
which involve the withdrawal of sizeable units of the police and fire
departments from those neighbourhoods. In theory, this line of criticism
runs, the large acreage of devastated terrain thus abandoned will become
ripe for profitable redevelopment at a future date, and in the meantime
the process of depopulation will push the poor—and their service

burdens—out of the city.

No effective governmental jurisdiction exists to effectuate what is needed: a more equitable redistribution of service costs and public benefits over the entire NYMR, and the nation. Yet a governmental instrument (the federal government) in fact is redistributing from the NYMR to the nation. Only in the courts has some limited progress been made in cases which have attacked the critical inequities of the property tax system and the use of zoning for the purpose of excluding the residences of the poor from a municipality. The progress is more apparent than real, however, as legal opinions concur that it will be years before there can be any practical and limited application of their results (Rose and Kaplan 1978). In the state legislatures, the numerous representatives of the suburban municipal baronies oppose an effective NYMR planning structure with stubborn persistence.

The NYMR and Energy Consumption

The NYMR consumes less energy per capita than the United States as a whole.

> With 9.7 percent of the nation's population and 12 percent of its money income, the New York Urban Region consumes 6.6 percent of the nation's energy. . . . Per dollar of money income energy consumption in the City is 46 percent, and in the environs 60 percent of the national level. (RPA 1974)

Two factors contribute to this relative energy efficiency in the NYMR. The first is its distinctive economic mix. With an economy tending less towards manufacturing than elsewhere in the nation, it imports many manufactured goods. The energy requisites for these commodities were expended elsewhere—as in Detroit, for example, in the case of motor cars.

Over and above this consideration, however, there is a real factor of efficiency present in the region's transportation expenditures. Owing to the fact that the NYMR has a higher density of residential and industrial development than other comparable regions in the United States, per capita use of energy for transportation in the region is about 72 per cent of the national level.

Within the NYMR, as well, energy efficiency varies generally with density by county. If daytime work populations as well as residential

populations are reckoned into the calculation, Manhattan presents us
with the lowest per capita consumption of any regional county. While
part of this is due to the tendency of energy-intensive manufacturers to
locate further out from the core, transportation efficiency realised by a
combination of compact settlement and the utilisation of mass transit
plays the major role.

Nevertheless, the trends in energy use are not encouraging. During
the decade 1960-70, energy consumption per capita grew by 56.8 per
cent, a rate which was almost twice as fast as the growth of person-miles
of travel. This reflects the accelerating propensity of regional residents
to use motor-cars for commutation as the regional deconcentration of
residence proceeds.

A similar tendency is revealed in the increase in industrial energy consumption of 24 per cent during the same period. This may be compared
to the 15.7 per cent increase of value added by manufacture and a 2.3
per cent decline in manufacturing employment over the same 1960-70
decade. Manufacturing industry in the region, having substituted mechanical energy for human work over the period, lost efficiency from the
standpoint of energy use, while it gained efficiency in terms of profit-
ability during an era of inexpensive energy. Today, however, confronted
by high energy costs, it is caught in a difficult squeeze as the canon of
economic efficiency is tending downward towards the lower level of
energy efficiency to which many firms became committed. This is
clearly related to the previously noted downward trend of manufacturing employment in the NYMR.

These difficulties are rendered more acute by the fact that during
1960-70, the region's utilities were shifting towards costlier and rarer
energy forms. Table 1.6 presents a regional summary.

Table 1.6: Growth of Energy Consumption by Energy Form, NYMR:
Annual Percentage Growth, 1960-70

Form	Annual % growth
Electricity	5.2
Gas (except for electricity generation)	4.4
Coal (.. .. ..)	-11.5
Transportation fuels (gasoline and kerosene)	4.0
Fuel for electricity imported into region	14.9

Source: RPA, 1974.

The shift to electricity means that to the energy losses incident upon primary fuel combustion must be added further losses as the heat thus produced is converted into electricity and transported through transmission lines — involving further line loss, to be used in an appliance which itself is often inefficient. Since the NYMR's power plants in 1970 were only 29.9 per cent efficient compared to the 32.7 per cent level prevailing in the rest of the United States, because of greater average age and technical obsolescence, the RPA estimates that only 27.6 per cent of the heat value of the fuel burned reached the consumer as electricity. Thus, 'Heat rejected by power plants now (1974) exceeds the total produced by residential fuel oil in the Region.' (RPA 1974)

At the same time, to satisfy these energy demands the region shifted from domestically available coal to imported oil and to natural gas. By 1970, about one-fifth of all oil and natural gas brought into the NYMR was devoted to the inefficient production of electricity.

Thus, over the years, the NYMR has developed towards a more energy-wasteful mode of operation from one that at the outset had the potential for energy conservation. Contributing to this was the availability of cheap petroleum-based fuels before 1975. The region shifted structurally in a number of ways:

1. Residential dispersion of affluent, largely white families contributed to single-family-housing heating-plant inefficiencies and automobile use.
2. Manufacturing plants moving to perimeter industrial parks shifted to mechanical energy and away from human labour.
3. The shift to electricity and away from the direct use of fuels imposed severe inefficiencies.
4. The shift away from coal (for environmental reasons) engendered greater regional reliance upon oil, destined to rise in price.
5. The failure of the region to upgrade the efficiency of its older fossil-fuel electricity generating plants promoted inefficiency.

It will be apparent that these trends and tendencies interlock with the other tendencies commented upon previously: the decline of the core cities, the segregation of blacks and Hispanics, the shift of durable goods manufacturing out of the NYMR, the lagging regional capital-investments in plant modernisation, and the fierce jurisdictional competition among local governments for tax rateables together with their search for the means to spill costs over into their neighbours. Since the energy pattern is related to the regional environmental quality problem, it is appropriate to discuss that next.

Environmental Quality in the NYMR

There is no question but that the physical environment of the NYMR is under substantial stress. The air receives a daily flow of pollutants from the increasingly automobile-reliant commutershed, from the numerous small heating plants serving its increasingly dispersed and de-concentrated housing pattern and from the industrial use of fuel. The waters of the region's rivers, bays, estuaries and the adjoining maritime continental shelf receive the impact of numerous domestic and industrial sewage outfalls — many technically illegal — along with hundreds of bargeloads daily of partly treated solid waste and sludge dumped into the ocean offshore from the entrance to the harbour. Most of the solid wastes in the region are dumped into marshland repositories and covered over with layers of dirt, to leach their effluents into the realms of soil and water. These sites are designated euphemistically as 'sanitary landfills'.

The key to the process of pollution prevalent in the region lies in the same kind of strategy previously noted in connection with the competition among municipalities to concentrate benefits and slough off costs externally. In this case, the potential clean-up costs of thousands of facilities are dumped into the air, water and upon the land in the form of gaseous, liquid and solid wastes. To the private firm, the benefit accrues in the form of a larger margin between revenues and costs, and the possibility of greater profit. To the municipal polluter, the benefit accrues in the form of lower tax rates in the absence of the need to invest in capital development for the purpose of treating and neutralising wastes.

A study of air quality in the NYMR by Zupan (1973) showed that the overall quality of air, which was among the worst in the United States' metropolitan regions in the 1960s, had improved somewhat by 1973. The improvement was largely in sulphur dioxide content and smokeshade, which Zupan attributes to the pattern of regional conversions to fuel with lower sulphur content. This is related to the tendencies previously noted to shift from coal and high sulphur oil as a source of energy — a shift which is now under strong economic challenge.

But the air pollution impact is not equal upon all, and thus the incentive to clean the air may vary from affected group to unaffected group.

... all analyses point to the same general conclusions. Persons of low income live in areas of poorer air quality than persons of high income. Persons of middle income also live in areas of poorer air quality than persons of high income, but not to the same degree as for the low income people. (Zupan 1973)

The controversy over NYMR energy policy is thus often cast in a framework where major polluting institutions argue that the reduction in profits arising from greater investment in clean air measures will influence them to leave the region or curtail their activities there. The lower income half of the population is thus confronted with a dilemma: the erosion of their job opportunities *v.* deleterious health effects from pollution for themselves and their families. The upper income portion of the population has less to reckon with in terms of pollution effects and a greater grasp on the levers of decision making.

Nevertheless, much regional progress has been made largely as a result of the activity of federal and state agencies. According to Parvin and Finch (1978)

Air quality in the New York region has improved tremendously in the last fifteen years (1963-1978). . . . However even with these reductions, the region's air quality is among the worst in the United States. . . . The suburban New York values [of air pollution variables] , of course are much more acceptable. . . . a relaxation of the regulations concerning the sulfur content of fuel burned in New York would make the New York sulfur dioxide levels far higher than those of other metropolitan regions.

Most recently, the public concern over the propriety of locating nuclear generation facilities in metropolitan regions and world trends in increasing low sulphur fuel prices have led precisely to a demand that these regulations be eased.

Water quality is poor and not improving. According to Mytelka and Thomson (1978) of the Interstate Sanitation Commission

Data from the [automatic water quality] monitors show that the waters of the area rarely meet the requirements for dissolved oxygen during warm weather months at some stations. These data indicate the effects of raw sewage and poorly treated municipal and industrial wastes on the receiving waters. . . . The graphs show that during the past several years, no appreciable changes have occurred in the dissolved oxygen content of the waters. Indeed, none will be apparent until some of the major secondary treatment plants that are presently under construction or being upgraded have been completed. Thus, it will not be until at least the mid-1980s that any appreciable improvement in the dissolved oxygen content of the core waters will occur.

Also contributing to the problem is the developing 'dead sea' of sewage sludge and waste barged offshore into the Atlantic, and the loads borne by the regional rivers, all of which have serious pollution problems. Of the major NYMR waterways only the upper Hudson has made significant improvement in water quality.

The amount of solid municipal wastes in the form of garbage and trash which the NYMR generates is colossal. A 1978 report of the Department of Environmental Protection of New Jersey reveals that more than 17,000 tons per day of solid wastes are generated in the NYMR portion of that state—over and above sanitary wastes (State of New Jersey 1978). Landfill operations are facing closure and the region is facing a crisis. By 1981, the federal government is committed by international treaty to the curtailment or elimination of ocean dumping (Greenberg and O'Neil 1978).

Belatedly, the region is turning to solutions which will simultaneously address the energy, pollution and employment questions. The Port Authority (1979) in a study of the possibility of the creation of 'resource recovery parks' where burnable solid wastes will be utilised to create energy while metals and other materials are recycled from the remainder, estimates that 30 per cent of the industrial energy requirements of the New York-New Jersey sub-regions can be realised in this way. Furthermore, since the most desirable sites for these activities are close to the core counties at the centre of the 'garbage-shed', employment spinoffs will benefit the unemployed workers of the old cities.

Three such parks are being planned for Brooklyn, Jersey City and Newark respectively. These would provide recovery facilities not only for basic energy and materials, but also for plants in the categories set forth in Table 1.7, which anticipate using recovered resources and energy as raw materials of production.

This sum involves the generation of payrolls amounting to $295.7 million, and would be augmented by a factor of 4,000 jobs at a payroll of $60 million for construction. This effort, although commendable, is small in relation to the overall employment problem of the region. It does, however, offer promise in relation to the goals of alleviating

Table 1.7: Projected Facility Profile: Resource Recovery Parks in Brooklyn, Newark and Jersey City, PANYNJ

Plant category	Number of plants
Food processing	6
Wood products	4
Furniture	4
Paper	9
Chemicals and plastics	8
Fabricated metal	8
Industrial electrical machinery	11
Instruments	8
Other	5
Total	63

By this means the following employment would be generated:	
On-site employment	14,825 jobs
Off-site support jobs	4,892
Induced jobs (neighbourhood effects to retailers, local merchants)	6,400
Total	26,117

Source: Port Authority, 1978.

environmental stress caused by solid waste disposal and producing energy by fuels which will substitute for imported oil.

The 700 tons per day of sewage sludge generated in the region poses as serious a problem. By the mid-1980s when projected plants are completed, the sludge output will probably rise to more than 1,500 tons per day (Greenberg and O'Neil 1978). It will no doubt become mandatory for the NYMR to develop plans for the co-disposal of dry sludge and burnable solid waste, for pyrolysis, and for composting on a large scale to deal with it. Barring the way to these options at present is the fact that many sewage treatment plants in heavily industrialised locations in the region like Newtown Creek in Brooklyn, and the Passaic Valley Plant in Newark, produce sludge with a lethal industrial chemical component, for which means of extraction must be found before recycling residues to air, water or earth.

Housing

Unlike many other advanced industrialised societies in the world, most
of the housing in the United States as a whole and the NYMR in particular is built by private sector developers for profit. Those developers
find their strongest market among the more affluent portion of the
NYMR population. Thus, suburban housing at low density has been
built throughout the region, providing for those affluent enough to
afford it, while apartment housing construction at rentals suitable for
the poorer portion of the population has languished. In theory, the
units vacated by the prosperous are supposed to 'filter down' to the
poor meeting their needs through free market mechanisms. In practice,
the filter is clogged (Carey 1976).

If a building available to filtering is structurally sound and of
basically good design it is more likely to filter up than down, as affluent
families occupy it for the purpose of rehabilitating it into an urban town-
house or cooperative. If it is in a declining state the owners, faced with
rising maintenance costs, are likely to milk it for revenue as long as
possible and ultimately abandon it.

Moreover, since many of those in need of housing are of minority-
group status in the five centres of non-white concentration, they are
excluded from the 'free market' by discriminatory real-estate practices,
as noted by the RPA study of July 1979 (*RPA News* no. 104, 1979).
Nor may they improve the housing stock where they live, since the
practice of 'redlining' is rampant there.

Financial institutions withdraw their credit-giving functions from
redlined neighbourhoods and insurance companies often follow suit.
Through an exquisite mechanism which fosters neighbourhood suicide,
however, these banks will accept deposits from the black residents of,
say, Newark, and lend them out to finance lucrative suburban developments. Thus, the thrifty Newark black may help to finance the destruction
of his own neighbourhood through the free market (Marshall 1974).

In such European countries as the United Kingdom, the Netherlands
and Sweden, where much housing is built through public sector efforts,
the growth of housing supply is often slow and painful. The citizen of,
say, Amsterdam who has a satisfactory income may chafe at the delay
on housing lists which may cost him a wait of two or more years for a
comfortable accommodation. In the United States, he might satisfy his
demand at once.

The poorer citizen of the NYMR — and many middle-income minority
citizens — may have to wait much longer than two years for decent

housing: perhaps a lifetime. As the economist John M. Quigley (1978) tells us:

> a sizeable fraction of the New York Region are simply too poor to afford decent, safe, and sanitary housing;
> the relative concentration of these households in central cities, especially New York City, is increasing;
> the relative ability of these households to purchase housing services has declined in the past decade (1968-78).

And as inflation, rising land prices, rising municipal real estate taxes, the increasing cost of credit for housing, the inability of cities to fund themselves through borrowing and the inequalities in income and wealth distribution in the regional population widen, increasing numbers of families find themselves slipping below the threshold of housing market participation. Fainstein and Fainstein (1978), in a study which compares European housing practice to that of the United States, hint that the New York City administration (like the banks) may have embarked on a bit of redlining on its own: ' . . . New York has large areas which the city government has deemed past salvation and in which it will invest no more housing funds'.

Thus, in the words of Quigley (1978) 'It should be recognized that the principal cause of inadequate housing conditions (in the NYMR) is low levels of disposable income.' Since a large and growing section of the NYMR (and the American) population is priced out of housing, it seems inescapable that a major public sector commitment must be organised. Recently, there has been some interest in the development of a National Mutual Housing Corporation, with similarities to the Western European council housing model. In introducing legislation in Congress to provide a framework for such an effort, Congressman Jonathan Bingham (1979), from a New York City district in the Bronx which is suffering greatly from the housing cost-income bind, stated:

> The principal strategies developed by the Federal Government to deal with [low and moderate income housing] problems are public housing and subsidies to private developers to build multifamily housing. Both approaches have had, at best, mixed results. Public housing has been very expensive to build, and management has often been poor and bogged down by red tape. Private developers are most interested in earning the profit from building the housing. The high cost of maintenance often results in poor management

once tenants move in. Mutual housing, a form of housing extensively developed in Western European countries and Canada, is a workable alternative to these two approaches in the United States.

It remains to be seen whether the enabling bill can be enacted against the wishes of private real-estate developers and whether, if enacted, it can be effective in a real-estate market whose prices are unregulated by effective government control and subject to regressive forms of taxation such as the property tax which, as Netzer (1974) has observed, amounts to the equivalent of a sales tax of 25 per cent or more on housing.

A Region in Need of Effective Planning

The cumulative significance of all the problems thus far discussed amounts to the description of a public sector chaos in which the absence of a mechanism for comprehensive, effective regional planning has thrown municipalities back on their own resources to survive. This has led to a competitive 'beggar-thy-neighbour' philosophy among municipalities which has been grievously exacerbated by the leakage of federal taxes out of the region. Vital needs such as housing for the low-income segment of the population, which cannot be profitably addressed by the private sector, go unmet. Perhaps the most critical example of this is the region's physical infrastructure. A study conducted by the Port Authority (1979) puts it well:

> While there has been some publicity of late, the periodic hand-wringing about the sorry state of our regional infrastructure, no problem in the region has been so systematically deferred and disregarded as this one.
> The physical infrastructure of the region—roads, bridges, sewers, water systems and public transit facilities—constitute the lifeline upon which we depend for our very survival.
> And yet, apart from the need for new infrastructure components, our existing systems are not being rebuilt. Breakdowns occur with increasing frequency. Reconstruction of these vital support systems is an absolute requirement if the region is to be economically competitive and healthy.

Yet the scale of the problem is staggering compared to the resources of the jurisdictions involved. Table 1.8 presents us with the estimates which pertain to the cities of the regional core.

Table 1.8(a): Required v. Actual Capital Expenditures for Water, Sewers and Streets in Millions of Dollars

	New York City	Newark	Jersey City	Elizabeth	Total
Average annual capital needs for next decade	$800	33	44	14	891
Average annual capital expended during past decade (not adjusted to current dollars)	90	6	4.4	1	101

(b): Required v. Recent Actual Replacement Rates for Water, Sewers, and Streets

Required replacement rates	Actual Rates			
	New York City	Newark	Jersey City	Elizabeth
Water lines (every 75 years)	250-300 yrs	300-400 yrs	400-500 yrs	300-400 yrs
Sewer lines (every 100 years)	250-300 yrs	300-400 yrs	500-600 yrs	600-800 yrs
Streets (every 40 years)	150-200 yrs	300-400 yrs	300-400 yrs	400-500 yrs

Source: Port Authority 1979.

These figures need no elaboration. When to them are added the other infrastructural needs of the New York and New Jersey sub-regions, the total problem suggests the need for a infrastructural renewal programme of $40 billion over ten years.

To address this problem alone would require the federal tax leakage to be plugged. It would also require a comprehensive planning structure for the region. At present, it does not exist.

The RPA which produces studies of great interest and considerable value is, of course, only a private nonprofit public interest organisation. The Port Authority is limited in its jurisdiction to the port area of the region. The Tri-State Planning Commission comes closest to a comprehensive planning agency, and yet it has its deficiencies.

The Federal Regional Council (of representatives from the federal agency programme operating in the NYMR) commissioned the RPA in 1975 to study Tri-State with regard to its effectiveness in implementing regional planning in the NYMR. The results of the study were not very supportive of Tri-State.

Starting with the premise that the fundamental question at stake was the question of who should decide land use for the region, it emphasised that:

> It is clear that without regional planning development patterns will not provide for public transportation, energy conservation, opportunities for all, open space preservation, an adequate housing supply, or renewed economic functions for the nation's old cities—all goals the nation professes. (RPA 1975)

Tri-State was not filling the need very well. It was pointed out that, instead of taking the initiative to seek out crucial issues to solve, it performed like a consulting firm, waiting for other agencies to bring matters to it. When matters did come before it, Tri-State made little effort to sound out public opinion through public meetings and public communications. The decisions tended to be made in closed session: thus they often proved publicly unacceptable and were shelved. The commission itself was composed of commissioners who were not only representatives from the three state governments concerned but usually also line agency heads in those states. Thus, ' . . . the Commission seems to function like a three-state confederation, with members speaking for the interests of their states or, at times, their agencies' (RPA 1975). The US Department of Health, Education and Welfare, furthermore, argues that comprehensive planning agencies should undertake social planning in conjunction with land use plans. It was felt by several persons interviewed by RPA that Tri-State does not consider social problems adequately.

Thus, for Tri-State to move towards the goal of becoming an effective regional planning agency it would have to shoulder the burden of public presentation and participation in decision making through the creation of a strong communications arm. A revision of the commission's structure away from state house and state agency domination is also indicated. Furthermore, an aggressive policy of identifying and proposing solutions for problems and campaigning for their acceptance and implementation is indicated—with due consideration of social issues and equity. Obviously for this to occur a major budgetary commitment should be forthcoming, along with a mechanism for funding plans which are accepted.

In contrast, the present mood of the nation is towards parsimony in government, towards budget cutting and towards local autonomy rather than regional planning. If these trends operate strongly within the NYMR the type of process which has contributed to the present crisis will continue, in all probability deepening it.

The American economy is known worldwide for its propensity to consume a disproportionate share of the world's materials and energy. One of its most pervasive contributions to material life has been the disposable food or beverage container. Perhaps the old core cities of the NYMR are to become pioneering examples of the city as a disposable cultural container. Or else the container is to be emptied of its contents in the form of the lower-income fraction of the population – who will scatter to poverty pockets elsewhere – and be recycled for the benefit of the more affluent. It does not seem likely that a major regional planning effort intended to address all of the economic, technical and social needs set forth in this chapter will be forthcoming.

References

Albion, R.G. (1970) *The Rise of New York Port*, Scribners, New York

Bergman, E.F. and T.W. Pohl (1975) *A Geography of the New York Metropolitan Region*, Kendall/Hunt Co., Dubuque, Iowa

Bingham, J. Member of Congress (2 Aug. 1979) 'A National Mutual Housing Corporation', *The Congressional Record of the United States: House of Representatives*, H 7166- H 7168, Washington, DC

Carey, G.W. (1976) *New York/New Jersey, a Vignette of the Metropolitan Region*, Ballinger, Cambridge, Mass.

—— and M. Greenberg (1974) 'Towards a Geographical Theory of Hypocritical Decision Making', *Human Ecology 2(4)*, 243-57

Fainstein, S.F. and N.I. Fainstein (1978) 'National Policy and Urban Development', *Social Problems, 36(2)*, 125-46

Gottman, J. (1961) *Megalopolis*, MIT Press, Cambridge, Mass.

Greenberg, M. and T.F. O'Neil (1978) 'Solid Waste: The End of the Bottomless Pit', *New York Affairs, 5(2)*, 114-29

Hall, P. (1966) *The World Cities*, World University Library, New York

Hardin, G. (1968) 'The Tragedy of the Commons', *Science, 162*, 1243-8

Holden, M. Jr. (1964) 'The Governance of the Metropolis as a Problem in Diplomacy', *The Journal of Politics, XXVI(3)*, 627-47

Hughes, J. (1974) 'Realtors, Bankers and Politicians', *Society, 11(4)*, 63-70

Marshall, R.D. (1974) 'The Flight of the Thrift Institution: One More Invitation to Inner-City Disaster', *Rutgers Law Review, 28(1)*, 113-25

Mytelka, A.I. and R. Thomson (1978) 'Water Quality: Floundering About', *New York Affairs, 5(2)*, 130-7

Netzer, D. (1974) *Economics and Urban Problems*, Basic Books, New York
Parvin, M. and S.J. Finch (1978) 'Air Quality: A Policy Model', *New York Affairs,*
    5(2), 138-50
Piven, F.F. (1972) 'Whom Does the Advocate Planner Serve?' in S.S. Fainstein and
    N.I. Fainstein (eds.); *The View From Below; Urban Politics and Social Policy*,
    Little, Brown and Co., Boston, pp. 228-33
Port Authority of New York and New Jersey, (1978) *Industrial Revitalization in
    the New York and New Jersey Region*, New York
Port Authority of New York and New Jersey, (1979) *Regional Recovery: the
    Business of the Eighties*, New York
Quigley, J.M. (1978) 'Housing: Providing Appropriate Incentives', *New York
    Affairs, 5(2)*, 91-103
Regional Plan Association, (1928) *Regional Survey of New York and Its Environs*,
    8 volumes, R.M. Haig and R.C. McCrea (eds.), New York:
    1, *Major Economic Factors in Metropolitan Growth and Arrangement*
    2, *Population, Land Values and Government*
    3, *Highway Traffic*
    4, *Transit and Transportation—Including a Study of Port and Industrial Areas*
    5, *Public Recreation*
    6, *Buildings*
    7, *Planning and Development of Land*
    8, *Public Services and Miscellaneous*
—— (1975) *Implementing Regional Planning in the Tri-State New York Region*,
    New York
—— (1977) *The Region's Money Flows (1), Government Accounts*, New York
—— (1979) *The Region's Money Flows (2), Business Accounts*, New York
Regional Plan Association and the Graduate School of Public Administration,
    Harvard University (1959-61) *The New York Metropolitan Regional Study*, 9
    volumes, Harvard University Press, Cambridge, Mass:
    1, E.M. Hoover and R. Vernon, *Anatomy of a Metropolis*
    2, M. Hall, R.B. Helfgott, W.E. Gustafson and J.M. Hund, *Made in New York*
    3, O. Handlin, *The Newcomers*
    4, M. Segal, *Wages in the Metropolis*
    5, S.M. Robbins and N. Terleckyj, *Money Metropolis*
    6, B. Chinitz, *Freight and the Metropolis*
    7, R.M. Lichtenberg, *One Tenth of a Nation*
    8, R.C. Wood, *1400 Governments*
    9, R. Vernon, *Metropolis, 1985*
Regional Plan Association and Resources for the Future, (1974) *Regional Energy
    Consumption*, New York
Regional Plan Association News, No. 101 (1977) 'The State of the Region, 1977'
—— No. 104 (1979) 'Segregation and Opportunity in the Region's Housing'
—— No. 105 (1979) 'New Cities'
Rose, J.G. and S.R. Kaplan (1978) 'Which Rural Municipalities (if Any) Have to
    Provide a Fair Share of Regional Housing Needs?' *New Jersey Municipalities*,
    pp. 12-15
Rosenwaike, I. (1972) *Population History of New York City*, Syracuse University
    Press, Syracuse, NY
State of New Jersey Department of Energy, (1978) Preliminary Policy Statement,
    Solid Waste: Its Energy Conservation and Production Potential, Trenton, NJ
Zupan, J.M. (1973) *The Distribution of Air Quality in the New York Region*,
    Resources for the Future, Johns Hopkins Univ. Press, Baltimore, Md.

2 MELBOURNE

P.W. Newton and R.J. Johnston

Australia has only a few large cities, of which the five mainland state capitals are dominant in terms of both population size (containing 60 per cent of the nation's 14 million inhabitants) and economic power (and probably political power too, although the seat of the federal government is at a smaller, inland city—Canberra). These five cities share a number of major characteristics, including their origins as seaport capitals of independent colonies, their lack of heavy industry, large tracts of low density suburbia, and a fragmented local government structure. Although this essay concentrates on one of the cities, the general patterns and problems to be discussed are typical of them all (Logan *et al.* 1975).

Melbourne was founded in 1835 by pastoralists from Tasmania. Nineteen years later, by which time it was the capital of the colony of Victoria, its population was recorded by the first Australian census as a little over 70,000. By the late 1930s it had more than one million inhabitants, and this total had doubled by the mid 1960s. The latest population census, in 1976, gave the Melbourne Statistical Division (Figure 2.1) a population of 2.6 million, in an area of some 6,110 square kilometres. Melbourne's growth has been extremely rapid; in the context of the State of Victoria as a whole it has been phenomenal. Table 2.1 depicts the state's settlement history and indicates how, in size at least, Melbourne has dominated the state since its foundation. It now contains some 70 per cent of the population compared to its nearest rival, Geelong, which only has 3.5 per cent. During the twentieth century there has been no challenge at all to Melbourne's hegemony within Victoria, and for the first three decades it was also the capital of the fledgling Commonwealth of Australia.

The Pattern of Melbourne

The original settlement of Melbourne (now the city's Central Business District) was on the northern banks of the Yarra River, some seven kilometres inland from its mouth in Port Phillip Bay. The Yarra here marks a major physical boundary. To the north and west are the edges

71

Figure 2.1: Melbourne: Built-up Area and Administrative Divisions

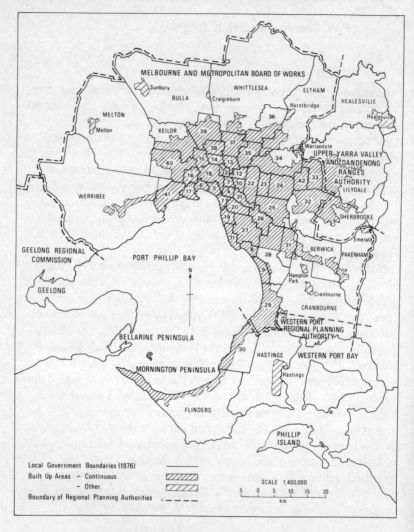

1. Fitzroy 2. Collingwood 3. Richmond 4. Prahran 5. South Melbourne 6. Port Melbourne 7. St Kilda 8. Mordialloc 9. Chelsea 10. Hawthorn 11. Sandringham 12. Kew 13. Northcote 14. Brunswick 15. Essendon 16. Footscray 17. Williamstown 18. Melbourne 19. Brighton 20. Caulfield 21. Malvern 22. Camberwell 23.Boxhill 24. Nunawading 25. Waverley 26. Oakleigh 27. Moorabbin 28. Springvale 29. Frankston 30. Mornington 31. Dandenong 32. Knox 33. Croydon 34. Doncaster and Templestowe 35. Heidelberg 36. Diamond Valley 37. Preston 38. Coburg 39. Broadmeadows 40. Sunshine 41. Altona 42. Ringwood

Table 2.1: Distribution of Victorian Towns by Size Categories, 1841-1976

	1000-1999	2000-4999	5000-9999	10,000-19,999	20,000-49,999	50,000-149,999	>150,000	Population of Victoria ('000)	Population of Melbourne ('000)
1841		1						20	4
1846	1			1				38	12
1851	2			1	1			97	23
1854	9	2	1	1	1	1		284	77
1857	11	6	2	1	1	1		457	110
1861	15	10		2	2	1		540	140
1871	30	14	3	3	3		1	746	216
1881	27	15	3	3	3		1	874	288
1891	31	18	3	3	3		1	1158	487
1901	36	22	4	3	3		1	1210	502
1911	64	32	5	3	3		1	1340	612
1921	67	36	8	3	3		1	1551	801
1933	69	36	12	2	3		1	1824	996
1947	61	46	13	2	3		1	2063	1228
1954	63	43	21	4	2	1	1	2478	1524
1961	63	46	19	8	1	2	1	2955	1984
1966	42	34	14	8	2	2	1	3250	2231
1971	38	34	13	10	2	2	1	3536	2503
1976	37	36	14	9	2	3	1	3746	2604

Source: Urlich Cloher (1979) for the period 1841-91; various census publications for the period 1901-76.

of a flat basalt plain; to the south and east is undulating hill country across which suburbia has spread for some 50 kilometres to the south and 40 to the east.

Melbourne's morphology is typical of the urban patterns which developed in the British settler colonies of Australasia and North America. The inhabitants came from a densely-peopled, closely-settled land run by a strictly hierarchical society in which access to property was very restricted. They encountered a new environment in which land was plentiful, an economic situation which made that land relatively cheap, and an evolving social system in which land ownership was encouraged for all. Out of these interacting forces developed an urban population characterised by a desire for low density living, in homes which they built for themselves (literally in many cases) on land they were able to buy. The land survey process laid out suburban plots and 'the cult of the quarter acre section' emerged ('section' being the local term for an individual building plot).

Initial expansion of the urban area was hindered by relative immobility and the residential districts which developed in Melbourne's first few decades were of fairly high density. Nevertheless, the affluent had both the time and the money to afford low density suburban living and the associated commuting, and they soon established themselves in large mansions, with accompanying grounds, on the slopes of South Yarra, Prahran and Toorak to the south of the Yarra. Parts of this area, even some of its original homes, still form the core of Melbourne's most exclusive residential districts (Johnston 1966). The lower income residents were confined to higher density developments, mainly to the north and east of the city centre, but here the townscape that was built up was very different from that being developed contemporaneously in Britain (Johnston 1968a; 1969). There were no large estates of standard terraced homes created by single developers; rather housing was built by small firms in small blocks, often of only two or three homes, and most of the terraces are mixtures of styles and dates.

Spatial segregation of social groups was established early in Melbourne, therefore, and was clearly reflected in the townscape. The nature of the segregation was to remain, but as the city grew the townscape was markedly transformed. The main stimulus to this change was development in the transport system, which allowed a large segment of the population to aspire to a detached home (usually a bungalow) on a relatively cheap quarter-acre section. Initially the expanding form of the metropolitan area was established by the tentacle-like extensions of the suburban railway system in the late nineteenth century (Johnston 1968b);

some very early railway construction allowed the establishment of independent suburbs on the coast south of the city proper. In the early twentieth century this railway network was complemented by a tramway system (still in operation) that allowed the infilling of areas between the tentacles. And then came the major impetus to suburban sprawl, the motor car. By 1932 there was about one car to every ten Melbournians; today the ratio exceeds four cars per ten persons, and household access to cars is very high (in 1976 only 17 per cent of Melbourne households had no access to a motor vehicle).[1]

The conclusion of World War II was to herald the beginning of a 25-year period of sustained urban growth unmatched in Melbourne's preceding 30 years: a doubling of the city's population to 2.5 million by 1971, covering an area twice that of London. A combination of inter-related factors was responsible for this development. There was a continued expansion of industry behind a tariff wall under a policy which saw the development of manufacturing as heavily tied to a local market. This is a process which, up to a point, produces its own momentum: the markets become manufacturing centres which in turn become bigger markets and so on (Brennan 1967)—the incentive for new industries to locate in the major cities, close to labour and markets, is strong. And the incentive to expand production and develop new lines of manufacture existed in order to satisfy the demand which followed a low level of consumer-oriented production during the war years.

The decision of state and federal governments in 1946 to embark on a large scale immigration programme reflected the need for an expanded workforce and a larger home market for locally produced goods, as well as a humanitarian response to individuals and families seeking resettlement from war-torn Europe. In 1947 125,000 persons, 9 per cent of Melbourne's population, were born overseas. By 1976 the overseas-born figure had reached 700,000 persons or 27 per cent of the population (almost 50 per cent of Melbournians were either born overseas or had at least one parent born overseas). Major birthplaces of the non-Australian born in 1976 were the United Kingdom and the Republic of Ireland 216,000, Italy 103,000, Greece 73,000, Yugoslavia 49,000, Germany 28,000, the Netherlands 21,000 and Poland 20,000. The inner city was the initial reception area for most migrants, but in like manner to other Australian cities (Galvin 1974) it is the southern European groups (Greek, Italian, Yugoslav) which are most heavily concentrated in Melbourne's inner residential areas. The British-born are more evenly distributed throughout the city reflecting their closer cultural affinity

with the host community, their higher level of occupational status and
greater ease of operating within the housing market (their tendency to
settle in newly-developed suburbs closely follows the pattern of the
host society). Settlement in outer suburbia, especially the outer
industrial suburbs, has been common among German, Polish and Dutch
migrants; and it is not uncommon for smaller communities of southern
Europeans to locate in the industrial suburbs also. The locational
pattern of all foreign-born residents of Melbourne (Figure 2.2) reveals a

Figure 2.2: Distribution of Foreign-born Population, 1976

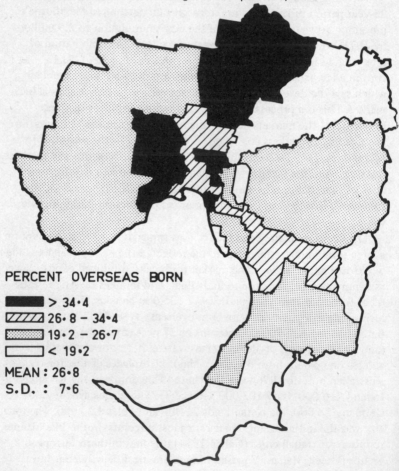

PERCENT OVERSEAS BORN

■■■ > 34·4
▨▨▨ 26· 8 – 34·4
▒▒▒ 19·2 – 26·7
☐ < 19·2

MEAN : 26·8
S.D. : 7·6

concentration of migrants in the central city. In addition, many of them have conformed to the Australian ethos of home ownership and have joined the suburban legions (note the extensions into the relatively low-status suburbs south-east into Oakleigh, Springvale and Dandenong, northwards through Preston into Whittlesea, and westwards to Werribee).

The socio-spatial pattern of Melbourne can be divided, in simplest terms, into the relatively affluent areas of the southern and eastern sectors, including the shores of Port Phillip Bay, and the working class northern and western sectors on the relatively flat, unattractive and tree-less basalt plains. This is confirmed by income and occupational data for 1976 (Figures 2.3a and b), which also highlight the continued high status of those early suburbs south and east of the city centre.

The generalisation in the previous paragraph is an oversimplification, especially with regard to the southern and eastern sectors, which contain major pockets of lower status populations. Many of these are associated with the development of suburban industrial areas along the main railway and highway routes leading out of the city; there are, for example, major nodes in the cities of Dandenong, Waverley, Oakleigh and Springvale on the south-eastern edge of the built-up area which include many large machinery and vehicle factories. Because industrial-isation came relatively late to Melbourne, the pattern of factory employment is dispersed and there is a relative lack of large, inner city plants. Much of the major industry is associated with the port, and is concentrated in Port Melbourne and in Footscray, Williamstown and Altona to the west of the estuary. Many small firms, especially in the traditional industries (clothing, jewellery, printing etc.) are concentrated in and around the city centre, but others can be found in most municipalities (Rimmer 1969).

The suburban spread of industry and the relative decline of the inner areas in the provision of jobs have been more than matched by the con-current decentralisation of retailing (Johnston and Rimmer 1969). Melbourne's Central Business District (CBD) has been in relative decline for many decades, with the development of suburban shopping centres to meet the local inhabitants' daily and weekly needs (Table 2.2). But in recent decades it has been in absolute decline too, as its department and speciality stores face competition from the newly-established region-al shopping centres in the suburbs which provide easy access by car and a pleasant atmosphere for shopping. The first of these centres was estab-lished in the south-eastern suburbs in 1960, alongside a major highway; there are now twelve such centres within the metropolitan area.

The system of housing provision in Australia is achieved primarily

Figure 2.3a: Distribution of Professional Workers, 1976

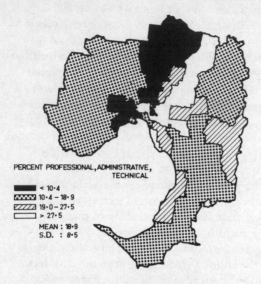

PERCENT PROFESSIONAL, ADMINISTRATIVE, TECHNICAL

- ■ < 10·4
- 10·4 – 18·9
- 19·0 – 27·5
- □ > 27·5

MEAN : 18·9
S.D. : 8·5

b: Income Distribution by Local Government Area, 1971

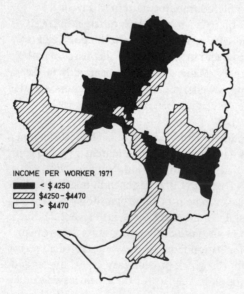

INCOME PER WORKER 1971

- ■ < $ 4250
- $4250 – $4470
- □ > $4470

Table 2.2: Pattern of Retail Development, Melbourne: 1968/9-1973/4

		Establishments		Employment						Wages		Retail Sales	
				Males		Females		Persons		Value		Value	
		N	%MSD	N	%MSD	N	%MSD	N	%MSD	($'000)	%MSD	($'000)	%MSD
CBD[a]	1968/69	1,917	6.3	12,415	12.9	17,239	19.4	29,654	16.0	70,242	22.4	345,178	14.5
	1973/4	1,651	5.7	10,017	10.4	15,185	15.9	25,202	13.1	100,526	19.1	435,871	11.3
Remainder of inner city[b]	1968/9	6,059	20.1	21,054	21.9	15,349	17.2	36,403	19.7	63,135	20.1	413,205	17.3
	1973/4	5,381	18.5	18,570	19.3	13,958	14.6	32,528	16.9	93,700	17.8	572,680	14.9
Middle suburbs[c]	1968/9	17,509	58.1	49,100	51.1	44,179	49.7	93,279	50.4	142,637	45.4	1,267,741	53.2
	1973/4	16,455	56.5	49,738	51.7	48,222	50.3	97,960	51.0	243,312	46.1	2,046,457	53.3
Outer suburbs[d]	1968/9	4,669	15.5	13,577	14.1	12,183	13.7	25,760	13.9	37,870	12.1	357,614	15.0
	1973/4	5,613	19.3	17,876	18.6	18,438	19.2	36,314	18.9	89,561	17.0	785,893	20.5

Note: a. Defined as bounded by Flinders, Spring, LaTrobe and Spencer Streets.
b. Includes remainder of the City of Melbourne not included in CBD, plus the municipalities of Collingwood, Fitzroy, Prahran, Richmond, St. Kilda, South Melbourne, Port Melbourne.
c. Includes the following 26 municipalities: Altona, Box Hill, Brighton, Broadmeadows, Brunswick, Camberwell, Caulfield Coburg, Doncaster and Templestowe, Essendon, Footscray, Hawthorn, Heidelberg, Keilor, Kew, Malvern, Moorabbin, Mordialloc, Northcote, Nunawading, Oakleigh, Preston, Sandringham, Sunshine, Waverley, Williamstown.
d. Includes the remaining 22 municipalities within the Melbourne Statistical Division (MSD).
Source: Australian Bureau of Statistics: Census of Retail Establishments and Selected Service Establishments 1968/9, 1973/4.

within the private sector which has been progressively increasing its share of the Victorian market from 80 per cent of new dwellings constructed in 1956 to 90 per cent in 1975. Currently the Housing Commission of Victoria is accommodating close to 350,000 people (9 per cent of the state's population) in public housing; its programme has, since 1938, been designed to provide low rental accommodation for families on limited incomes and pensioners who formerly had to live in the sub-standard dwellings of depressed areas.[2] For the early part of its history, the Housing Commission concentrated on building houses. There was a reversion of this policy in the 1960s during which time a dozen blocks of forty-storey family flats were erected as part of an urban renewal programme in the inner city suburbs. These developments have sub-sequently attracted a good deal of criticism, dealing with their inappropriateness for families with children and the difficulty in providing adequate levels of social infrastructure for such population densities, their complete displacement of existing neighbourhood communities, and their plain ugliness (Stretton 1971). Subsequent con-struction has reverted to the detached house and a variety of medium density residential developments — dwelling forms more closely aligned with the overall metropolitan residential pattern, where low density owner-occupied suburban housing is extensive with three-quarters of all dwellings being detached; 23 per cent are medium density flats or units.

Prior to 1960, 90 per cent of new dwellings constructed within Melbourne each year were detached single family structures. This figure declined to 57 per cent per annum in 1969 but has now risen to over 70 per cent, and only 2 per cent of current developments exceed 3 storeys in height. The flat boom of the 1960s and early 1970s was for the most part an inner suburban phenomenon. In response to the maturation of the baby boom generation of the immediate post-World War II period, the increased potential for new household formation was realised with the tendency for the majority of young people to leave their parents' home. This was also a period of rising real incomes, per-mitting a greater degree of economic independence for younger (as well as elderly) people; a period when levels of overseas immigration reached a peak; and a period when the organisation of family life (divorce, re-marriage, solo-parenting, working couples), and its concomitant stimulus as an agent in new household formation, was undergoing transformation. Since that time, as inner areas have become more highly developed, suit-able land less readily available, and the requirements of local councils more stringent, the trend was altered to building groups of single storey villa units in less central locations.[3]

In common with trends in other Western industrial countries the price of land, housing and related services has experienced significant inflation since the mid 1960s (see Table 2.3), a response, in part, to the demand forces outlined above. The pattern of change within Melbourne has been even more dramatic, as results from the National Committee of Inquiry into Housing Costs (1978) reveal. In 1970/1 the average house/land package cost $A14,200; this had increased to $41,300 by 1977/8. The proportional increase in the cost of new housing lagged behind increases in average annual earnings from 1966/7 to 1971/2, but between 1971/2 and 1976/7 housing cost increases outpaced rising incomes, with important implications for levels of home-ownership (the period 1971/6 saw a decline in levels of home-ownership, both nationally and in Melbourne).

Table 2.3: Trends in Housing and Economic Indicators (Melbourne)

Indicator	% increase	
	1966-7/1971-2	1971-2/1976-7
Wholesale price of materials used in building	19	88
Average annual earnings	46	104
Average value of new houses	31	130
CPI	20	81

Source: National Committee of Inquiry into Housing Costs (1978).

Of greater significance, perhaps, has been the recent emergence of a trend which could be the first indication of a major redistribution of population within Australia's major urban areas. This trend concerns changes in the price of land at centre and periphery. The gradient of land prices with distance from the CBD is well established and holds for Melbourne (Figure 2.4a). However Figure 2.4b shows that outer suburban land prices were rising faster than inner city land prices between 1972 and 1976, followed by a reversal in 1976/7. Falling transport costs over the 1960-76 period contributed to increases in outer suburban land prices (Sharpe 1980), but the reverse trend set by 1977 land prices is likely to be maintained under the recent rise in transport costs. A considerable proportion of recent investment by life insurance groups has been in CBD properties, principally office development (Kilmartin and Thorns 1978a); and there has been considerable speculative activity in inner city residential properties since the early 1970s. Because inner city

Figure 2.4a: Vacant Residential Land Price in Melbourne (least squares regression significant at 1% level)

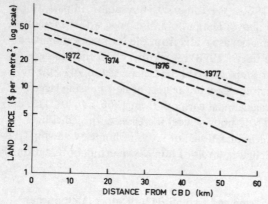

b: Rates of Change of Vacant Residential Land Price

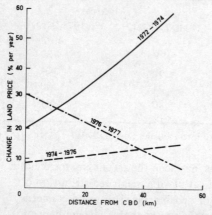

property had been undervalued in the post-World War II 'suburbanisation' years, the boom in house sales which began in Melbourne in 1973 had its greatest impact on inner city prices (Howe 1979). Yet during this time, it has been a policy of the state government to assist home buyers by developing land (and for public tenants, housing estates) at the metropolitan fringe where land is cheap. Such a policy could place a burden on future homeowners (and tenants) if the savings made on land are quickly eroded by higher transport costs generated by future petrol increases, the latter being a current federal government policy.

One final aspect of Melbourne's geography requiring comment here concerns its political organisation. The city of Melbourne itself is but a small part of the metropolitan areas defined for statistical and other purposes (31 square kilometres out of 6,110) and in 1976 it housed only 65,000 residents, 2.5 per cent of the metropolitan total. Several of the districts which are now suburbs within the metropolitan area were formerly separate settlements, such as the port at Williamstown, the market town at Dandenong, and the seaside 'resort' at Brighton. Not surprisingly, these acquired separate municipal status early in their history and have resisted any efforts to remove it. But it was not only these separate early settlements which acquired independent municipal status within the network of shires which formed the basic unit of local government in rural Victoria. As the built-up area expanded so the residents of the suburban integuments petitioned for independent municipal status, which was usually granted. Thus the metropolitan area today comprises 56 separate territorial authorities (see Figure 2.1), including 42 cities.

Planning Melbourne

At the federal level, the decades since World War II have been characterised by a political environment largely antagonistic to the concepts of detailed economic and spatial planning, producing a general belief that the country's morphology should be determined by the largely unfettered operation of free-market forces. This ethos has been even stronger in the relatively conservative State of Victoria so that, for example, planning for Melbourne was advanced later than that for Sydney (for which the County of Cumberland Plan was produced in 1948). Nevertheless, a large and sprawling city must be organised, at least for the provision of basic public utilities such as transport, water and sewage disposal systems. Thus the Melbourne and Metropolitan Board of Works (MMBW) was empowered in 1949 to produce a plan for the metropolitan area, which it did in 1954 and again in 1971.

Despite the general antagonism to planning in state political circles, therefore, it has been found necessary to plan for Melbourne in a variety of ways. (Indeed, there are over 35 separate state government bodies concerned with some aspect of the urban environment: Kilmartin and Thorns 1978b). There are now some 17,000 persons employed in local government within the metropolitan area. Their tasks are largely those of integrating the vast urban complex and providing a liveable environment. Five inter-related problem areas can be identified.

1. The Organisation of Planning

a) *Federal Government Relations.* Government involvement in urban affairs occurs principally at state level within Australia, the prime reason being that under the Australian federation it is the states that have the control of land and therefore of land use planning, as well as of local government (Logan 1979). An equally significant reason has been a dominance of federal politics by a coalition of the Liberal and Country Parties (L-CP), which bring to bear a combination of *laissez-faire* and neo-capitalist philosophies on the subjects of national, regional and urban development. In the three decades since 1950, for example, these parties (or government coalitions) have held office for 27 years; the three-year gap (1972-75) represents an interregnum when the Labor Party briefly held power (Wilmoth *et al.* 1976).

Between 1950 and 1972 federal L-CP governments held firmly to the views that planning in general represented unwarranted interference with market forces (Newton 1980), and metropolitan planning was not a concern for a federal government. This is not to say that federal policies had no effect on urban areas. On the contrary, the federal immigration programme resulted in large numbers of immigrants settling in Australia's metropolitan areas, particularly during the later 1960s. It was in this period of rapid change that state governments were required to take the initiative for directing development — and it came largely in the form of plans for accommodating metropolitan growth in the primate cities (rather than channelling growth to the smaller cities and towns).

The first direct incursion into urban affairs by federal government came in 1972 when the L-CP government set up (as a pre-election counter to Opposition initiatives: Whitlam 1971; 1972) the National Urban and Regional Development Authority (NURDA). This organisation was intended to advise on the formulation of urban and regional development policies. However, NURDA was shortlived and was replaced by a new Ministry and Department of Urban and Regional Development (DURD) when the Labor Party took office early in the following year.

Labor's new Department of Urban and Regional Development introduced a range of programmes, providing funds to the states to redress what they believed to be specific metropolitan problems:

1. the need to connect many of the more than 25 per cent of
   Melbourne households currently without any connection to

      mains sewerage (over 25 million dollars of federal funds was allocated for this task in 1975);

2. the need to decentralise tertiary employment from central city concentrations (a first step was to have been the relocation of several federal offices to certain of Melbourne's outer suburbs, e.g. Ringwood);

3. the need to stabilise land prices (government organisation and development of land, tied to particular locations, was seen to have the dual benefits of dampening land costs and redirecting growth);

4. the need to improve the quality of housing in inner city areas (the inner city programmes were primarily concerned with rehabilitation — in contrast to state government renewal programmes of the preceding decade — and aimed at preserving and enhancing existing communities).

In addition to these programmes there was a broader regional strategy concerned with directing future metropolitan growth away from the primate cities to selected cities and towns in the middle (and largely vacant) tier of the nation's urban hierarchy, the reasoning being that

> the rapid growth rates of Sydney and Melbourne were seen as causing inequalities amongst some community groups and inefficiencies in the allocation of national resources. Thus the slowing down of these growth rates became one of the major policies for achieving a national redistribution of population. (MMBW 1977a, p. 77)

The border towns of Albury-Wodonga were selected as Victoria's first growth centre.[4] (Albury is in NSW, across the River Murray from Wodonga.) A target population of 300,000 by the year 2000 was adopted (the 1971 population was 56,000, Wodonga's share being 11,000). A Development Corporation was established as a statutory authority to plan and develop the areas designated for growth (a principal function being to acquire, hold, manage, and provide land in areas designated for development). Growth was to be stimulated by relocating government departments and offices from the central areas of capital cities. By 1976, Wodonga's population was 14,000. A major setback has been federal government's withdrawal (since the defeat of the Labor Party in December 1975) from active participation in urban and regional planning and development.[5] Sharp cuts have been made to the growth centres programme and to the urban projects financed by the federal Labor government under the L-CP's 'new federalism' policy whereby the Australian government returns the responsibility for urban and regional development to the states. Unlike the situation under the Labor government (1972-75), when purpose-specific grants were used to advance redistributive policies, federal grants to the states are now no longer tied to specific projects.

b) State Government Relations. The structure of political power in a city is a fundamental determinant of resource allocation between suburban localities. In Australia the consensus is (see Bowman 1978) that local government is state government writ small, performing functions (at community level) which the state parliament has decided shall be provided (local government functions in Victoria encompass suburban road construction and maintenance, drainage, sanitation, certain recreational facilities, a limited range of welfare services, and town planning; all are financed in part by levying rates on property). State government, in contrast, is involved in the provision of health facilities (principally hospitals), public housing, utilities, public transport, education, and fire and police services. In all, over 40 state government agencies are involved in the provision of services to any one local government authority in the Melbourne metropolitan area. Co-ordination of this plethora of agencies, and a range of additional statutory authorities (e.g. West Gate Bridge Authority, Metropolitan Fire Brigades Board, Melbourne and Metropolitan Tramways Board, Melbourne Harbour Trust, Melbourne Underground Rail Loop Authority) presents a major problem in metropolitan governance. Figure 2.5, which shows the responsibility structure of one of these bodies, the Port Phillip Authority, clearly demonstrates the complexity of relations which exist within most state government agencies.

How services and facilities are allocated by the state among residential communities within the metropolitan area determines, to a significant extent, the relative levels of welfare or illfare which can be expected to accrue to residents by virtue of their relative access to (or lack of) facilities. There are several commentators who suggest that the power structure at state level and the spatial pattern of electoral representation among government (as contrasted with opposition) parliamentarians provides an important indicator to who gets what, where. In terms of electoral representation, the grip of social class on Melbourne's voting pattern is striking. Comparison of suburb socio-economic status (Figure 2.3) with Labor or Liberal-held electorates (Figure 2.6) reveals that the

Figure 2.5: Responsibility Structure for the Port Phillip Bay Authority

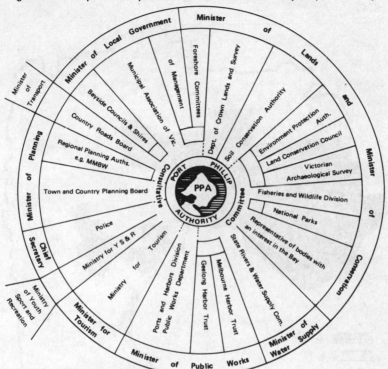

city's voters divide fairly simply: Labor votes are concentrated heavily in the inner city zone and suburban areas immediately west and north of the CBD. At the most recent (1979) election there has been an incursion of Labor support into the newer working class and outer industrial suburbs to the south-east: Oakleigh, Springvale and Dandenong. Liberal supporters congregate in the traditionally upper and middle class suburbs east of the Yarra river, extending outward to the newer middle class suburbs in the east and south.

The Victorian Liberal Party, like their federal counterparts, have enjoyed considerable political success (often with the assistance of a CP coalition), holding office continuously since 1955. The pattern of post-World War II development in Melbourne is therefore in large measure a product of the locational decisions made by this one political party in response to its perception of the role of the state in promoting a particular form of urban economic development — and in response to its acknowledged locus of electoral support within the metropolitan

Figure 2.6: Melbourne's Political Configuration at State Level Elections, 1979

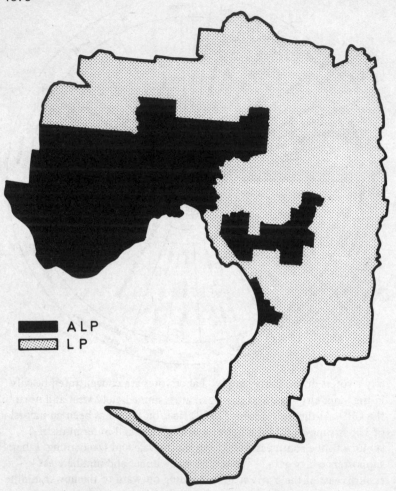

area (Table 2.4). Locational bias is revealed in a number of instances. One case concerns tertiary institutions where, taking the CBD as a focus for dividing the east of the city from the west, all three universities lie to the east as do 11 of the 13 state colleges of advanced education. Noxious land uses are predominantly west of centre: Melbourne's international airport, the city's two power stations, a majority of the city's chemical plants, the major sewerage farm (which treats 165,000 megalitres — or 70 per cent — of metropolitan sewerage, which is subsequently

Table 2.4: Structure of the Victorian Parliament, 1979

	Location of Member's Constituency								
	Melbourne			Remainder of State			State		
	ALP	LP	NPa	ALP	LP	NP	ALP	LP	NP
Legislative Councilb	12	16	0	1	11	4	13	27	4
Legislative Assembly	29	26	0	3	15	8	32	41	8

Notes: a. ALP—Australian Labor Party
         LP — Liberal Party
         NP — National (formerly Country) Party
b. The Legislative Council (upper house) is essentially a house of review for the Assembly. It is the Legislative Assembly which holds power to originate money bills. Both houses are elected on the basis of universal adult franchise with preferential voting; however, MLAs are elected for 3 years whereas MLCs can hold office for 6.
Source: Victoria, 48th Parliament, Members of the Legislative Council, 8 November 1979. Victoria, 48th Parliament, Members of the Legislative Assembly, 20th February 1980.

discharged, after treatment, into Port Phillip Bay) — and this is a region housing over a quarter of Melbourne's residents, many of whom have no option but to accept the negative externalities associated with the area. The acquiescence of working class and migrant residents to such developments in the 1950s and early 1960s has changed over the last decade and a half, with major corporations and state government being made aware of the importance that the public attaches to the maintenance of a quality of environment. The 'green bans' movement was a uniquely Australian phenomenon which involved combined action on the part of the Builders Labourers Federation—who imposed work bans—and conservation and resident groups to halt action on urban development projects which threatened certain residential communities, historic buildings, parkland and so forth (see Hardman and Manning 1976).[6]

More numerous but less well organised than the management and labour groups are consumer and resident groups which began to appear in the early 1960s in response to a growing dissatisfaction with the planning philosophies and public participation provisions associated with all levels of government and a call for greater citizen involvement in metropolitan decision-making. Of these, the local Residents' Associations committed to the protection of inner suburban areas have been particularly active (for example the Carlton Association, formed in 1969 to counter the 'bulldozer' approach to inner city renewal of large urban institutions such as the State Housing Commission: see Holmes 1976).

c) *Local Government Relations.* With its 56 local councils ranging in
population from 9,600 (Port Melbourne) to 120,000 (Waverley),
Melbourne has become the nation's giant in terms of the number of
governmental units within a metropolitan area.[7] This pattern of
fragmentation is common to North American cities (Mercer 1979) where,
it is argued, local autonomy is highly valued and entrenched — a reflection
of the strength of privatism as a basic value in the society. The desire for
control of local territory by the resident population has been inherent
in the creation of local government areas in Australia:

> For the most part the initiative for incorporation of local govern-
> ments in Australia was left with the private citizens . . . the Australian
> States have . . . not presided over the establishment of units of local
> government . . . nor established regulations which introduce change
> when, as has happened in every metropolitan area in Australia, units
> grow together or surround other units. (Leach 1977)

The failure to make arrangements for city-level government has meant
that area-wide problems (e.g. conflict between inner city and outer suburban residents over freeway construction, class-based exclusionary
zoning which sees the virtual exclusion of industrial land from a band
of several eastern municipalities extending out as far as Ringwood
(MMBW 1971)) in some instances cannot satisfactorily be approached,
let alone be solved.

To some extent the needs of an area larger than that encompassed
by a single municipality are met by arrangements made between two or
more councils for the joint provision of services — some of the most
common involve library services, boundary road maintenance, garbage
disposal, water supply and parks. These represent rather minor aspects
of local government responsibility and for the most part councils are
involved in not more than one or two joint arrangements. A more
formal association of local government authorities was proposed in
1973 by the federal Labor government as a means of making submissions for financial assistance to combat area-wide problems; however,
these programmes were abandoned with the defeat of the Labor Party
in 1975.

So, apart from these minor perturbations, individual councils have
remained stubbornly independent, each responding to its own constit-
uency and concerned chiefly with its own local problems and

development. Yet almost without exception those who survey the local government scene in Victoria comment on the need for amalgamation of local councils (Holmes 1976; Leach 1977; Bowman 1978). Boundaries drawn in the nineteenth century bear little relation to present-day patterns of development; for example, 'as urban growth has proceeded, population and industrial and commercial activity spilled out over local boundaries and no one local governing authority had the power to follow them' (Leach 1977). Nor does the proliferation of councils make sense from an organisational point of view (in some municipalities the costs of administration take a large share of revenue; there is unnecessary duplication of assets, under-utilisation of plant and equipment and an inability to provide the qualified expert staff required by present-day councils). In addition, there are gross disparities between authorities in terms of the resources available (e.g. via rating of property) to them to meet their responsibilities.

2. Planning the Sprawling City

a) Metropolitan Planning Framework.

Although Victoria shared with other states the enthusiasm and reforming zeal of the early town planning movement, it has been tardy in giving legislative support to planning ideas. Victoria waited until 1944 for its first planning legislation, until 1954 for its first plan (Melbourne's Metropolitan Planning Scheme) and until 1968 for this plan to be given statutory force. (Sandercock 1975)

The growth of population in Melbourne during the two decades following World War II, combined with expectations for ever greater expansion by the end of the century (a figure of 5 million was advanced for the city: TCPB 1967; MMBW 1967) meant that by the latter part of the 1960s the state government found itself forced to take steps concerning the planning of metropolitan Melbourne.[8] This move was precipitated to a degree by the friction and uncertainty surrounding the existence of *two* planning authorities with overlapping but uncoordinated responsibilities for the city's development: the Town and Country Planning Board of Victoria (TCPB) which was commissioned in 1946 to make reports and recommendations to the government on planning schemes (which it could itself prepare) and town planning matters generally; and the Melbourne and Metropolitan Board of Works (MMBW), an instrumentality constituted in 1890 to control and manage the metropolitan water supply and sewage system and which, in 1949, gained responsibility for the preparation of a planning scheme for metropolitan Melbourne.

The state government's response was a major amendment in 1968 to the Town and Country Planning Act (1961) establishing a three-tier planning system which continues to the present:

i) State Planning. Involved here is broad, strategic planning by the TCPB, culminating generally in Statements of Planning Policy.[9] These are prepared by the Board in consultation with the State Co-ordination Council (SCC), a body comprising heads of government departments and major statutory authorities. This link between the TCPB and the Premier's Department allows full expression of the state government's development priorities and programmes in Statements of Planning Policy and their subsequent transmission to regional and local government authorities for enforcement within their particular systems of planning and development control.

ii) Regional Planning. Regional Planning Authorities (RPA) were established to prepare planning schemes and control development for any specified area extending beyond the boundaries of any one municipality. Four RPAs have jurisdiction in the Melbourne-Port Phillip Bay district (see Figure 2.1): the MMBW, which is the regional authority for 52 of Melbourne's 56 municipalities, the Western Port RPA and Geelong RPA (both constituted in 1969; the latter became the Geelong Regional Commission in 1977) and the Upper Yarra Valley and Dandenong Ranges Authority (constituted 1977).

iii) Local Planning. Basically, municipalities have control over development within their areas, extending to the preparation of their own planning schemes. However, this power is delegated by many to either a regional authority or the TCPB. In commenting upon the role of municipalities in the planning process, Holmes (1976) was prophetic in speculating that councils would have a diminished planning responsibility once the regional authorities were strongly established.

b) Melbourne's Metropolitan Plans. Despite the recent emergence of regional planning authorities for Geelong, Western Port and Yarra/ Dandenong, the major force in metropolitan planning remains, as has been the case since 1949, the MMBW. Of its several published reports concerning the plans for Melbourne's development, the first, *Melbourne Metropolitan Planning Scheme 1954: Report*, has received most positive

comment: 'Hardly a problem of Melbourne as we know it today was
not covered in that Report, although some of the suggested solutions
we now know to have been infeasible' (Joy 1977).

A reading of the 1954 Report reveals some of the principal concerns:

i) The sprawling, low density development, which has added
substantially to the cost of providing the normal utility services,
to the cost of transportation, and to the time taken to travel
from one part of the city to another.

ii) The decline in the residential amenities of the inner suburban
area due to the obsolescence and low standard of many homes
and to the encroachment of industry and other non-residential
uses.

iii) The expansion of industry and its guidance to locations which
will be convenient for both industrialists and workers, and
which will bring about an adjustment of the present unbalanced
distribution of places of residence and work.

iv) The congestion resulting from the increasing concentration of
activities within and adjoining the central business area.

v) The increasing difficulty in the movement of people and goods
throughout the planning area due partly to the increase in the
population, but more particularly to the increasing use of
motor vehicles.

vi) The difficulty of securing sufficiently large sites for schools
within convenient distances of the children's homes and for
hospitals in suitable locations.

vii) The lack of sufficient parklands and playing fields to meet the
needs of the growing population.

These were to be redressed as far as possible by establishing several
guiding principles (strategies) which were to provide a foundation for
detailed local planning. For instance: limiting the outward growth of
the city by the provision of a rural zone which surrounds the area set
aside for urban development (to contain a projected 2 million people by
1980-85) extending to the metropolitan boundaries; decentralising
population, commercial and industrial activity—to satellite towns, and,
perhaps most interestingly, to five 'district centres' within the metropolitan area (at Footscray, Preston, Box Hill, Moorabbin and Dandenong)
to relieve congestion in the central city and reduce commuting distances
to work and shops; increasing residential densities by encouraging flat
development; facilitating greater public transport usage by employing a

system of feeder bus services from outer suburbs to the nearest railway station; provision of an arterial road system (ring road to by-pass CBD; intersuburban; radial) to permit an uninterrupted movement of the increasing volume of road traffic; and exclusive zoning of areas for specific land uses.

In the 15 years which followed the release of the 1954 Report, Melbourne experienced rapid population growth (Table 2.5) (through natural increase and overseas immigration), passing the planners' ultimate population forecast 10-15 years earlier than expected; low density suburbanisation intensified as rural and green belt land was rezoned for extensive residential development,[10] and a high level of personal mobility was achieved via the automobile (while development of public transport stagnated). With this as background, the MMBW planning reports of 1967 and 1971 both reflect an expectation of continued high rates of population and economic growth.

In its 1971 report *Planning Policies for the Melbourne Metropolitan Region* the MMBW outlined a number of assumptions, policies and predictions which were fundamental to the plan which was ultimately adopted. Briefly these were as follows (after Logan 1977):

1. the population projections prepared by the MMBW indicated that the population of the Melbourne Statistical Division could reach 3.7 millions by 1985 and 5 millions by the year 2000;

2. 'the major part of the population growth would have to occur through new development outside the existing built up area . . . Areas shown as urban corridors . . . would contain all future outward urban expansion of the city . . . the wedges of non-urban land between the corridors would be retained substantially in their present non-urban character' (Figure 2.7);

3. the MMBW advocated a policy of maintaining the CBD as the most dominant centre in the metropolitan region. Although there was reference to a form of concentrated development within the corridors, the concept of metropolitan sub-centre development was clearly rejected;

4. the report argued that 'Melbourne for a long time has been the most industrialised capital, where manufacturing industry employs almost four out of ten workers'. Although the suburbanisation process was clearly recognized there was little questioning of the long run significance of manufacturing as a provider of jobs in the future.

Table 2.5: Population and Housing Profiles for Melbourne Statistical Division[a], 1954-76

	1954	1961	1966	1971	1976
Total population	1,589,185	1,984,815	2,230,580	2,503,450	2,604,035
Total population as per cent of Victorian total	64.8	67.7	69.3	71.5	71.4
Annual inter-censal growth rate (%)	2.5	3.2	2.4	2.3	0.8
Age of population (years):					
% 0-4	9.7	9.9	9.5	9.7	8.6
% 5-14	16.2	18.2	18.0	18.1	18.0
% 15-24	12.4	14.4	16.8	17.5	17.3
% 25-34	16.3	13.9	13.0	14.1	15.8
% 35-44	14.6	14.4	13.9	12.3	11.7
% 45-54	12.4	12.0	11.6	11.5	11.5
% 55-64	9.8	8.7	8.6	8.5	8.5
% ⩾ 65	8.9	8.8	8.7	8.2	8.7
Marital status:					
% Never married	44.4	46.6	46.9	46.1	45.4
% Married	47.5	46.0	45.5	46.2	46.1
% Separated	1.6	1.6	1.6	1.6	2.0
% Divorced	0.8	0.8	0.8	1.0	1.5
% Widowed	5.8	5.2	5.2	5.1	5.0
Birthplace:					
% Australia	83.1	77.1	74.5	72.5	72.9
% Outside Australia	17.2	23.1	25.5	27.5	27.1
Women in Work-force:					
(as % of women 15-64)	37.3	40.4	46.4	47.3	53.6
Fertility ratio					
(children 0-4 as ratio of women 15-44 times 100)	45.4	47.3	44.6	44.9	38.4
Occupational status (males)					
% Employer	6.7	5.9	5.5	4.8	) 10.9
% Self-employed	7.2	6.1	5.7	5.2	)
% Employed	84.8	83.5	87.5	88.5	85.9

	1954	1961	1966	1971	1976
Industry of occupation (males):					
% Primary production	2.9	2.1	1.6	1.1	0.9
% Mining	0.3	0.3	0.3	0.4	0.3
% Manufacturing	39.3	37.7	38.2	32.4	29.8
% Electricity	2.9	2.9	2.9	2.9	2.3
% Construction	10.0	11.1	10.8	9.3	9.7
% Commerce	15.7	15.3	15.0	17.9	17.6
% Transport, storage	7.8	7.4	7.0	6.5	6.6
% Communication	2.6	2.7	2.6	2.3	2.4
% Finance, property	2.9	3.4	3.7	6.9	7.4
% Public admin., defence	(b)	(b)	4.9	5.6	5.8
% Community services	(b)	(b)	7.5	6.3	8.1
% Entertainment	4.0	4.0	4.0	2.9	3.0
Class of dwelling:					
% Self-contained flat	5.9	8.8	13.3	15.1	(b)
Nature of occupancy:					
% Owner	63.7	70.7	73.1	69.6	69.6
% Tenant—SHA	3.5	3.2	3.5	3.6	2.9
% Tenant—other	24.9	17.6	21.6	22.5	20.1
Motor vehicles per dwelling:					
% No vehicle	—	—	26.5	22.5	17.3
% 1 vehicle	—	—	70.2	75.2	78.5

Notes: a. The tabled figures relate to the area covered by the Melbourne Statistical Division as defined at 30 June 1971; the maintenance of a constant area base has necessitated some data estimation for 1954 and 1961.
b. Comparable figures not available.

Yet at the time the 1971 report was being issued a number of fundamental economic, technological and social changes were already in train, which would produce a pattern of development substantially different to that experienced previously. The changes hinge on the following factors.

Figure 2.7: MMBW Framework Plan for the Melbourne Region, 1971

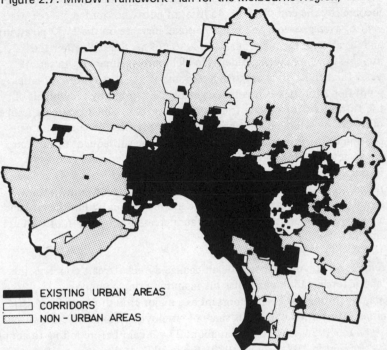

EXISTING URBAN AREAS
CORRIDORS
NON – URBAN AREAS

Energy. The major phase of suburbanisation within Australia's cities occurred during a 25 year period following World War II when there was a steady decline in real motoring costs approaching 1 per cent per year (taking the petrol component: in 1972, 45 litres – or 10 gallons – of petrol cost only 4.9 per cent of average weekly earnings, compared with 15.3 per cent in 1949; Bureau of Transport Economics 1975). In this time, car ownership has rapidly increased from 0.2 cars per capita in 1960 to 0.4 in 1976. The growth of automobile traffic has been a direct contributing factor in the low urban density characteristic of Australian cities, since it is estimated that 35 to 45 per cent of urban space is consumed by the private transport system for roads and freeways, car parks, service stations and motor industries (Sharpe 1980) – notwithstanding the indirect contribution made by facilitating the proliferation of the (single family) detached home on its sixth-of-an-acre block of land (and permitting increased separation of home and work).

The increasing price of petroleum since 1973 (and the possibilities of interruptions to supply) has the potential for changing the competitive position of modes of transport and location within the city. The extent and speed of change will hinge upon the price of fuel in relation to real income (by the end of 1979, 45 litres of petrol accounted for 6.7 per cent of average weekly earnings—a small increase on the 1972 position)— and, as always, the individual's valuation of his time. Whether the increase in white collar residents in Melbourne's inner city in recent years (Maher 1978) is as much a response to the distribution of employment opportunities as it is to a changing perception by individuals of the future cost of private transport is uncertain. The increase in number of inner city white collar jobs, however, is a result of a corporate perception of the importance of the CBD and the subsequent upsurge in construction of high rise office blocks. The market place is already responding to the rising importance of centrality (Figure 2.4); a continuation, and perhaps an intensification, of this trend could witness a significant rearrangement of socio-economic groups within the city and a change in the housing stock with an increasing proportion of medium and high density units.

Employment. Another significant change in recent years concerns the labour force, and in particular the manufacturing component. Manufacturing has been important as a major growth factor for Australia's cities. At a national level, its share of employment expanded between 1947 and 1954, levelling off at about 27 per cent before falling to about 24 per cent in 1971 (Linge 1979). Since 1971 decline in manufacturing has continued due in part to the economic recession and to tariff cuts in 1973 of the order of 25 per cent, but also to technological and structural change. There is no prospect for a return to earlier rates of increase in manufacturing and factories have ceased to be a dynamic element of growth in the cities. In making this point, Logan (1977) reveals that before 1970 much of the population growth was attracted to the suburbs by the establishment of new factories there and also by the relocation of factories from central city suburbs.

At the moment growth in employment is being generated most strongly within the tertiary sector. There has been considerable decentralisation of retailing employment within Melbourne during the 1960s and 1970s not only in traditional suburban arrangements but also in free standing regional shopping centres.[11] However, the decentralisation of employment has not extended as strongly to office work, which remains firmly tied to the city centre and if North American and European trends are any guide will continue to do so (Gottmann 1979), with the prospects for central city revival being based largely on continued concentration of office work with a concomitant relocation of white collar employees in inner city locations.

Population. The expectation that Melbourne's population could reach 5 million by the turn of the century was being replaced in the mid-1970s by forecasts which indicated that 3.5 million may be closer to the mark (Birrell 1975). Several factors are responsible for this downturn: a decline in the birth rate, a slowing down of immigration, and a net loss of internal migrants to other state capitals (Rowland 1979). From a distributional point of view, the pattern of population change over the period 1971-6 clearly reveals a continued evolution of a dispersed, low density city – despite a lower rate of overall metropolitan growth. In this context, although Melbourne's growth rate has declined, for the next decade or so the rate of household formation will generate a need for new housing at least as great as the past 10 years or so (National Population Inquiry 1978) – and most of this new stock will be located on the periphery. To a large extent this will occur because the planners have already zoned considerably more urban land than was or is needed (Birrell 1975); a response, it has been argued by some (Sandercock 1979) to the pressure exerted by developers to release fringe land for residential use ('The plan can become little more than a guide to developers as to where to acquire land around the periphery of the city': Logan 1977).

So one of the major briefs which Melbourne's first regional planning authority was given in 1949 still remains – controlling the outward growth of the city. Considerable uncertainty surrounds current thinking within the MMBW concerning the future shape of Melbourne; an understandable situation perhaps, given the force of criticism (from residents, councils, private corporations, academics) which descends on the planning authority following release of its planning reports and the fact that the state government appears a reluctant partner when planning decisions are required (as an example: in December 1978 the state government gave final approval to a corridor growth plan for Melbourne which has been under consideration for almost 10 years: *The Age* 1978).

Within the approved corridor concept, the MMBW has developed a series of views ('strategic options') on how Melbourne should develop. The principal options are outlined here (drawn from MMBW 1979a, b, c) as they are speculative options, awaiting reaction from a range of quarters: private and public, individual and corporate.

i) Dispersing Growth. This option is based on a continuation of the trends towards the dispersal of population and activities which were evident up to and including the 1976 census. It would entail accelerated development of land in the defined corridors. Population levels in inner and middle suburbs would probably continue to fall. There are several implications of such a strategy: a greater reliance on private motor vehicles and a continued reduction in the proportion of trips by public transport. Increased use of the rail system may occur for longer distance radial movements. The functioning of the city would therefore be particularly sensitive to disruption to liquid fuel supplies or major increases in fuel prices. Whilst this alternative may well meet the current aspirations of a significant proportion of Melbourne's residents, those who would prefer to locate in proximity to public transport and the diverse urban services established within the present built-up area may be progressively disadvantaged through lack of opportunity to obtain accommodation. Public sector investment in inner area facilities would be underutilised, although, as Logan (1977) points out, this situation has been produced by a pattern of state government investment which favours the central city (underground rail loop: $300 million; arts centre: $110 million; Westgate Bridge: $200 million and so on) in comparison with the continually expanding suburbs. Under a dispersing growth scenario, public expenditure must also decentralise.

The use of existing services and facilities would decrease and there would be additional costs involved in servicing the areas on the fringe of the urban area. Reserve servicing capacity would be available, particularly in the middle suburbs. There could be an increase in opportunities to provide a variety of new facilities in suburban areas. Present housing trends would continue and little change would be involved in the pressures on buildings and environments of architectural and historic significance. Employment opportunities would be more dispersed throughout the urban area. Further development on the urban fringe would entail a loss of land now being used or capable of use for agricultural production which contributes to the rural vista adjacent to the city.

ii) Centralised Growth. Relative emphasis would be given to the CBD as the focus of commercial activity rather than the further growth of centres in suburban areas, and to the effective use of radial public transport networks rather than the provision of major road improvements in suburban areas. Additional inner city populations would have to be accommodated through infill development in existing residential areas, accompanying rehabilitation and redevelopment on a large scale as well as redevelopment of vacated industrial areas as residential districts.

The implications of this concept include major changes in the life styles and housing choices available to Melbourne residents — particularly lower income groups. There would be reduced growth in the reliance on private transport. There would also be potential for increased public transport use in inner areas, probably generating increased traffic congestion and air pollution there. Continuing public and private sector investment in the inner area would be more effectively utilised than in other options. Increased public sector investment would be needed to upgrade some services and facilities within the inner area. Public sector action would also be required in some cases for land assembly and the subsidisation of land costs. The established community networks of the inner city would be disrupted. Whilst the provision of some additional housing might service demands, substantial redevelopment of existing residential areas would threaten areas of historic and architectural significance, family housing and low cost housing.

The curtailment of development in the outer areas would be needed, limiting the option now available for those who desire to live in outer areas. Developers who speculated on fringe land would be in line for significant losses.

iii) Suburban Growth Centres (Multi-Nodal Development). This entails an emphasis on growth of activities and services at locations accessible to suburban housing, thus enhancing local job opportunities. There are several views as to the form which this might take. One is that activities should be encouraged to locate at selected centres, associated with the fixed rail network and surrounded by intensive housing development. Another is that encouragement should be given to the development of localised activities in residential areas. Such views are not necessarily in conflict but rather suggest differing degrees of emphasis. Within this context it has been suggested that population dispersal from inner areas can reduce the pressure on housing there and thus allow the areas to evolve as balanced and viable communities. However, accelerated reduction in population and employment levels within inner areas would result in underuse of the diverse facilities and further reductions in nearby job opportunities for the local unskilled work force. Overall, accelerated movement of activities out from the central area would result in a greater reliance on road travel but a concentration of activities at selected centres associated with the radial rail network would provide opportunities for enhanced use of the rail system and bus networks focused on those centres.

Melbourne is already a multi-centred metropolis in which activities have increasingly been locating within suburban areas. Thus the issue here is not whether such a pattern of suburbanisation should be developed but whether it is desirable to accelerate its development—and whether it is desirable to encourage an increased degree of concentration of activities at selected centres, rather than an increasing spread of activity centres as is now occurring.

Since its inception, the Metropolitan Scheme has made provision for District Business Centres at key locations throughout the metropolitan area. Although these proposals have generally been maintained, the level of public sector action at such centres has not been sufficient to attract the range and extent of facilities originally envisaged and major retail centres have been established elsewhere in some cases. Fragmented land ownership, cost cost, congestion and lack of parking and amenity at established centres have contributed to this situation. In view of these circumstances, it is evident that proposals for an increased emphasis on the development of selected suburban centres would require increased levels of public intervention in assisting the development of such centres and, in at least some cases, an increased limitation on developments beyond such centres.

3. Linking the Parts: the Transport Problems

It is generally conceded that at least until the late 1950s the various modes of public transport (railway, street trams and buses) provided an adequate level of accessibility within Melbourne. The first phase of what became a massive transition to private transport was associated with the accelerated growth of the city and the manner in which this growth was accommodated. Population growth was accommodated by extending Melbourne's area, with residential densities in the newer suburbs in most instances less than those in the established areas. Consequently, the public transport accessibility of the entire urban area was declining with every new development. The spread of industries to the outer suburbs also meant a change from the period prior to the mid-1950s when most workplaces, blue or white collar, were accessible by public transport. For an increasing proportion of the non-CBD workforce, public transport was not a feasible alternative to the car (Joy 1977). This response—essentially utilitarian in nature—was reinforced by many workers for whom public transport was available (e.g. those employed in the CBD) opting to commute in the comfort and convenience of their private automobile.

By the early 1960s it was evident that public transport in Melbourne could not compete with the automobile in the sprawling, thinly inhabited suburbs. In highlighting the popular view that public transport failed to keep pace with the development of the city, Joy (1977) points out that

> . . . even if the community had been prepared to pay for enough public transport infrastructure to maintain accessibility in the newer suburbs at the level achieved back with the tramway boundaries [Melbourne's tram routes generally operate no more than 10 or 12 kilometres from the CBD, and mostly to the north and east], the new dwellers were not prepared to use it.

It is always easier to speak with hindsight rather than with forethought, and it is doubtful whether Melbourne's future transport pattern could have been markedly different had different conclusions been reached and priorities assigned more than a decade ago when the city's first (and to date, only) Transportation Plan was being formulated. In 1963 the state government set up a Melbourne Metropolitan Transportation Committee to advise on the future development of transport in the metropolis and its environs. The plan was published in 1969 (Melbourne Transportation Study 1969). It has as one of its primary aims: 'the effecting of a balance between all forms of transport. Emphasis has been placed on giving the public transport services the capacity to win increased patronage despite the expected increase in car ownership' (MTS 1969).

In documenting its proposals to 1985 the Melbourne Transportation Study contains plans for the rail, tram and bus networks, as well as highway proposals. The costs given are $242 million for railways, $113 million for trams and buses and $2,221 million, or 86 per cent of the total outlay, for highways. Furthermore, $140 million of the public transport costs were for rolling stock rather than new infrastructure. Principal features of the railway plan include the CBD's underground rail loop ($80 million) and three new lines, two of which are radial (Figure 2.8). Of these proposals, only the underground loop, with its objective of dispensing passengers around the CBD and hopefully stimulating added private development therein, has been undertaken, and is due for completion late in 1980. Proposed extensions to the tramway network (520 route kilometres in 1964) were about 3 per cent; the length of bus routes was to be extended 64 per cent from a 1964 level of 1,800 kilometres (to date there has been only a 12 per cent increase).

A transportation plan which for the most part acquiesced to the onslaught of the private automobile must take some responsibility for the increasingly poor performance of public transport in Melbourne. From

Figure 2.8: Melbourne's Transportation Plan, 1969

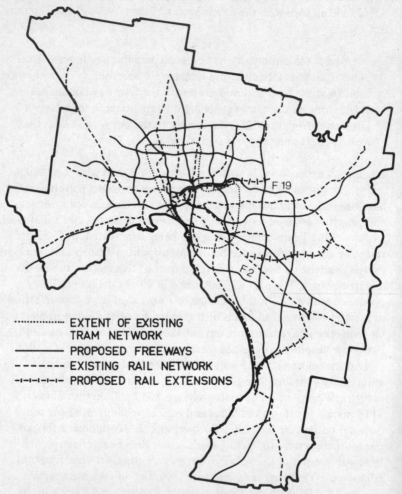

```
················  EXTENT OF EXISTING
                  TRAM NETWORK
──────────────  PROPOSED FREEWAYS
── ── ── ── ──  EXISTING RAIL NETWORK
-ı-ı-ı-ı-ı-ı-  PROPOSED RAIL EXTENSIONS
```

1962 to the present there has been a 40 per cent decline in metropolitan passenger journeys for both rail (148 million per year down to 90 million) and tram (167 million to 101 million), with a 36 per cent decline for government-operated buses (31 million to 20 million); privately operated buses have fared no better with a 26 per cent decline in passengers carried between 1973 (74 million) and 1978 (55 million). Meanwhile, government subsidies to these operations have increased to cover the gap between revenue and expenditure, which is currently about 50 per cent of operating costs for both rail and tram.

The Melbourne Transportation Committee, in formulating its high-way plan to 1985, followed the lead of the MMBW in basing its proposals on certain expectations of rapid growth within Melbourne: 85 per cent increase in population to 3.75 million; 95 per cent increase in employment; 50 per cent increase in built-up area; and 100 per cent increase in number of automobiles (with attendant increases in auto-mobile trips and trip lengths—a trebling of traffic volumes being expected). In arguing that road construction was required to keep pace with travel demand generated by the private automobile, the highway plan, and indeed the entire transport plan, was reactionary:

> This is not a matter in which there are alternatives. Either a large scale programme such as is recommended in the [highway] plan is instituted and maintained over a long-term period or traffic con-gestion and greatly increased transport costs would become chronic features of the metropolitan road system. (MTS 1969)

The principal feature of the road plan was massive freeway construction. The freeway network was to comprise a completely new system of roads imposed on the urban area, with a total route mileage of 500 kilometres (Figure 2.8), which represented 52 per cent of the new route mileage contained in the highway plan. Only 5 per cent of new routes involved road widening to accommodate public transport movement.

The reaction to the highway component of the 1969 Melbourne Transportation Plan has been severe, and continues to the present. The plan has been criticised for its narrow focus: a wider range of options should have been investigated, including car pooling, express bus lanes, modern trains, restricted access roads, higher parking fees, increased petrol taxes, pay as you drive charges, lowered fares, transferrable tickets, new fare structures, special amenities for particular groups such as the elderly and mothers, encouragement for smaller cars, new trams, 'light rail vehicles', commuter bus clubs, jointly owned vehicles, multiple hire taxis, bicycle facilities at stations, power assisted bicycles, and special bike paths.

Major concern, however, focused upon the substantial expenditure of public funds (this concern extended from public reaction within the state to federal government decisions to cut back substantially on its allocation of funds to Victoria for freeway construction, stressing the need to improve urban public transport) and the land acquisition required to build the highways (650 hectares for new arterial roads and 5,000 hectares for freeways). It was against the latter that Citizens

Against Freeways was formed, comprising a committee of representatives from residents' associations, councils and other bodies, to coordinate the fight to save residential communities threatened by several freeways (principally the F19 and F2).

In 1973, reacting to heavy public pressure, the state government halved the 1969 freeway plan to 250 kilometres and announced new guidelines for the construction of freeways in urban areas (one of which was to cease freeway construction in inner areas). This move cast doubt on the philosophy underlying the plan and reduced its recommendations to an unlinked collection of freeway segments which did not serve their desired function. It has been argued (Freeway Fighter 1977) that this situation is being used by the Country Roads Board as a justification for more freeway construction via the linking of the existing freeway segments. As an editorial in *The Age* (11 March 1978) outlines:

> The Government, after calling a halt to the 1969 freeway master plan, now has recognized that leaving gaps between lengths of freeway already built compounds the problem. Concentrated traffic has to find a way and tends to saturate an entire residential neighbourhood. In these circumstances, to complete a freeway may be more sensible than to leave a gap.

The state government apparently came to this conclusion in March 1978 when they finally decided that a freeway link would be built through Malvern to link two existing freeway segments.

There seems to be considerable uncertainty among those government departments and regional authorities which have a responsibility for directing Melbourne's development as to the future shape of the city. Uncertainty within Melbourne's principal regional planning authority concerns the desirability of either centralising or dispersing growth and encouraging multi-centred development (MMBW 1979b). The transport network, existing and planned, is a major force in shaping the city. Melbourne's 1969 Transport Plan contained a range of recommendations which if implemented would have amounted, in Thomson's (1978) terms, to a weak-centre strategy for the metropolis; namely a highway system which not only served the city centre but included ring roads for inter-suburban movement between residence and workplace, with public transport being restricted to a few radial railway lines to accommodate peak-hour commuters to the centre. With a combination of ring and radial freeways (Figure 2.8), industrial and commercial development outside the city centre would be powerfully attracted to the interchange points between the rings and radials, and this should generate the growth of strategic intra-urban centres. There is some evidence to suggest that several 'sub-regional foci' are developing within Melbourne at the present time (O'Connor and Maher 1979).

Not unexpectedly, there was opposition to some of the likely consequences of a weak-centre transport strategy, such as a decline in the importance of the city centre and the need for extensive, and costly, freeway building. By initiating construction of the underground rail loop and assigning radial freeways a higher priority than ring routes in the foreshortened Highway Plan, the state government was turning back towards a strong-centre strategy characteristic of an earlier era in Melbourne's development.

4. Social Planning

Melbourne's private housing market (which comprises more than 95 per cent of the city's total stock) operates so that a household's economic position is the major factor in determining its residential location. The ensuing patterns of income and socio-economic status segregation reflect the differential ability of groups to compete for particular areas within the city. A concern of social planners for some time has been whether location in particular low income sectors of a city actually increases the extent of inequality for those living in such areas (e.g. if there are lower standard schools in low-income suburbs, they may help to create a 'culture of poverty'). There are some reasons for believing that it might:

> . . . segregation *permits* differences in the quality of local public services between rich and poor areas. Without segregation the rich and poor, old and young, migrant and native-born have the same garbage services, use the same parks, swimming pools, roads and footpaths and patronise the same shops. With segregation these can all be better in the areas where the rich and powerful live. Segregation, then, is necessary before there can be variations in the quality of local public services available to different income and social groups. (Neutze 1978)

The concept of social mix has long existed as a town planning philosophy which sought the establishment of socially balanced neighbourhoods, although the degree of mix and the means of achieving it were never spelled out very clearly (Sarkissian 1976). It is a concept which has recently been embraced with some enthusiasm by a number of the state's public housing authorities whose estate policies up until the 1970s had produced homogeneous islands of low income housing, albeit across a range of locations within the city (social mix at municipality and metropolitan level increases, but not at the scale of the neighbourhood). Future public housing is likely to be much less obtrusive than it has been in the past with housing authority purchases of existing stock in established suburbs in addition to the mingling of public housing in new private developments. Public housing, with its small share of the market, has a limited role to play in redistributing groups within the city. But as Neutze (1978) points out, there are other ways to improve the residential milieux of poor families; for instance, a redistribution of income so that households can afford to buy into areas with better services and environments.

Another welfare approach involves the equality of access by resident groups to needed urban services and amenities. Neutze (1978) highlights the fact that most services—e.g. health centres, schools—have to be supplied in discrete units. In providing such services in only a limited number of locations, those who live close by are favoured. With the spatial segregation of different groups, decisions about where to locate services (and the quality to be offered) influence the distribution of welfare between groups. Problems of equal access are likely to be greatest in cities which are fragmented into a large number of small local government areas and where such authorities have important service-related responsibilities, so that local government permits at least the wealthy people to group together to provide the local public goods and services they choose. In Australia, most of the important urban services (such as schools, police, hospitals, major roads, water supply, sewerage, fire safety) are provided by either state governments or special-purpose metropolitan authorities which are in a position to supply services of equal quality city-wide.

The extent of spatial variations in the distribution of a range of both private and public services within Melbourne will be briefly examined for education and health. Studies of access to health care within Australasian cities (Barnett and Newton 1977; Donald 1975) have indicated that the distribution of services (general practitioners, specialists, hospitals, nursing homes) is far from equitable. In a review of health services in Melbourne in 1972, Donald (1975) revealed that although the metropolitan area had a ratio of 1.02 general practitioners per thousand people, 55 per cent of Melbourne's municipalities had practitioner ratios of less than the Australian Medical Association (AMA)

Figure 2.9: Distribution of General Practitioners, 1975

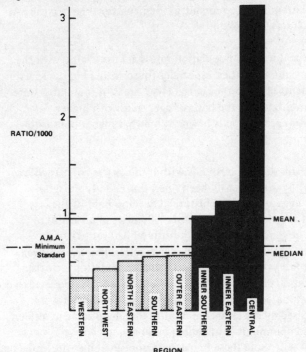

Central: South Melbourne, Port Melbourne, Melbourne, St. Kilda, Prahran,
                Richmond, Collingwood, Fitzroy.
Inner Eastern: Doncaster and Templestowe, Box Hill, Waverley, Nunawading,
                Camberwell, Kew, Hawthorn.
Inner Southern: Malvern, Caulfield, Brighton, Sandringham, Oakleigh, Moorabbin,
                Mordialloc.
Outer Eastern: Ringwood, Knox, Croydon, Sherbrooke, Lilydale, Healesville.
Southern: Dandenong, Berwick, Packenham, Springvale, Chelsea, Frankston.
North Eastern: Northcote, Heidelberg, Preston, Diamond Valley, Eltham,
                Whittlesea.
North Western: Brunswick, Essendon, Coburg, Broadmeadows, Keilor, Bulla.
Western: Williamstown, Footscray, Sunshine, Altona, Melton, Werribee.

standard (Figure 2.9). In particular, the western region's ratio of 0.34
per thousand and the north-western region's ratio of 0.43 per thousand
residents indicate a very real undersupply of key medical care providers.
Hospital bed distribution is highly centralised, with a ratio of 49 beds
per thousand persons in the Melbourne City municipality in contrast to
ratios of less than one bed per thousand in one-third of the city's 56
municipalities (the distribution of medical specialists is also bound
closely to that of the major central hospitals).

Doctors apparently evaluate any potential place of practice in terms of their own social, economic and environmental preferences, coupled with an appreciation of the community's demand for their services. As Donald (1975) states for Melbourne:

> ... the highest doctor-to-population ratios are associated with the more affluent municipalities, especially those with a high proportion of aged residents close to the central city. Areas of low status were mainly differentiated on the basis of age, areas with higher proportions of aged residents having somewhat higher doctor-to-population ratios.

As far as the distribution of hospitals within the city is concerned, two principal factors have apparently been operating. Firstly, hospital distribution strongly reflects the historical development of the city (high ecological associations can be observed between measures of population density and centrality with hospital bed ratios), with allocation of public funds for hospital construction requiring proven demand (construction consequently lags behind population growth). Secondly, the Hospitals and Charities Commission requires that at least one-quarter of the estimated cost of capital works for a new hospital or extensions by raised by the local community, thereby placing wealthier, older-established communities at a distinct advantage.

Prospects for redressing these imbalances appear slim at present. The AMA and other health-professional unions have continued to resist any attempt at government control over their activities, and in the case of hospitals there appears to be little concern with the question of equity — hospital investment continues to centre on the major hospitals near the CBD at the expense of the suburbs.

If access to health care contributes directly to the level of physical well-being of the population, access to education has an equally important and perhaps more lasting contribution to make to material well-being. Much has been written about the role of education in socialising the individual into his role in life. Restricted access to education for certain groups (through lack of information, parental influence or finance) or variations in the quality of education throughout a region become principal contributing factors to both the establishment and perpetuation of social differences. In Melbourne, 200 schools have been designated by the State Education Department as disadvantaged and eligible for statutory grants, and the number of such schools is four times higher in the central city area than in the outer suburbs (MMBW 1977a). A broader perspective on educational deprivation is provided by a study of school life expectancy in Melbourne (Batten and Lenthal 1977). School life expectancy is defined as the average number of school years remaining to persons who are just entering the formal education system, and for the Melbourne statistical division the average is 9.5 years. The municipalities of Brighton and Camberwell have the highest levels of school participation with averages of 10.5 years—a marked contrast to Collingwood with 7.5 years. This difference of three years provides one measure of the highly variable degree of educational participation within the metropolitan area; the highest levels of participation are in the eastern and southern bayside suburbs, which contain concentrations of white collar workers on above average incomes.

Melbourne's planners have appeared reluctant to include equity considerations in their proposals for the city's future growth and development. They were absent from the 1971 strategy plan (MMBW 1971), included as an attachment to the subsequent report on general concept objections to the plan (MMBW 1974), but absent from a March 1979 review of Melbourne's planning options (MMBW 1979a) where the Chairman of the MMBW stated:

> The first step in this review has been to look at alternative strategic options which, in view of recent trends in the development of Metropolitan Melbourne, cannot be adequately discussed unless the changing strategic issues of the four E's, namely Energy, Efficiency, Employment and Environment, are fully examined.

By October 1979, the omission of the fifth E, equity, had been highlighted by critiques from several quarters and was duly reinstated in subsequent reports:

> The issue of equity is related to a concern to provide, as far as is practicable, enhanced opportunities for access to community facilities, services and to the benefits of living in an urban area for all sections of the community. (MMBW 1979b)

There is a degree of caution, however, in the planning authority's perception of its role in this area. They proceeded to argue:

> It is accepted that the issue of equity may be tackled more directly and perhaps more efficiently by means not directly related to urban form. However, decisions regarding urban form do have equity implications and these need to be recognised and taken into account

during the decision-making process.

5. The Quality of Melbourne's Physical Environment

The continued growth of Melbourne and the likely intensification of development in Geelong and Western Port regions under recent industry drives (Western Port Regional Planning Authority 1979; Geelong Regional Planning Authority 1976) points to the emergence of continuous urban development stretching from the tip of the Mornington Peninsula to deep into the Bellarine Peninsula by the end of this century. The progress of such development has already adversely affected the quality of the natural environment—the city's 'breathing spaces'—in several important respects.

a) Decline in Recreational and Resource Land. The Bellarine and Mornington Peninsulas have traditionally been Melbourne's holiday and recreational zones dominated by weekender cottages, camping grounds, and open space with access to beach areas. With the growing demand for building sites in environmentally attractive locations and the penetration of freeways, both areas have witnessed typically suburban transitions and a growth in permanent residences.

Forty kilometres to the east of the CBD, the Dandenong Ranges provide Melbourne residents with considerable recreational amenity. The close proximity of Melbourne and its expansion eastward exposes the Dandenongs to the encroachment of urban development on a scale detrimental to landscape conservation. Between 1971 and 1976, for example, the municipalities which largely comprise that portion of the Dandenongs within the Melbourne Statistical Division experienced rates of population and dwelling growth of about 35 per cent. The TCPB Statement of Planning Policy on Dandenong Ranges (1971) and the more recent formation of the Upper Yarra Valley and Dandenong Ranges Authority (1977) and its formulation of a draft regional strategy plan (1979) represent attempts to protect scenic and bushland environments for recreation and conservation within a framework which will permit further, albeit constrained, residential development.

b) Increasing Pollution of Beaches and Bay. Contamination of Port Phillip Bay and its beaches by human sanitary wastes is one of the major consequences of rapid urban growth. Bacteriological sampling of Melbourne's bayside beaches by the Environment Protection Authority in 1973-4 revealed E. Coli counts exceeding 1,000 per 100 ml,[12] at

locations stretching from Altona to Brighton, and Mordialloc to
Frankston plus a number of discrete locations from there to south of
Mornington. The major cause of this contamination is drainage from
the some 150,000 premises within the Bay catchment which remain
unsewered, together with storm water drainage from the entire urban
area, whether sewered or not, and sewerage wastes from shipping.

Prospects for future improvement are not particularly good according to Birrell *et al.* (1974), for several reasons: the substantial number
(65,000 in 1973) of vacant sections in unsewered areas subdivided prior
to the (1970 for MMBW areas) sewerage requirement; the significant
number (27,750 in 1972) of households for which sewerage is available
but no connection has been made or enforced; and the shortage of
finance for such major undertakings.

c) Air Pollution. Melbourne is fortunate in having a variable climate in
which prolonged episodes of air pollution are rare. Nevertheless, its
capacity to generate a range of pollutants is increasingly well-
documented. For example, Le Roy *et al.* (1976) reviewed the occurrence
of photo-chemical smog in Melbourne and noted its emergence as a
major air pollution problem requiring attention. Measurements of ozone
show that WHO's air quality criterion is exceeded on 20 to 30 days
each year in the city (Sawford 1976). Motor vehicle emissions have
been identified as the prime source of photo-chemical smog as well as
a range of other pollutants (90 per cent of carbon monoxide within
cities is generated from motor vehicles, as are 65 per cent of hydro-
carbons, 55 per cent of nitrogen oxides and significant quantities of
lead: Commonwealth Department of Transport 1977). Consequently,
it is not surprising to find that in those areas where pollution levels have
been monitored for a period of time increases in concentrations of
certain oxidants have been detected (Galbally 1972).

The populations most at risk are those resident in the inner city
suburbs adjacent to the major arterial roads, and those near to industrial
plant (where dust and smoke fallout impact most severely on an
immediate environment). Since 1973 the Environment Protection
Authority of Victoria has had the tasks of monitoring pollution levels
for Melbourne and undertaking environmental management — a recent
(1979) thrust being a draft state environment protection policy for air
quality. The state has responded to pressure for environmental protection
and management on a range of fronts during the 1970s; its response to
date has largely been in the formation of agencies, a number of which
have initiated draft legislation. The 1980s will test the state's willingness

(i.e. in enacting and enforcing legislation) to pursue an active platform of environmentally sensitive development.

Conclusions

There are many aspects of Melbourne's urban development, patterns and problems which it shares in common with Adelaide, Brisbane, Perth and Sydney. It is a very large urban area, both in population and in land covered—the latter because of the low density of much of the residential mosaic. It occupies a coastal site, with attendant difficulties of coordination, especially with regard to traffic. Rapid growth in recent decades, associated with economic prosperity, immigration, and car ownership, has encouraged the suburbanisation of residences, jobs, and commercial and other facilities. Coordinating this rapid sprawl is proving extremely difficult, given the traditions of *laissez-faire*, minimal government involvement in planning, the federal-state conflict, and local government balkanisation. In attempting such coordination and in putting forward means to counter the increasing range of perceived metropolitan problems, Melbourne's planners face a mammoth task. One thing is clear: there is little or no chance of decanting population and jobs to the state's other towns—they are too small to offer viable locations. The boom years may be over, and Melbourne may never reach the population of 5 millions forecast for 2000, but the problems will not go away. One fears that in an increasingly gloomy economic future they—like those of most large cities—may be accentuated, and the potential to handle them substantially reduced as governments try to disengage themselves from planning activities.

Notes

1. Considerable variation exists in the pattern of access to vehicles across the city. In 1976 there were 10 inner city LGAs where 30 to 40 per cent of households had no motor vehicle; a marked contrast to more than 20 LGAs where less than 10 per cent of households are in a similar position.

2. The waiting list for public housing is long—over 21,000 in 1976 (and normally does not include those requiring short-term emergency housing, estimated at 31,000 persons per year in Victoria—80 per cent Melbourne-based: Shelter 1978).

3. Construction of the villa unit (cluster) form gathered pace when the Strata Titles Act was passed in 1968. This enabled individual ownership of each dwelling in a group under separate title and its popularity is shown by the number of plans

lodged – 460 in 1968, increasing to 2,300 in 1977.

4. Other designated growth centres included Monarto (South Australia) and Bathurst-Orange (NSW).

5. This is reflected in the merging of DURD with the Departments of Environment and Housing, of Construction into the Department of Environment, Housing and Community Development (1976), and the abolition of EHCD in November 1978 with its functions variously transferred to the Departments of Housing and Construction, Science and Environment, Employment, and National Development among others.

6. Producer/employer groups such as the Victorian Chamber of Manufacturers and the Melbourne Chamber of Commerce have for a long period lobbied state and local government on proposed legislation or planning policies. For example, the latter group was influential in persuading the Melbourne City Council to introduce long term strategic planning in Melbourne's inner areas which would protect members' property interests; it also supported the underground rail loop project designed to improve the public transport services in central, commercial Melbourne (the loop is a continuation of an existing line which bounded the entire southern and part of the western side of Melbourne's CBD, and when completed will provide rail access to all 4 boundaries of the CBD); and it was a major influence on recent state government moves to limit the corporate development of regional shopping centres in established retail districts.

7. Brisbane statistical division, population 867,784, comprises 9 LGAs (with Brisbane city council responsible for over 700,000 – an exception to the traditional pattern); Sydney (2,807,828) 41; Newcastle (351,087) 8; Adelaide (842,693) 32; Perth (703,199) 26; Hobart (153,216) 7.

8. For a study of town planning developments in Melbourne prior to 1945, see Sandercock (1975, chapter 3).

9. To date, nine Statements of Planning Policy have been issued by the TCPB: Western Port (1970); Mornington Peninsula(1970); Dandenong Ranges (1971); Yarra River (1971); Highway Areas (1973); Macedon Ranges and Surrounds (1975); Central Gippsland (1975). Others for the Melbourne metropolitan area and the entire Victorian coastline are being prepared.

10. A recent study by the MMBW (1977b) reveals an absolute decline in numbers of owners, employees, numbers and acreages of rural holdings between 1966 and 1973 in the outer municipalities of Whittlesea, Werribee, Keilor, Knox, Sherbrooke and Springvale; a related study (MMBW 1977c) reveals a 33 per cent decline in number of dairy farms within the metropolitan area between 1971 and 1975 while retaining its position in this period as a major supplier to the state of orchard, berry and vegetable produce.

11. Currently there is a state government embargo on the approval of new regional shopping centres within Melbourne awaiting the outcome of a study designed to determine their impact on established suburban retail centres.

12. The standard chosen by international health authorities above which bathing waters are considered unsafe is water with more than 400 E. Coli per 100 millilitres on 10 per cent of samples taken (Birrell *et al.* 1974, pp. 8-11).

References

Alexander, I. (1979a) 'Job Location and Journey to Work: Three Australian Cities, 1961-1971', *Australian Geographical Studies, 17*, 155-74
––––– (1979b) *Office Location and Public Policy*, Longman, London

—— and J. Dawson (1979) 'Suburbanisation of Retailing Sales and Employment in Australian Cities', *Australian Geographical Studies, 17*, 76-83

Archer, R.W. (1978) 'The Market for New Multi-Unit Housing in Sydney and Melbourne', Paper presented at National Housing Economics Conference, Sydney (available as Staff Paper, Research Directorate, EHCD, Canberra)

Badcock, B.A. and D.V. Cloher (1979) 'An Approach to the Formulation and Implementation of Marginal Housing Policy: the Low-Rent Boarding and Lodging Sector, City of Adelaide, 1977-78', in P.W. Newton (ed.) *Housing Research for Housing Authorities: 1. Processes Influencing Low Income Housing*, Australian Housing Research Council, Melbourne

Barnett, J.R. and P.W. Newton, (1977) 'Intra-Urban Disparities in the Provision of Primary Health Care', *Australian and N.Z. Journal of Sociology, 13*, 60-8

Barr, L.R. (1978) 'Conflict Resolution in Environmental Management: The Newport Power Station Controversy', *Australian Geographical Studies, 16(1)*, 43-52

Batten, D.F. and J.F. Lenthall (1977) 'Regional Indicators of Educational Participation', Proceedings of the Australian and NZ Section of the Regional Science Association, Sydney

Birrell, R. (1975) 'Population and Planning: the Consequences of Ignoring Demographic Realities', *Royal Australian Planning Institute Journal*, October, 87-94

—— et al. (1974) *Port Phillip Bay: The Case for Alarm*, Progress Press, Melbourne

Bowman, N. (1978) *Local Government in the Australian States*, AGPS, Canberra

Brennan, T. (1967) 'Urban Communities', in A.F. Davies and S. Encel (eds.) *Australian Society*, Cheshire, Melbourne

Bromilow, F.J. (1977) 'What is an Affordable House', in *Productivity and the Affordable House*, Housing Industry Association, Melbourne

Brotchie, J.F. (1979) *On Economic Sizes of Cities*, CSIRO Division of Building Research, Melbourne

Bureau of Transport Economics, (1975) *Transport and Energy in Australia Part 1 – Review*, AGPS, Canberra

Centre for Urban Research and Action, (CURA) (1977) *The Displaced: A Study of Housing Conflict in Melbourne's Inner City*, Australian Housing Research Council, Melbourne

Commonwealth Department of Transport, (1977) 'Transport Pollution Control', in Institution of Engineers, Australia, *The Politics, Economics and Technology of Pollution Control*, Canberra

Donald, O.D. 1975 *Medical Services in Melbourne: A Geographical Analysis*, Geography No. 12, Monash Publications, Melbourne

Freeway Fighter, (1977) 'Why Melbourne Needs a Transport Plan', September, p. 5

Galbally, I.E. (1972) 'Ozone and Oxidants in the Surface Air Near Melbourne, Victoria', Proceedings of the International Clean Air Conference, Melbourne

Galvin, J.P. (1974) 'Origin and Settlement of Non-British Migrants in Newcastle', *The Australian Geographer, 12*, 517-30

Geelong Regional Planning Authority (1976) *The Geelong Region: An Industrial Location*, Geelong

Gottmann, J. (1979) 'Office Work and the Evolution of Cities', *Ekistics, 46* (274), 4-7

Government of Victoria, (1972) *Report of Board of Inquiry into Local Government Finance in Victoria*, Victorian Government Printer, Melbourne

—— (1978) *Report of the Board of Inquiry into the Melbourne and Metropolitan Board of Works*, Melbourne

Hardman, M. and P. Manning (1976) *Green Bans. The Story of an Australian Phenomenon*, Australian Conservation Foundation, Melbourne
Harvey, D. (1973) *Social Justice and the City*, Edward Arnold, London
—— (1975) 'Class Structure in a Capitalist Society and the Theory of Residential Differentiation', in R. Peel *et al.* (eds.) *Processes in Physical and Human Geography*, London
Holmes, J. (1976) *The Government of Victoria*, Queensland University Press, Brisbane
Howe, R. (1979) 'Housing Displacement in Inner City Melbourne', in P.W. Newton (ed.) *Housing Research for Housing Authorities 1. Processes Influencing Low Income Housing*, Australian Housing Research Council, Melbourne
Interplan Pty Ltd, (1973) *City of Melbourne Strategy Plan: Development Problems and Constraints*, Melbourne
Johnston, R.J. (1965) 'Sales in Australian Central Business Areas', *The Australian Geographer, 9*, 380-1
—— (1966) 'The Location of High Status Residential Areas', *Geografiska Annaler, 48B*, 23-35
—— (1968a) 'An Outline of the Development of Melbourne's Street Pattern', *The Australian Geographer, 10*, 453-65
—— (1968b) 'Railways, Urban Growth, and Central Place Patterns', *Tijdschrift voor Economische en Sociale Geografie, 59*, 33-41
—— (1969) 'Towards an Analytical Study of the Townscape: the Residential Building Fabric', *Geografiska Annaler, 51B*, 20-32
—— and P.J. Rimmer (1969) *Retailing in Melbourne*, Department of Human Geography, Australian National University, Canberra
Joy, S. (1977) 'Evaluating Melbourne's Planning: Criteria and Criticisms', in G. Seddon (ed.), pp. 28-33
Kendig, H. (1979) *New Life for Old Suburbs*, George Allen and Unwin, Sydney
Kilmartin, L. and D. Thorns (1978a) 'The Heart Possessed: Ownership of Central Business Areas in Australasia', Paper presented at SAANZ conference, Brisbane (mimeo)
—— and D. Thorns (1978b) *Cities Unlimited: The Sociology of Urban Development in Australia and New Zealand*, George Allen and Unwin, Sydney
LeRoy, P.A., W. Lau, and G. Holden (1976) *The Occurrence and Control of Photo-Chemical Smog in Melbourne*, Smog '76, Clean Air Society of Australia and New Zealand
Leach, R.H. (1977) *The Governance of Metropolitan Areas in Australia with Lessons from Canadian and American Experience*, Centre for Research on Federal Financial Relations, Research Monograph 21, ANU, Canberra
Linge, G.J.R. (1979) 'Australian Manufacturing in Recession: A Review of the Spatial Implications', *Environment and Planning A, 11*, 1405-30
Logan, A. (1979) 'Recent Directions of Regional Policy in Australia', *Regional Studies, 13*, 153-60
Logan, M.I. (1977) 'Evaluating Melbourne's Planning: Regional Implications', in G. Seddon (ed.), pp. 40-4
—— *et al.* (1975) *Urban and Regional Australia*, Sorrell, Melbourne
Maher, C.A. (1978) 'The Changing Residential Role of the Inner City: The Example of Inner Melbourne', *Australian Geographer, 14*, 112-22
May, J.D. (1975) 'Rural Over-Representation', *Journal of Commonwealth and Comparative Politics, 13*, 132-45
Melbourne Transportation Study (MTS), (1969) *Melbourne Transportation Study Volume 3: The Transportation Plan*, Melbourne
Mercer, J. (1979) 'On Continentalism, Distinctiveness and Comparative Urban

Geography: Canadian and American Cities', *The Canadian Geographer, 13(2)*, 119-39

MMBW, (1954) *Melbourne Metropolitan Planning Scheme: Report*, Melbourne

—— (1967) *The Future Growth of Melbourne*, A Report to the Minister of Local Government on Melbourne's Future Growth and its Planning Administration, Melbourne

—— (1971) *Planning Policies for the Melbourne Metropolitan Region*, Melbourne

—— (1974) *Report on General Concept Objections*, Melbourne

—— (1977a) *Melbourne's Inner Area. A Position Statement*, Melbourne

—— (1977b) *Review of Planning Policies for the Non-Urban Zones*, Melbourne

—— (1977c) *Metropolitan Farming Study*, Melbourne

—— (1979a) *The Challenge of Change: A Review of Metropolitan Melbourne's Planning Options*, Melbourne

—— (1979b) *Alternative Strategies for Metropolitan Melbourne*, Melbourne

—— (1979c) *Alternative Strategies for Metropolitan Melbourne: Background Papers*, Melbourne

MMBW Planning Branch, (1974) *Social Dysfunction and Relative Poverty in Metropolitan Melbourne*, Research Report No. 1, Melbourne

National Committee of Inquiry into Housing Costs, (1978) *The Cost of Housing: Volume 1*, Canberra

National Population Inquiry, (1978) *Population and Australia: Recent Demographic Trends and Their Implications*, AGPS, Canberra

Neutze, M. (1977) *Urban Development in Australia*, George Allen and Unwin, Sydney

—— (1978) *Australian Urban Policy*, George Allen and Unwin, Sydney

Newton, P.W. (1977) *Patterns of Population Movement in an Australian City*, CSIRO Division of Building Research, Technical Paper 19, Melbourne

—— (1980) 'New Towns in Isolated Settings in Australia', in R. Lonsdale and J. Holmes (eds.) *Settlement Systems in Sparsely Settled Regions: The United States and Australia*, Pergamon, NY

—— and B.S. Coe (1980) 'The Existing Stock of Housing: Structure and Distribution', in F.A. Blakey and J.F. Nicholas (eds.) *Options in Housing*, CSIRO, Melbourne

O'Connor, K. (1978) 'The Journey to Work of Inner City Residents in Melbourne, 1966 and 1971', *Australian Geographical Studies, 16(1)*, 73-81

—— and C.A. Maher (1979) 'Change in the Spatial Structure of a Metropolitan Region: Work-Residence Relationships in Melbourne, 1961-1971', *Regional Studies, 13*, 361-80

Podder, N. (1972) 'Distribution of Household Income in Australia', *The Economic Record, 48*, 181-200

Richardson, S. (1979) 'Income Distribution, Poverty and Redistributive Policies', in F. Gruen (ed.) *Surveys of Australian Economics Vol. 2*, George Allen and Unwin, Sydney

Rimmer, P.J. (1969) *Manufacturing in Melbourne*, Department of Human Geography, Australian National University, Canberra

—— (1976) 'Politicians, Public Servants and Petitioners: Aspects of Transport in Australia 1851-1901', in J.M. Powell and M. Williams (eds.) *Australian Space, Australian Time*, Oxford University Press, Melbourne, pp. 182-225.

Rowland, D.T. (1979) *Internal Migration in Australia*, Australian Bureau of Statistics, Canberra

Sandercock, L. (1975) *Cities for Sale, Property, Politics and Urban Planning in Australia*, Melbourne University Press, Melbourne

—— (1979) *The Land Racket: The Real Cost of Property Speculation*, Silverfish Books, Melbourne

Sarkissian, W. (1976) 'The Idea of Social Mix in Town Planning: an Historical Review', *Urban Studies, 13*, 231-46

Sawford, B.L. (1976) 'Meteorological Aspects of Pollution Dispersal in the Atmosphere', in Institution of Engineers, Australia, *Management of Urban Air Quality*, Melbourne

Searle, G. (1980) 'Manufacturing Company Change within Melbourne, 1970 to 1973', Paper presented at Institute of Australian Geographers conference, Newcastle

Seddon, G. (ed.) (1977) *Urbanisation*, Centre for Environmental Studies, University of Melbourne

Sharpe, R. (1980) 'Improving Energy Efficiency in Community Land Use – Transportation Systems', *Environment and Planning A, 12*, 203-16

Shelter, (1978) *Emergency Housing Report*, Melbourne

Stilwell, F.J.B. (1976) 'Sharing the Economic Cake: Inequality of Income and Wealth in Australia', in T. Van Dugteren (ed.) *Who Gets What? The Distribution of Wealth and Power in Australia*, Hodder and Stoughton, Sydney

Stretton, H. (1971) *Ideas for Australian Cities*, Georgian House, Melbourne

Taylor, P.J. and G. Gudgin (1977) 'Antipodean Remises of Labour', in R.J. Johnston (ed.) *People, Places and Votes*, Department of Geography, University of New England, Armidale, pp. 111-20

TCPB, (1967) *Organisation for Strategic Planning*, Report to the Minister for Local Government on the Future Growth of Melbourne, Melbourne

The Age (21 Dec. 1978) 'Corridor Plan Approved at Last'

Thomson, J.M. (1978) *Great Cities and Their Traffic*, Penguin, Harmondsworth

Urlich Cloher, D. (1979) 'Urban Settlement Process in Lands of "Recent Settlement" – an Australian Example', *Journal of Historical Geography, 5*, 297-314

Western Port Regional Planning Authority, (1979) *Review of Operations of the Western Port Regional Planning Authority 1969-1979*

Whitlam, E.G. (1971) 'A New Federalism', *Australian Quarterly, 43*

—— (1972) *Australian Labor Party Policy Speech*

Wilmoth, D., R. Purdon, A. Strickland and M. Logan (1976) 'Towards a National Strategy for Urban and Regional Development', in J. McMaster and G. Webb (eds.) *Australian Urban Economics*, ANZ Book Co., Sydney

3 TOKYO

M.E. Witherick

Japan has experienced a speed and scale of urbanisation probably unmatched anywhere else in the developed world and to the degree that over half the Japanese people now live in cities with populations in excess of 100,000 inhabitants (Figure 3.1). An economic revolution, ignited and still substantially fuelled by industrialisation, has in less

Figure 3.1: Population Growth and Urbanisation in Japan, 1920-75

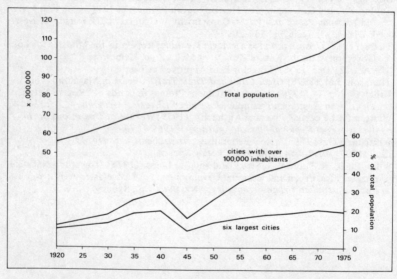

than a century transformed Japan from an introverted, largely rural country with a meagre material resource-base into one of the most powerful and successful nations in the international community. An integral part of this revolution has been the remarkable growth of the Tokyo metropolis, propelled by a dynamic mix of industry and commerce, providing leadership in so many facets of national life and epitomising the fruits of an uninhibited capitalism. Today Tokyo not only enjoys an unchallenged pre-eminence in the Japanese urban system, but its economic progress has raised it to the status of a leading world

120

city (Hall 1977). However, as in other countries, economic success has
generated its wake of societal problems, such as housing shortages,
traffic congestion and deterioration of the physical and biotic environment. The desired solution of these and other problems has prompted
the gradual emergence in Japan of an essentially 'ameliorative' mode
of planning (Berry 1973). Much less forthcoming has been recognition
of the need for a more positive calibre of planning oriented rather more
towards the formulation of developmental policies and which takes a
longer-term view of Tokyo's growth and its repercussions on the rest
of the country.

This chapter is concerned with post-war Tokyo and in particular with
the two master plans which from the mid-1950s to the late 1970s have
sought to cope with the more pressing issues raised by Tokyo's persistent
advancement as a strong-centred metropolis. It is hoped that this
appraisal will signal not only the achievements of those plans, but also
indicate lessons to be incorporated in programmes of planning action
for the 1980s.

Background

The National Capital Region

Planning at a metropolitan level has been practised in Japan since 1956
when the decision was taken to effect the planning of Tokyo and its
neighbouring city-port of Yokohama in the wider spatial context of
what is now known as the National Capital Region, with planning
authority vested in a National Capital Region Development Commission.
At the time of its inception, the region accounted for 10 per cent of the
Japanese land area and 24 per cent of the nation's population.

The boundaries of the National Capital Region were extended in
1966, so that it now covers an area of approximately 36,500 km^2 lying
within a 150-km radius of central Tokyo. Administratively, the region
comprises the Kanto District, which is made up of seven prefectures
(Chiba, Gumma, Ibaraki, Kanagawa, Saitama, Tochigi and Tokyo),
together with the prefecture of Yamanashi (Figure 3.2). Within the
core area of the region, three territorial divisions are frequently encountered in the contexts of government and planning, and it is
important that these spatial units should be clearly defined at the outset.
The first is known as the *Ward Area* of Tokyo and constitutes the
historic nucleus of the city; it is currently made up of 23 wards and
contains a residential population of around 8 millions. Secondly, there

Figure 3.2: The National Capital Region and its Subdivisions

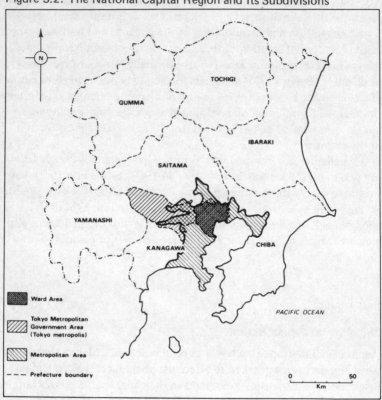

is the administrative area of the Tokyo metropolitan government which is widely referred to as the *Tokyo Metropolis*. In fact, it coincides exactly with the prefecture of Tokyo and embraces the Ward Area together with a large suburban appendage reaching out to the west of the city centre; at present some 11.5 million people live within its borders. Finally, the Japanese Census defines what is called the *Metropolitan Area* which includes the cities of Tokyo and Yokohama and their suburbs; as such, it closely matches the outer limits of the present built-up zone generated by these two cities. According to the 1970 Census, this area contained 15 million people.

Post-war Recovery and the First Master Plan (1958)

The post-war economic recovery of Japan has been fully recorded and analysed elsewhere (e.g. Allen 1965; Broadbridge 1966; Kornhauser 1976;

Yamamura 1967). Consequently, it is sufficient in this study merely to stress that a spectacular expansion of commercial and industrial activity (particularly of quaternary industries), a proliferation of governmental institutions and a marked concentration of educational and cultural establishments provided the vital fuel for a greatly accelerated urban-isation and macro-scale urban growth (what the Japanese planners call 'metropolitanisation'). At the same time, the widespread devastation wrought during the closing stages of World War II presented the oppor-tunity, in theory at least, to build anew and relatively unfettered by the constraints of the pre-war infrastructure. By 1955, 16 per cent of the Japanese population lived in the six largest cities and 35 per cent in cities with more than 100,000 inhabitants (Figure 3.1).

Between 1945 and 1955 the population of the Tokyo Metropolitan Government Area more than doubled and as such provides a single indication of the gathering momentum and magnetism of the metro-politan economy (Table 3.1). No doubt, Tokyo's recovery had been stimulated by the National Capital Reconstruction Act (1950) which made the rebuilding of Tokyo a top national priority. The decision which was taken six years later to set up the National Capital Region Development Commission and to adopt a more macro-scale approach to the planning of the capital's growth, appears to have been somewhat tardy. None the less, in 1958 the first Master Plan (National Capital Region Development Commission 1958) was published for immediate implementation, its basic strategy being to corset Tokyo within an 11-km-wide green belt circumscribed at a radius of about 16 km from the city centre (Tokyo Metropolitan Government 1978). The core thus com-prised the Ward Area of Tokyo together with the cities of Kawasaki, Yokohama and Kawaguchi and the scope it offered for the accom-modation of further growth was severely limited. Whilst the green belt was drawn to inhibit suburban sprawl and to firm-up the edge of the metropolitan area, any further growth drawn to the National Capital Region was to be encouraged to locate in the peripheral zone beyond the green belt. To this end, the plan proposed the construction of 13 satellite towns which would also accommodate decentralised people and jobs. The 'Law for Town Development', enacted in the same year, sought to provide the legal powers and make the financial provisions necessary for the implementation of this part of the Master Plan.

During the two years it took to prepare the Master Plan, the basic dimensions of growth in the National Capital Region were beginning to change to a scale and at a rate which far exceeded the projections prefacing the plan. It was not long before the plan's whole viability was

Table 3.1: Population Distribution in the National Capital Region, by Prefectures, 1945-75 (population in millions)

Prefecture	1945	1955	1965	1975
Tokyo	3.5	8.0	10.9	11.7
Kanagawa	1.9	2.9	4.4	6.4
Chiba	2.0	2.2	2.7	4.1
Saitama	2.0	2.3	3.0	4.8
Gumma	1.5	1.6	1.6	1.8
Ibaraki	2.0	2.1	2.1	2.3
Tochigi	1.5	1.5	1.5	1.7
Yamanashi	0.8	0.8	0.8	0.8
NCR	15.2	21.4	27.0	33.6

Source: Bureau of Statistics (1977)

being brought into question, as the National Capital Region began to account for over half of all the population and employment growth in the country and as its more central prefectures—Chiba, Kanagawa, Saitama and Tokyo—regularly showed levels of population growth in excess of 2 per cent per annum (Table 3.1). Intolerable pressures and congestion were thus generated within the core area and the green belt soon fell victim to the rapacious spread of Tokyo. The general inefficacy of the plan was also precipitated by the fact that the metropolitan planners did not at the time fully command the legal powers and financial resources necessary for its prompt and decisive implement-ation. Slowly, and far too belatedly, the required legislation was passed by the Diet, as for example, the 'Law concerning Restrictions on Industries' in 1959, and in 1966 the 'Law concerning Preservation of Suburban Green zones' and the 'Law concerning Special Measures on National Finance for the National Capital Region'.

Official recognition that the situation had become out of control was indicated in 1962 when a minor revision of the plan was instituted, but it was not until 1966 that the Development Commission was instructed to undertake a comprehensive reappraisal of developments within an enlarged National Capital Region and to prepare a wholly new plan in tune with the rather different circumstances which now prevailed. Thus in October 1968 the second Master Plan was published, so designed to achieve a reconciliation between the need to enable Tokyo to fulfil its role of leadership in the national context and the need to solve the problems of overcongestion normally associated with the execution of that function.

1968 Master Plan

The revised assumptions and forecasts providing the fundamental dimensions for the second Master Plan related for the most part to developments anticipated during the period 1965-75, but with frequent reference being made to 1985 projections. Specifically the plan assumed that the population of the National Capital Region would increase from 26.9 to 33.1 millions by 1975 and to 38 millions by 1985, thus extending the built-up area from 1,430 to 2,600 km². In the early phases of the plan implementation, it was expected that net in-migration would account for more than half the total population increase, whereas in the 1980s its share was thought likely to decline to about one-third. Mirroring the demographic growth, the regional labour

Table 3.2: Projected Employment Changes in the National Capital Region, 1965-85

Sector	1965		1975		1985	
	Employees (millions)	% of total employed	Employees (millions)	% of total employed	Employees (millions)	% of total employed
Primary	2.1	16	1.6	9	1.1	6
Secondary	4.9	37	6.6	40	7.7	42
Tertiary	6.2	47	8.3	51	9.6	52
NCR	13.2		16.5		18.4	

Source: National Capital Region Development Commission (1968)

force was projected to increase from 13.2 to 16.5 millions by 1975 and to 18.4 millions by 1985; this growth was to be accompanied by significant shifts in the sectoral balance of the regional economy (Table 3.2).

The primary objective of the second Master Plan was to alleviate the already acute pressure on the central areas of Tokyo by encouraging selective decentralisation from the core, and at the same time endeavouring to ensure that growth gravitating towards the National Capital Region from other parts of Japan would be directed as much as possible to peripheral sub-centres rather than to the core itself. The strategy to be adopted, therefore, aimed to open out the pattern of metropolitan development in a manner which bore some resemblance to that already pursued in connection with London and South-East England (Hall 1974). Compared with the 1958 Master Plan, the whole character of the strategy was more expansionist, being founded on a more realistic appraisal of Tokyo's growth potential. In pursuit of its basic objective, the second Master Plan sought to coordinate three distinct programmes of action, one for each of three major subdivisions of the National Capital Region, namely 1) the Built-up District, 2) the Suburban Re-development District and 3) the Outer Development District (Figure 3.3).

Built-up District

This core division of the National Capital Region embraces the 23 wards of Tokyo (an area extending to a little more than 10 km from the city centre) together with the adjoining city areas of Yokohama, Kawasaki, Musashino, Mitaka and Kawaguchi (Figure 3.3). More than anything, this district represented the dynamism of post-war Tokyo, where excessively-concentrated growth had given rise to that plethora of problems which tend to characterise so many world cities — traffic congestion, high land values, large volumes of commuting, an acute shortage of space for business growth, etc. Yet despite the enormous competition for space, the amount of vertical development has probably been less in Tokyo than in any other leading capital city. Much of the explanation lies in the 1923 earthquake which destroyed so much of Tokyo and which persuaded the Japanese government to impose a height limit of around 40 m on all vertical development. Under pressure from business firms, the ban was eventually lifted in 1963, faith being placed in the ability of modern building technology to construct high-rise accommodation capable of withstanding the destructive impact of earthquakes. Thus belatedly the central-city skyline of the Built-up District has been increasingly punctuated by prestigious office blocks which rise to over 250 m.

Although such vertical development along with lateral encroachment into residential areas has undoubtedly helped to increase the capacity of the inner area, the plan recognised the impossibility of adequately accommodating all the centripetal growth pressures impinging upon Tokyo. For this reason, the plan called for a policy of selective decentralisation, whereby 'non-pivotal' activities should be removed to less central locations to make proper room for those high-order activities vital to Tokyo's further enhancement as the pivotal point of political, economic, social and cultural life in Japan. Specifically, the plan recommended the dispersal of production and circulation functions, together with research and educational establishments. In pursuit of this objective, the plan sought to take advantage of the 'Law Restricting Industrial and Educational Establishments in the Built-up Area' which had been enacted in 1959.

A crucial part of the planning strategy for the Built-up District was the comprehensive redevelopment and reorganisation of its spatial structure in such a way as to ultimately create a multi-centred metropolis (Witherick 1972a). Such a goal had previously been defined in the 1958 Redevelopment Plan for the Built-up District. Three new business centres were to be constructed, each comprising a mix of high-order shops, commercial offices and professional premises and each located in conjunction with a major terminal station on Tokyo's railway network. These new business nodes at Ikebukuro, Shibuya and Shinjuku, along with an enlargement and redevelopment of Yokohama's central business district, were intended to help relieve some of the acute pressure on the Maranouchi and Yurakucho areas, the long-established business quarters of Tokyo.

Although the plan referred rather vaguely to the relocation of factories and the abatement of public nuisances (presumably stemming from industrial development), it was strangely silent as to the future of those major industrial concentrations lying within and close to the core, namely the great factory zone on the low-lying flats along the Sumida River, the heavy port-related industries at Yokohama and the manufacturing district around Kawasaki. Instead, attention was directed rather more towards the need to achieve a finer segregation of housing from this industry. It also highlighted the need to undertake the comprehensive redevelopment of large areas of obsolete housing, where the densely-packed, wooden and mainly single-storey dwellings would be replaced by 5- to 7-storey concrete apartment blocks. Such renewal would inevitably involve a general reduction in the residential population of the Built-up District and the removal of a proportion of existing residents to either housing projects in the suburbs or satellite towns located further out into the National Capital Region.

Suburban Redevelopment District

Beyond the Built-up District, and reaching out to some 50 km from the centre of Tokyo, was the second subdivision of the National Capital Region entitled, not altogether appropriately, the Suburban Redevelopment District (Figure 3.3). This was the part of the metropolitan region which had been so badly ravaged by the virtually uncontrolled suburban

Figure 3.3: The Second (1968) Master Plan for the National Capital Region

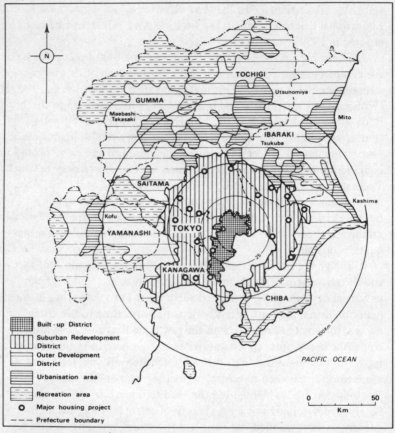

boom of the 1950s and early 1960s. During these years, its residential development had acquired a host of undesirable characteristics. Little regard had been paid to the quality of agricultural land, for example, for in many areas precious grade 1 and grade 2 land had been built over. Insufficient attention had been given to basic infrastructure, particularly to proper water supply and sanitary sewage disposal; and, reflecting the gross inflation of the costs of building land, individual dwelling units were intolerably small and densely packed. The establishment of commercial and social services had lagged a long way behind the growth of population in the rashes of residential development fingering out along the transport arteries leading from central Tokyo. Above all else it was the extension and improvement of public transport services which had facilitated this suburban sprawl and the increasing spatial dislocation of workplace and residence. Ironically, the first Master Plan had designated much of this district as a green belt wrapping around the Built-up District, but so great had been the growth in the demand for housing and so ineffectual had been the planning controls that by 1965 much of the belt had already been built over. The National Capital Region Development Commission had no option but to officially abandon the green belt.

In this district, the plan aimed to exert a more careful control over the location and standards of future residential development. What was envisaged was the construction of 18 very large housing projects with target populations ranging from 60,000 to 350,000 persons and modelled on schemes already successfully undertaken by the Japan Housing Corporation (Witherick 1972b). Some of these projects were in fact already under way, having been initiated as 'satellite towns' under the terms of the first Master Plan. By concentrating residential development in this way and by the designation of some 50,000 ha of 'green zones', it was hoped to obviate the suburban sprawl which had characterised the growth of Tokyo during the earlier post-war period. Added to which, those 'green zones' (some of them relics of the 1958 green belt) would serve a valuable amenity and recreational role. To help meet the shortage of building land that would ensue from this designation of green zones and the belated preservation of the remaining high-grade agricultural land, the plan proposed the reclamation of 10,000 ha of land from Tokyo Bay by 1975 and a doubling of that amount by 1990, at which time approximately one-eighth of the bay will have been converted into land.

The plan anticipated the creation of relatively little new employment within the suburban belt. Clearly the service needs of the growing residential population would generate a certain amount of employment within the tertiary sector, as would the deliberate creation of a series of 'commodity circulation centres' at strategic intersections between the proposed Tokyo Loop Highway and the major radial expressways, where wholesaling, storage and other distributional activities decanted from the core were to become concentrated (Figure 3.4). Furthermore, the plan admitted that a limited amount of industrial development would have to be tolerated, as for example the growth of industries which 'for unavoidable reasons must be located near large cities and located with reference to the major routeways', or industries which were considered 'to produce tolerably small public nuisance'. Also countenanced was encroachment by a certain amount of port-related and largely heavy

Figure 3.4: Transportation Proposals of the 1968 Master Plan

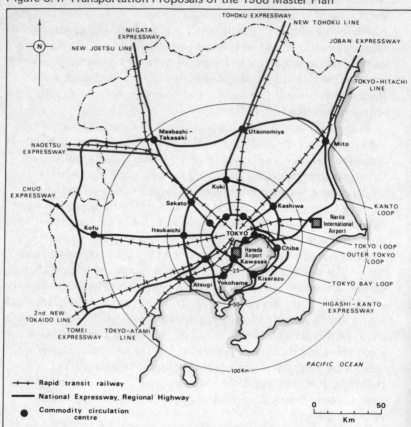

industry spreading out along the shores of Tokyo Bay from the Built-up District.

Outer Development District

The Outer Development District, accounting for the remainder of the National Capital Region, was defined ostensibly to function as a reception area both for those activities and people displaced from the Built-up District and for the new growth moving towards the metropolis from other parts of the country. The plan designated 16 'urbanisation areas', located between 50 and 100 km from central Tokyo, in which most future growth in this part of the National Capital Region was to become concentrated (Figure 3.3). The majority of them are located in the three northernmost prefectures. Eight of the proposed schemes

(Kamagaya, Koga, Maebashi-Takasaki, Mito, Ota, Oyama, Tsuchiura and Utsonomiya) had been initiated as 'satellite towns' as part of the first Master Plan, along with five others which, by virtue of being situated much closer to Tokyo, had been conveniently recast by the 1968 Master Plan as housing projects located within the Suburban Redevelopment District. The term 'urbanisation area' conveys little about the aims and objectives of the projects. In most cases the designated area embraced a localised grouping of essentially low-order urban centres, so that an important purpose of the scheme would be to integrate these existing settlements into a single high-order urban centre which would at the very least merit the label of 'new town'. In four of the schemes, however, the aspirations were possibly deserving of titles implying a higher status. At Mito, Kofu, Maebashi-Takasaki and Utsonomiya, through a combination of industrial growth and the development of a major 'commodity circulation centre', the aim was to nurture a large 'multifunctional centre' (Figure 3.4). In all but one of the remaining 'urbanisation area' schemes not only was the scale generally smaller, but also the developmental emphasis was to be almost exclusively upon industrial growth, with great reliance being placed on provisions made in the 'Law for Promoting the Construction of New Industrial Cities' enacted in 1962. In stark contrast, the Tsukuba project in Ibaraki Prefecture was to contain no industrial development whatsoever; initiated in 1963, its single objective was to accommodate research and educational establishments decentralised from the Built-up District.

The spatial concentration of growth as advocated in the 1968 Master Plan was intended not only to preserve as much agricultural land as possible, but also to leave large tracts of countryside available for recreational purposes. To this end, the plan designated some seven 'recreation areas' (Figure 3.3). In some, as around the lakes of Kasumiga-ura and Kita-ura in Ibaraki, priority would be placed upon the conservation of the natural environment, whilst in others more weight would be given to the development of a tourist infrastructure, as in the northern piedmont of Fuji and along parts of the coast in Chiba Prefecture. The recreational and tourist potential of the Outer Development District was recognised as being of considerable diversity, ranging for example from hot springs to ski slopes, from shrines and temples to golf courses, from mountain lakes to sandy coasts. Clearly, with increasing affluence and leisure time the exploitation of such resources would become increasingly crucial to the general well-being of the metropolitan population and a vital part of that exploitation would involve improved access from Tokyo.

The 1975 Review

Since 1975 had been set as the terminal date for the application of the
second Master Plan, a review of developments within the National
Capital Region was set in train by the Megalopolis Region Reorganisation
Bureau of the National Land Agency, an organisation which in the
previous year had superseded the National Capital Region Development
Commission as the planning authority for the Tokyo Metropolis. This
change in the planning arrangements was significant on two counts. Firstly,
it represented an important step towards a more macro-scale approach
to urban and regional planning, and secondly, it now allows the Prime
Minister and the Japanese Cabinet a much more direct control over the
planning of Tokyo and two other leading cities, Osaka and Nagoya.

In 1976 the Bureau published a 'Basic Plan' to provide the essential
guidelines for the development of the National Capital Region over the
next 10 years. Despite the change in the general economic climate, the
basic projections and assumptions embodied in the new plan do not
differ significantly from those which had been suggested in its predecessor for the period 1975 to 1985. The similarity of the two plans
extends further, in that the 1976 Basic Plan seeks as a prime objective
to control the general distribution of employment and population. To
this end it uses the same threefold division of the National Capital
Region but with the first two more aptly referred to as the 'Inner Urban
Area' and the 'Suburban Development Area'. The intention is still to
create a 'multi-terminal' metropolitan structure and to nurture the
development of what are now openly referred to as 'satellite towns' in
the outer areas of the National Capital Region. One noteworthy departure evident in the 1976 plan is an increased emphasis on planning of a
more social complexion, reflecting a greater concern for the general
standards of the living environment and the general quality of life. This
aside, it is perhaps remarkable that the current plan does not incorporate
other changes in direction for, as the ensuing discussion endeavours to
demonstrate, despite its undoubted achievements, the 1968 plan was
ultimately shown to have deficiencies both in its theory and in its
application—shortcomings which are presumably to be perpetuated in
the 1980s.

Plan Implementation—A Critical Appraisal

In this next section an attempt is made to review the achievements and shortcomings of the planning which has been practised in the National Capital Region since the mid-1960s. Partly for reasons of data availability and partly because it represents a milestone in the evolution of Japanese metropolitan planning, the appraisal is made principally in terms of the state of affairs which existed in 1975, the terminal year prescribed for the second Master Plan. The evaluation considers in turn each of the three planning divisions of the National Capital Region, with particular emphasis being placed on what are deemed to be important planning issues or problems arising in each of those districts. In the Built-up District the major concerns are employment growth, traffic and environmental pollution, in the Suburban Redevelopment District housing is the key concern, whilst in the Outer Development District a fundamental consideration is the establishment and viability of the designated 'urbanisation areas'. In each planning division, one prefecture has been selected to furnish the bulk of the case-study material, thereby enabling the construction of a reasonably integrated image of progress made in three representative areas. By focusing on these sample prefectures of Tokyo, Chiba and Ibaraki, it is hoped that the overall review will be imbued with a greater degree of cohesion.

The General Performance of the National Capital Region (1965-75)

In terms of population growth, the National Capital Region as a whole performed very much as forecasted in the second Master Plan, the total population of 33.6 millions recorded in 1975 being only 0.5 million in excess of the projected figure. The suburban prefectures of Chiba and Saitama, together with the outer parts of Kanagawa, undoubtedly accommodated the greater part of the regional population increase (Table 3.1). However, the plan's prognoses for the development of the regional economy proved to be less in line with actual changes. Despite the scale of demographic growth, the regional labour force increased to only 15.8 millions, thus falling short of expectation by some 0.7 million workers (Table 3.2). A sectoral analysis of regional employment in 1975 shows that the secondary sector (including construction) accounted for only 35 per cent of total employed, 2 per cent less than it did in 1965; whereas a figure of 40 per cent had been forecasted (Tables 3.2 and 3.3). In stark contrast, the expansion of the tertiary sector was considerably in excess of that anticipated, its share of the regional workforce rising to 56 per cent. By the very nature and locational requirements of its component activities, the growth of this particular sector clearly had profound implications for the core area of the National Capital Region, to the extent that by 1975 it accounted for two in every three jobs in the Tokyo Metropolitan Government Area.

Table 3.3: Sectoral Analysis of Labour in the National Capital Region, 1975 (by place of residence)

Prefecture	Total employed (thousands)	Primary	Secondary (% of total employed)	Tertiary
Tokyo	5,618	1	34	65
Kanagawa	2,890	3	41	56
Chiba	1,886	14	32	54
Saitama	2,173	9	40	51
Gumma	870	20	36	44
Ibaraki	1,139	28	31	41
Tochigi	851	21	35	44
Yamanashi	385	22	31	47
NCR	15,812	9	35	56

Source: Bureau of Statistics (1977)

Major Issues in the Built-up District

a) Employment Growth. Although the total population of the Tokyo Metropolitan Government Area (cf. Tokyo Prefecture) increased by 0.8 million between 1965 and 1975, a significant distinction needs to be drawn between the Ward Area (constituting the commercial and industrial heart of Tokyo Metropolis) and the largely residential remainder of the prefecture. The modest decline in the residential population of the Ward Area since its peak in 1965 attests to the combined effects of lowered densities in residential renewal schemes and the continuing erosion of residential land by the expansion of non-residential land uses (Table 3.4). In the three central wards of Chiyoda, Chuo and Minato, however, the residential population had been reduced much more dramatically to total just over 0.3 million. Outside the Ward Area, population growth appears to have been sustained at a remarkably consistent rate of 0.5 million extra people every five years. No doubt the maintenance of this rate of increase was facilitated in the post-1965 period by the release of land which had previously been part of Tokyo's ill-fated green belt designated in the first Master Plan.

More worrying in terms of planning policy is the fact that during the

Table 3.4: Population Change in the Tokyo Metropolitan Government Area, 1955-75 (population in millions)

	1955	1965	1970	1975
Ward Area	7.0	8.9	8.8	8.6
Rest of prefecture	1.0	2.0	2.6	3.1

Source: Bureau of Statistics (1977)

decade under scrutiny, the daytime or working population of the Tokyo Metropolitan Government Area grew from 8.3 to 13.4 millions. Although the employment growth curve is now beginning to level off, clearly the record during the term of the 1968 Master Plan was irrefutably one of a massive and prolonged increase in jobs. In the three central wards alone, which effectively represent Japan's economic, political and cultural heart, the volume of in-coming commuters now numbers over 2 millions, as compared with a flow of 1.1 million at the beginning of the plan period. Admittedly, it was always the intention of the plan to permit the growth of high-order business and governmental functions, together with many of their ancillary services, and there can be no disappointment that this has not happened. But what has been achieved in terms of the aim to remove many distributive activities from the core area? Very little appears to have been accomplished as regards the decentralisation of wholesaling. The three central wards, together with Taito Ward to the north-west, still contain 52 per cent of all the wholesale establishments in Japan, 63 per cent of all employees and 83 per cent of the national annual sales. In slight contrast, the retailing situation has begun to show some signs of improvement in that the Ward Area's share of national totals has dropped to 9.5 per cent of all retail establishments, 11 per cent of all employees and 14.5 per cent of annual sales. In 1965, for example, the Ward Area accounted for nearly 12 per cent of Japan's total stock of retail establishments. Complementing this contraction, there has been a rise in retail turnover levels in adjacent prefectures as more department stores and the larger chain stores have moved in pursuit of the growing suburban clientele (Tokyo Metropolitan Government 1978).

In keeping with policy, the general standing of manufacturing in the economy of the Tokyo Metropolitan Government Area has diminished, albeit very slightly, during the plan period; the Keihin's (defined as a belt running from Chiba through Tokyo and Kawasaki to Yokohama) overall share of total industrial production in Japan has also shrunk

(Fisher and Sargent 1975). Manufacturing now accounts for 22 per cent of the prefectural labour force, as compared with a figure of 28 per cent for retailing and wholesaling; in 1965 the figures were 28 per cent and 26 per cent respectively. Although the agglomeration diseconomies of rocketing site-costs, traffic congestion and the introduction of restrictive laws have been instrumental in bringing about this small decrease, the spatial concentration of the information industries, the existence of a huge reservoir of labour and an immense consumer market still hold considerable attraction for manufacturing. One interesting development within the realms of manufacturing in the Ward Area is that, whilst on the one hand the number of large factories (employing 300 workers or more) has decreased from 450 to 300, on the other hand small factories (employing less than 10 workers) have increased from 58,500 to nearly 80,000. The latter type of establishment currently accounts for around 80 per cent of the total number of factories. Three types of manufacturing are becoming increasingly conspicuous in these small-scale operations, namely i) printing and publishing (a crucial part of the information industry), ii) the production of goods closely related to fashion (furniture, clothing, toys, leather goods, etc.) and iii) the making of parts and components (electrical, motor vehicles, etc.) under subcontract to larger assembly plants (Tokyo Metropolitan Government 1978).

Thus it would seem that the growth of employment in central Tokyo has exceeded the forecasts made in the 1968 plan and that it has done so principally because the intended decentralisation of manufacturing and distribution, in particular, has not proceeded to the extent that was originally planned. A lack of really effective restrictive legislation coupled with the inability to offer substantial inducements to firms to relocate elsewhere in the National Capital Region may be partly to blame, but why is it that both wholesaling and much manufacturing should be so apparently reluctant to quit their central-city strongholds? The idea of removing such activities to a contrived network of new sub-centres is fine in theory, but sub-centres by their very definition are suitable only for sub-central or sector functions. There are certain forms of manufacturing (clothing, printing and publishing for example), which are of a central rather than a sub-central calibre and which, even under pressure from planning, will refuse to abandon profitable central locations.

As a corollary to this review of the employment situation, it should be noted that the plan has probably been much more successful in controlling the general distribution of employment within the Built-up

District and that it has gone a long way to realising its aim of restructuring that part of the National Capital Region into 'a multi-centred
metropolis'. In the Ward Area, the three new business nodes at Ikebukuro,
Shibuya and Shinjuku are now all but complete. The dimensions of the
Shinjuku Business Centre, the first to be finished, are impressive. The
whole development, covering a ground-floor area of 96 ha, focuses on
Shinjuku Station, which, with nearly 4 million passengers passing through
it each day, is possibly the busiest terminal station in the whole of
Japan. A measure of the high degree of accessibility enjoyed by the site
is suggested by the fact that no less than seven different rail systems and
more than one hundred different bus services converge on the station
and its forecourt. The Centre is a fan-shaped development and occupies
a site twice the size of that of the long-established Marunouchi business
district (Figure 3.5). The main structure is the West Entrance, a two-
level square which serves essentially as a great concourse providing
interconnection between all the public transport services. To the north-
west, there are 11 street blocks set aside for high-rise office development.
Three of the blocks are owned by the Tokyo Metropolitan Government,
whilst the remaining 8 blocks are shared by 11 major companies. In all,
there are about 1,650 ha of office floor space available in this part of
the Centre. Also included in the development are large department
stores, hotels and a huge car park set alongside Metropolitan Highway
No. 4. Total employment in the Centre is in the order of 300,000 jobs.

b) Traffic and Transport. Although the construction of the new
business centres has helped to reduce the acute convergence of traffic
flows actually within the central parts of the Ward Area, the overall
growth in employment and services has had very profound implications
in terms of traffic generation and the strains which it has thrown on
Tokyo's transport system. During the plan period, commuter traffic
increased at an average rate of 5 per cent per annum, and it was estimated
that in 1975 roughly half of the employed people living within a 50-km
radius of central Tokyo commuted into the Ward Area. With a daily commuter flow of over 2 million people, few would question Tokyo's boast
that it experiences the largest commuter movements in the world (Tokyo
Metropolitan Government 1975).

Table 3.5, which refers to passenger movements within a 50-km radius
of central Tokyo, indicates that the railway network is now responsible
for carrying just over half the metropolitan passenger traffic. The network is shared by Japan National Railways (30 per cent of total
passengers in 1975) and 11 private railway companies (23 per cent of

Figure 3.5: Plan of the Shinjuku Business Centre

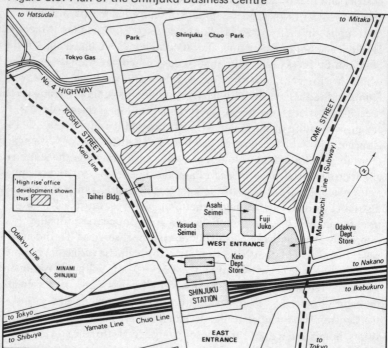

Table 3.5: Passenger Traffic within a 50-km Radius of Central Tokyo, 1960-75

Year	Total Passengers (millions)	Railways	Subways (% of total passengers)	Buses	Private Cars
1960	5,522	59	6	15	no data
1965	7,371	60	10	13	no data
1970	9,478	42	14	10	18
1975	9,776	53	17	10	14

Source: Bureau of Statistics (1977)

total passengers in 1975). The centre of the railway system is the Yamate Loop which runs through Tokyo Station and which encircles the central wards for a perimeter distance of about 30 km. The Loop not only provides a valuable orbital service through the employment-rich inner city areas, but it also allows the operation of through-services across the city centre. The private railway system does not penetrate inside the Loop, but most of the companies do have terminal stations located on it. Two-thirds of all the passengers carried by the total railway system are commuters and as such this means severe congestion at peak hours. During the last 10 years, in order to deal with the increased peak-hour travellers, the railway companies have adopted a range of relatively cheap ways of increasing their carrying capacities by increasing rolling stock and lengthening train units, by shortening train headways and by endeavouring to persuade offices, schools and colleges to stagger their working hours (Thomson 1978).

The subway system of Tokyo was started just before World War II, when the Ginza line was built to transport people in that part of central Tokyo lying within the Yamate Loop. Since 1945 a further seven lines have been constructed and during the plan period it is clear that the whole subway system assumed an increasingly important role (Table 3.5). The subways connect with the Japan National Railways system and through-train agreements are operated, thus allowing the two authorities to run trains in each other's tracks and saving passengers unnecessary interchanges. As Thomson (1978) has pointed out, the subway system is now fulfilling three important roles. It is meeting the need for efficient movement within the central wards; it is taking relatively short-distance traffic away from the railways (thus helping to ease peak-hour congestion); and it has replaced the old tramways, thereby helping to relieve congestion on the roads.

The tramways, which for decades served as an important mode of transport within the Ward Area, were superseded not only by the subways but also, to a lesser degree, by the introduction of bus services which are possibly more effective in the suburbs than the central area. Table 3.5 suggests that during the period of the 1968 plan there was a slight demise in the buses' share of total passenger traffic, possibly reflecting the impact of growing car ownership and the disruption of bus services prompted by recurrent traffic jams. The recent introduction of over 50 km of peak-hour bus priority lanes may go some way to help to revive the appeal of the bus for commuting purposes.

The figures in Table 3.5 give little indication of the tremendous increase in motor traffic and private car-ownership which took place during the 1970s (in the Tokyo Metropolis alone there are now around 3 million registered vehicles) and which has meant that traffic volumes have persistently exceeded the capacity of the metropolitan road network. The approach of the problem was recognised as long ago as 1959 when the metropolitan government decided to set up a Tokyo

Expressway Public Corporation (Tokyo Metropolitan Government 1975). Amongst other things, it was commissioned to undertake the construction of urban motorways intended for short-distance traffic and designed for high capacity; the emphasis was to be on achieving the smooth flow of large volumes of traffic rather than speed (Thomson 1978). Over 150 km of such motorway have been completed, the strategy of the corporation being to start its programme at the very centre of Tokyo and to gradually work outwards, ultimately to connect with eight motorways (entitled National Expressways) being built by the Japan Highway Public Corporation (Figure 3.4). A key part of the inner-city system is a ring road around the central wards into which the eight radial motorways will link.

The problems associated with the improvement of road transport in the densely-developed Ward Area and with the construction of urban motorways have been immense. A widely-adopted solution has been to elevate most of the motorways above existing roads. Although this practice helps to keep down the costs of land acquisition and the destruction of the urban fabric, the environmental costs have been enormous, bringing the roar of heavy traffic to within a few metres of bedroom windows and excluding daylight from those residential areas in the shadow of the elevated motorways. The situation is particularly bad at access points and motorway intersections. Furthermore, in order to reduce construction costs to an acceptable level, design standards have had to be lowered, so that the motorways typically have two-lane carriageways and are characterised by sharp bends, steep gradients and frequent access points, all of which conspire to boost the incidence of accidents and traffic jams.

What has become increasingly clear is that the spirit of optimism which prevailed at the time the motorway programme was drawn up has now given way to widespread disillusionment. The increased volume of road traffic still far exceeds the design capacity of the system, so that congestion and reduced traffic speeds have added substantially to the irrefutable environmental and social costs associated with Tokyo's 'motorisation'. As yet there is no indication that these costs, together with the user costs of expensive parking and of tolls which are charged on all motorways, are in any way serving to reduce the volume of vehicular traffic. By comparison, the developments with respect to the rail and subway systems seem to be considerable achievements, but for how much longer can elaboration of these successful systems continue to cope with the ever-increasing volumes of traffic which reflect the persistence of permissive attitudes towards the continued build-up of a strong-centred metropolis?

c) Environmental Pollution. It was during the 1960s that environmental
pollution in Tokyo rapidly reached crisis proportions, with a whole
range of indices clearly showing that in 1969 pollution of both
atmosphere and water was at its worst (Environmental Agency 1978).
Rapid and large-scale industrial growth, greatly swollen volumes of
vehicular traffic and a substantially increased production of domestic
effluent were the principal sources of pollution which, in conjunction
with the general shortage of space, collectively provoked a serious
deterioration in environmental quality in the inner areas of Tokyo.
Although 'public nuisance abatement and disaster prevention' had been
stipulated as planning objectives in the Built-up District even in the first
Master Plan, it was not until 1967 that the 'Basic Law for Pollution
Control' was enacted. This legislation and subsequent revisions of it
have done much to improve the general situation, but some of the
environmental problems still seem intractable (Fisher and Sargent 1975).
Initially the responsibility for pollution control rested with the Tokyo
metropolitan government, but in 1971 the Japanese government created
the Environmental Agency to undertake the nationwide coordination
of anti-pollution measures. Three years later, the metropolitan government once again took the initiative and introduced its own programme
'for defending metropolitan inhabitants from environmental pollution'.
In this it set for each major pollutant a target date for the reduction of
the nuisance to a specified acceptable level (Tokyo Metropolitan
Government 1977).

In 1977 the metropolitan government was able to report that levels
of sulphur dioxide and carbon monoxide in the atmosphere over the
Built-up District were now compliant with the target standards, but in
the case of nitrogen oxide emissions from vehicles and factories the
targets had not been achieved other than on a very localised basis (Tokyo
Metropolitan Government 1977). Giving rise to considerable concern
was the apparent failure of the programme to reduce the concentration
of photochemical oxidants in the air. With regard to water pollution,
the levels of noxious substances deemed to be detrimental to human
health—cadmium, cyanide, etc.—have been significantly lowered so as
to no longer constitute a problem in most of Tokyo's rivers. Unhappily
the situation in Tokyo Bay itself has not shown any real improvement;
the configuration of the bay is such that it does not readily facilitate
the dispersal of pollutants discharged from its feeder rivers. In the bay
there is not only direct pollution, but due to the raising of the

temperature of its water in summer, eutrophication commonly takes place, thereby giving rise to secondary pollution, such as the notorious 'red tide' (an algal 'bloom' encouraged by the concentration of nitrates and phosphates, which is followed by anaerobic conditions).

The pollutants considered so far are those which stem mainly from manufacturing industry and motor transport. It should be remembered, however, that even in the inner areas of Tokyo there is still a very large residential population whose effluents have contributed significantly to water pollution. In the Ward Area alone, for example, there is a residential population in excess of 8 millions. The second Master Plan had aimed by 1975 to service 90 per cent of all dwellings in the National Capital Region with piped water and proper refuse disposal facilities, whilst the target in the context of sewage treatment had been set at an altogether more modest level of about 50 per cent of the total built-up area to be provided with modern systems.

Modern Tokyo has certainly now learnt the lesson of neglecting this basic concept of development planning, namely that the setting down of sewage systems should precede the appearance of the built-up area. The Meiji Restoration, the Great Kanto Earthquake and World War II had all offered golden opportunities for carrying out the radical improvement of infrastructure, but such chances were not seized. The lag in the extension of the sewage system in Tokyo has been caused primarily by a lack of financial resources. The government's policies concerning the priority allocation of public funds have always been indifferent to sewage treatment schemes. In pre-war days, priority had been given to expenditure on public works related ultimately to industrial promotion, to such undertakings as the construction of roads, harbours and airports. The Japanese government's rationalisation of its long-held attitudes has been that the construction of sewage disposal schemes should be carried out at the expense of its beneficiaries (*Tokyo Municipal News* 1970). The construction of the present sewage system in Tokyo started in 1884 and up to 1951 it covered only 11 per cent of the Ward Area. It was not until the enforcement of the City Planning Law in 1969 that sewage treatment was added to the list of basic facilities required in built-up areas. In the Saitama area of Tokyo, close to the boundary with Yokohama and by no means an area of old housing, the sewage network as late as 1970 serviced only 7 per cent of the built-up area, but since then Tokyo metropolitan government, in conjunction with the local second-tier authorities, has set about the construction of a system for the whole of the Tama catchment. Completion has been set for 1985; of the construction costs for main sewers, pumping stations and treatment plants, 50 per cent will be borne by the central government and 25 per cent by the Tokyo metropolitan government. Intercepting sewers are constructed at the expense of the second-tier authorities.

Without question some progress has been made in Tokyo both with the extension of the sewage system and with control over the discharge of toxic substances into water bodies. But half the housing in the Ward Area still has no sewerage and the concomitant of this is that the two indices of organic water pollution—biological oxygen demand and chemical oxygen demand—still indicate an intolerably high level of pollution in the majority of Tokyo's rivers. Only in the Edo River and the upper reaches of the Tama River is water quality deemed to be acceptable, which is as well since both water courses contribute to the urban water supply.

According to the metropolitan government, the number of complaints received from the public about other forms of environmental pollution, such as noise, vibrations and offensive odours, continues to rise (Tokyo Metropolitan Government 1977). It is evident that the standards relating to motor vehicle noise have not been met and that measures to control aircraft and rail noise are only just beginning to take effect. Environmental problems of a somewhat different character are the risk of fire in those densely-developed areas of older and largely wooden housing and the consequences of land subsidence in the low-lying areas of Tokyo. The main cause of this subsidence is thought to be the compaction of soft clay strata resulting from an overpumping of groundwater. Land which formerly stood at 1 to 2 metres above sea-level has since sunk to below that datum, and bearing in mind that such areas in Tokyo contain a great many residents living at high densities, as well as much large-scale industrial development, it is clear that the construction of flood protection schemes has become a top priority. Although there is now strict control over groundwater pumping, subsidence still seems to be taking place, albeit at a slower rate than hitherto; the problem appears to be particularly resistant in some parts of Yokohama (Association of Japanese Geographers 1970; Environmental Agency 1978).

Thus this brief review of environmental pollution in Tokyo would concur with the conclusion that during the term of the second Master Plan 'a remarkable reaction has occurred. The severity of environmental problems . . . has been increasingly recognised by the Japanese themselves, and in recent years there has emerged a widespread consensus of opinion to the effect that, from now on, Japan must adjust to a less

hectic rate of economic expansion which will allow for increased spending . . . on measures aimed at coping with the environmental costs of . . .
growth' (Fisher and Sargent 1975).

Housing in the Suburban Redevelopment District

The National Capital Region has a mammoth multi-faceted housing
problem compounded principally from a rapid and substantial increase
in population, rising family income and aspirations, a persistent shortfall in the supply of adequate housing and a manifestly deficient
residential infrastructure. The precise complexion of the housing problem
does, however, vary somewhat within the region. In the Built-up District,
a major difficulty revolves around the renewal of large areas of outworn
housing and the general improvement of environment and infrastructure.
In the Suburban Redevelopment District concern centres rather more
on the construction of housing at a rate commensurate with demand
growth, on access to the new housing market and on the need to effect
much tighter control over the location and standards of new housing.

It had been forecast in the 1968 plan that provision would have to be
made for more than 11 million extra people by 1985. This, coupled with
the continuing decline in family size (from 3.9 persons in 1965 to an
expected 3.3 persons in 1985) and the need to replace a large heritage
of substandard housing, conditioned conservative estimates to put the
housing needs of the National Capital Region at 8.3 million new
dwellings. However, the Japanese government's own housing programme,
along with that of the Japan Housing Corporation, envisages the construction of a supply of new dwellings well short of the estimated
demand (Tokyo Metropolitan Government 1972). As a consequence,
responsibility for much of the required housing programme has had
to rest with private developers and individual households. Great reliance
is now being placed upon flat development as one way of offsetting the
general shortage and very high cost of building land. Although there has
been a certain amount of resistance to the flat as a dwelling mode, it
should be understood that access even to such modest accommodation,
either by means of mortgage or bank loan, is to all intents and purposes
only within the bidding competence of middle-income households.
Furthermore, the cost relationship between housing and incomes
deteriorated significantly during the 1970s with the inflation of housing
costs outstripping the rate of income increment by three times.

The weak development of the public sector is one aspect of the
Japanese housing situation which gives rise to considerable concern. In
the whole of the National Capital Region, only 7 per cent of all the

housing falls within that sector (Table 3.6). What is worse is that, because of high rents, much public sector accommodation is occupied by middle- rather than low-income households. Poorer families, particularly those in the Ward Area, are obliged to rely on privately-rented accommodation which is characterised by a high incidence of shared facilities, a high density of room occupation and a high proportion of substandard property.

Table 3.6: Dwelling Tenure and Age in the National Capital Region, 1975

Prefecture	Total Dwellings (000s)	Owned	Public Rented	Private Rented	Built 1966-75
			(% of total dwellings)		
Tokyo	3,715.6	36	9	41	46
Kanagawa	1,805.8	44	7	33	55
Chiba	1,140.3	53	7	22	57
Saitama	1,260.0	67	6	24	60
Gumma	453.4	67	5	19	42
Ibaraki	560.3	71	4	15	41
Tochigi	435.1	65	4	18	45
Yamanashi	202.9	75	6	17	37
NCR	9,653.4	48	7	31	50

Source: Bureau of Statistics (1977)

Chiba Prefecture, lying immediately to the east of the Ward Area and with a substantial part of its territory falling within the Suburban Re-development District, has recently become the scene of some very large-scale residential development. Between 1965 and 1975 the prefectural population increased by 50 per cent, requiring the provision of housing for some 1.4 million extra people (Table 3.1). Reflecting this demographic surge, well over half the housing in Chiba in 1975 had been constructed during the previous decade (Table 3.6).

Both the public- and private-rented sectors are less strongly developed there as compared with the Tokyo Metropolitan Government Area. The compensating higher incidence of owner-occupied housing implies that the new residential areas of Chiba, along with those of Saitama, are essentially middle-class districts of better housing. But the indices of housing conditions contained in Table 3.7 suggest that the situation is by no means clear-cut. Compared with the two 'core' prefectures of Tokyo and Kanagawa, there is a better showing in terms of average dwelling size and the possession of a bathroom, but this is offset by a poorer standing with regard to the two facilities of piped water and flush toilets. This latter comparison may well reflect the impact of anti-pollution measures adopted by the Tokyo metropolitan government and the Yokohama City Authority and a closer approach to the domestic services targets set in the 1968 plan.

Table 3.7: Housing Conditions in the National Capital Region, 1975 (% of dwellings)

Prefecture	Repair needed	Piped water	Flush toilet	Bathroom	Floor area/dwelling (m^2)
Tokyo	18	90	63	52	52
Kanagawa	17	90	45	69	59
Chiba	19	69	30	76	70
Saitama	17	83	27	74	68
Gumma	22	83	16	80	90
Ibaraki	22	53	9	84	83
Tochigi	21	55	10	81	84
Yamanashi	22	85	21	78	98
NCR	18	83	42	66	64

Source: Bureau of Statistics (1977)

In pursuit of the cause of better housing, considerable credit should be given to the Japan Housing Corporation which was set up in 1955 by the Japanese government for the specific purpose of alleviating the acute housing shortage (Witherick 1972b). The corporation is unusual in that it is financed both by central government funds and by private investment, and it exists to provide not just public housing to rent, but also housing for sale to owner-occupiers; about one-third of all the dwellings built by the corporation have fallen in that sector. The corporation also sells to firms accommodation which is subsequently let to their employees.

The Japan Housing Corporation has undertaken the construction of housing schemes throughout Japan, but inevitably its efforts have been most directed towards the provision of housing in the suburban rings of the country's major cities. An interesting and early venture completed by the corporation was at Sodegaura in Chiba (Witherick 1971). The scheme was noteworthy not because of its size—indeed it was com-paratively small, accommodating around 15,000 people—but rather that it was built on land reclaimed from the shores of Tokyo Bay. Clearly, this creation of building land by means of reclamation has been encouraged by the excessively high land prices and by the voracious and apparently insatiable demand for more urban space within the immediate orbit of Tokyo. Such reclamation is also very desirable in the sense that it should help to reduce the rate at which high-grade agricultural land has been lost to suburban growth.

Located some 25 km from the centre of Tokyo, Sodegaura occupies a site of 115 ha of former mudflat (Figure 3.6). Two-thirds of the residents live in concrete, 5-storey blocks of 2- and 3-bedroomed flats which are rented from the corporation. In addition, there are 1,000 owner-occupied dwellings and these are arranged into neighbour-hoods quite separate from the public housing. The completion of this part of the project involved a useful blend of public and private enterprise.

Figure 3.6: The Sodegaura Housing Project

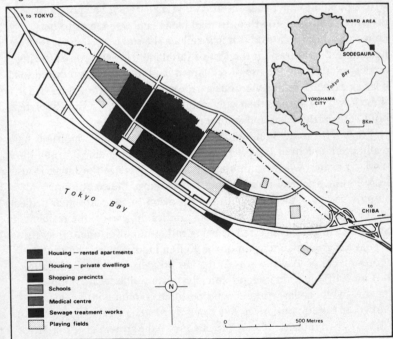

The corporation was responsible for setting down the street pattern, demarcating the building plots and providing the main services. The plots were then purchased from the corporation by prospective house-holders, who assumed the responsibility for having a dwelling con-constructed to suit the family accommodation needs and household income. In Sodegaura, as in most of the corporation's schemes, attention has not just been confined to the provision of decent housing. An attempt has been made to meet most of the service requirements of a modern residential community from shops to schools, from medical centres to sports facilities, and, reflecting the growing concern about environmental pollution, Sodegaura boasts its own sewage treatment works.

There is no doubt that housing projects like Sodegaura (now part of the much larger Kaihin New Town) have set higher residential standards for suburban Tokyo. Lessons learnt from them have been usefully employed in the design and construction of the much larger housing projects which were part of the second Master Plan, schemes like Chiba New Town (between Tokyo and the new international airport at Narita) and Tama New Town situated to the west of the Ward Area and now with a population in excess of 400,000 (Hall 1977). The policy of diverting suburban growth onto man-made land also seems to be eminently shrewd, in that it might reduce the site cost element in housing and cut down on the loss of farmland. However, one growing anxiety concerning the use of reclaimed land refers to the reduced load-bearing capacity during vigorous earthquakes. An additional hazard in these low-lying areas is their vulnerability to the tidal waves associated both with earthquakes and summer typhoons.

Finally, it should be noted that improved residential conditions have really been bought at the price of a physically-demanding journey-to-work on overcrowded commuter services, for it is not the Japan Housing Corporation's general policy either to encourage the creation of employment in association with their projects or to locate their projects with reference to employment opportunities. In theory, the residents of Sodegaura might be regarded as being rather more fortunate than most in that the gradual extension of the Keihin industrial belt around the shores of Tokyo Bay towards Chiba has brought work to the locality. But most of Sodegaura's economically-active residents are middle-income, white collar workers, who perforce commute into central Tokyo. In the circumstances, one can only rue the fact that neither of the first two master plans did much to encourage the growth of either office employment or 'clean' industry in the Suburban Redevelopment District.

Urbanisation Areas in the Outer Development District

It was during the period 1965-75 that the peripheral prefectures of the
National Capital Region showed the first signs of demographic expansion,
but the scale of that growth was so small as to amount to little more than
0.6 million people (Table 3.1). Most of the expansion was more or less
equally shared by three of the four prefectures, namely Gumma,
Ibaraki and Tochigi. Bearing in mind that all but one of the 16
designated 'urbanisation areas' are located within these four prefectures,
the demographic record must at face value stand as an unfavourable
comment on the achievements of the decentralisation programme
(Figure 3.3). The prefecture of Ibaraki, with only its south-western
margins falling within the Suburban Redevelopment District, will serve
as a reference area for the closer examination of the progress and
problems of planning in the Outer Development District.

Within its administrative limits, Ibaraki contains six 'urbanisation
areas', four of which had been designated during the operational term of
the first Master Plan. The legislation necessary for their creation had
been enacted in 1958 and they were referred to initially as 'city development areas'. In three of those projects, Ishioka, Koga and Tsuchiura, the
declared intention was to provide a focus for industrial development (the

Table 3.8: Urbanisation Areas in Ibaraki Prefecture

	Type and date of designation	Population at designation (000s)	Population (1975)	Designated area (ha)	Industrial use (ha)
Ishioka	Industrial satellite, 1964	35	44	2,470	333
Kashima	Industrial satellite, 1967	57	155	5,590	2,940
Koga	Industrial satellite, 1963	63	90	4,000	333
Mito	Multiple function, 1961	183	278	5,100	383
Tsuchiura	Industrial satellite, 1963	96	134	4,230	367
Tsukuba	Research & education, 1966	82	120	3,300	0
	Total	516	821	20,890	4,356

Sources: National Capital Region Development Commission (1968); Bureau of
Statistics (1977).

label 'industrial satellite' is attached in later planning documents), but the provision of land for this purpose, and the subsequent record of population growth do appear to have been rather meagre (Table 3.8).

Kashima is the only 'industrial satellite' to be designated in Ibaraki during the term of the second Master Plan and its later origins are perhaps reflected in its much larger dimensions. The aim is to create a large industrial city on the Pacific Coast, developed in conjunction with a new port capable of berthing 200,000 tonne tankers; the scale of the port is such that it is already capable of handling nearly twice as much cargo as Yokohama. The industrial emphasis is on petro-chemicals, but other important activities being built up include the manufacture of heavy machinery and electric-power generation. The population of Kashima is now estimated to have increased by over 100,000 people and thus the development appears to be fairly well on schedule to reach its target population of 300,000 people by 1985. Perhaps it is somewhat unflattering to refer to Kashima as an 'industrial satellite', for here more than in most of the other 'urbanisation areas' there is clear evidence of a sound and dynamic employment base which should serve to ensure a high degree of independence from Tokyo and, reinforced by distance, a low level of commuting into the metropolis.

The only other project in Ibaraki with its roots in the second Master Plan is the unique venture at Tsukuba, where a new town is being built in association with an agglomeration of research and high-order educational institutions, most of which, under pressure, have been re-located from the Built-up District. Finally, there is the Mito-Katsuta project, the largest in Ibaraki, which is one of four in the National Capital Region described as developing 'multiple urban functions'. Although provision has been made for industrial growth, the establishment of a 'commodity circulation centre' is intended to engender a more diversified economic base than is to be found in the prefecture's other 'urbanisation areas'. The same prescription has been made for Kofu (Yamanshi), Maebashi-Takasaki (Gumma) and Utsonomiya (Tochigi) and it is now within the bounds of longer-term plans that by the turn of the century all four centres will have graduated into million-cities.

An interesting feature which emerges from Table 3.8 is that the collective growth recorded in the six 'urbanisation areas' up to 1975 slightly exceeds the net population growth for Ibaraki as a whole. There is evidence that during the term of the second Master Plan, depopulation has been experienced in parts of the prefecture, particularly in the remoter and poorer rural areas, and that there may have been a small shift of people from these rural areas into the 'urbanisation areas', thereby effecting a greater spatial concentration of the prefectural pop- ulation (Bureau of Statistics 1976). But the tentative conclusion to be drawn from Tables 3.1 and 3.8 is that, if there have been decentralisation flows of any note from Tokyo into the Outer Development District, then these have been counterbalanced by an exodus from the prefecture, presumably in the general direction of the Suburban Redevelopment District. One might conjecture that had the outer boundary of the Suburban Redevelopment District been more tightly drawn around the agglomeration's built-up area, and possibly reinforced by an encircling green belt, then possibly the record of growth in the Outer Development District may by now have been rather better.

A very vital part of the 1968 Master Plan related to proposals for the general improvement of transport within the National Capital Region and between the metropolitan region and the rest of the country (Figure 3.4). The impressive programme for the construction of radial and ring expressways is well under way, although less progress has been made with the ambitious proposals to bridge Tokyo Bay both at its entrance and between Kisarazu and Kawasaki. The programme for the railway system is no less remarkable. Seven rapid-transit routes, similar to the Tokaido line, are under construction and these new services will put places situated 100 km out into the National Capital Region easily within an hour's travelling time of the central wards of Tokyo (Witherick 1972a). An inevitable product of this general reduction of time-distance values will be the gradual extension of Tokyo's commuter catchment towards the very boundaries of the National Capital Region. Unhappily, this improvement in accessibility does not appear as yet to have been very effective in persuading industrialists to abandon core sites in favour of more peripheral locations. This, coupled with the limited amount of land set aside in most for industrial purposes, has meant that decentralisation to many of the 'urbanisation areas' has so far tended to involve people rather than industrial jobs. Far from becoming self-sustaining counter-magnets, the greater number of those 16 projects, specifically the 'industrial satellites', are in real danger of developing into dormitory areas for Tokyo. Unhappily the planners in the Development Commission have not commanded the powers necessary to curb this further extension of Tokyo's sphere of commut- ing influence, that is powers of the type held by the development corporations of the British new towns. The potential appeal of the 'urbanisation areas' as distant suburbs for Tokyo is further enhanced by the fact that they will offer new and adequate housing at prices lower than those that pertain in the Suburban Redevelopment District for equivalent accommodation. Due to the cheapness of public transport, the saving in housing costs may well outweigh the additional travel costs associated with commuting from farther out in the National Capital Region.

For how much longer the improvements in transport within the National Capital Region will be able to cope with the increasing volumes of commuting which they have triggered from the outer half of the region is very much open to question. That time may well be fast approaching. However, the planners still prefer to direct their attentions to a further enlargement of the capacity of the regional transport system, possibly to include the development of new modes of public transport such as high-speed monorail. The prospect of 3 million jobs concentrated in the Ward Area of Tokyo alone is now a very real possibility. This will require doubling the capacity of the current system at the present level of overcrowding. It is clear that the great majority of these extra workers will have to be brought in by rail, but the ability of Tokyo's terminal stations to handle this increased volume of commuter traffic is in doubt, as is the ability of the subway and bus services to move this vast convergence of workers within the central wards. It does seem a little ironic that whilst much time and effort are being spent on research into ways of increasing the competence of the metropolitan transport system to deal with the future demands likely to be placed upon it by pursuit of a strong-centre strategy, much less attention is paid to the alternative of putting together a really convincing and effective regional decentralisation programme.

Conclusions and Prospects

The continued and seemingly relentless growth of population and employment in the National Capital Region, particularly in its more central areas, is a dominant feature of Japan's urban geography. Implementation of the 1968 Master Plan has done little or nothing to reduce the powerful magnetism of the core area. Indeed, that magnetism in terms of labour recruitment has been so intensified that its pull virtually reaches to the peripheries of the National Capital Region. As a consequence, the undoubted achievements within the realms of transportation appear somewhat paradoxical. On the one hand, transport might be perceived as the villain of the piece through its extension of Tokyo's commuter catchment area. On the other hand, the improvement of the regional transport system might justifiably be regarded as the one redeeming development which has maintained the highly-pressurised regional mechanisms in functioning order.

The small amount of growth which to date has taken place in the Outer Development District is hardly indicative of a substantial degree of regional decentralisation. Presumably once the vacant space within the Suburban Redevelopment District has been fully utilised, that situation may change quite dramatically. Most of the 'urbanisation areas' can be seen for what they really are, namely parasitic developments, potentially huge detached dormitories directly linked to the heart of the Tokyo metropolis. Neither do they appear to have been very successful in their other role of heading off 'immigrant' growth before it reaches Tokyo.

A benevolent interpretation of post-1968 events might suggest that the regional planners have been the victims of a framework of essentially impotent legislation which has repeatedly failed to provide the muscle either to curtail the pull of the core or to ensure the creation within the region of effective countermagnets to Tokyo. A less charitable view of the situation might suspect that the planners in the National Capital Region have not acted out of conviction and have paid only lip service to the avowed policy of regional decentralisation. Alternatively, it might be that the failure of many of the 'urbanisation areas' to gain a really significant momentum during the 1970s is symptomatic that the whole strategic notion of decentralisation to sub-centres is not the easy nor necessarily the appropriate solution to Tokyo's growth problems. Could it be that the events of the last two decades are to be read as conveying the message that rather than resist and redirect the growth pressures, every effort should be made instead to accommodate those pressures as fully as possible '*in situ*'?

The developments which took place in the National Capital Region up to 1975 were palatable so long as there was the prospect of continuing economic growth and provided the inhabitants of the Tokyo agglomeration were prepared to tolerate the undoubted social costs associated with the perpetuation of a strong-centre metropolis. However, should the current world economic recession persist, there may well be widespread regret that more stringent steps were not taken to achieve a measure of regional decentralisation as the metropolitan inhabitants may become more alive to the social costs which they have silently and perhaps unwittingly borne these last two decades. In this sense, the formulation of the 1976 Basic Plan might be regarded as timely and apposite, for although it will do little to change the supposed direction of the regional strategy, it should do rather more to improve the general quality of the environment and to raise welfare levels.

The very position of planning in modern Japanese society appears to be an uneasy one, perhaps to the point of even being ambivalent. Capitalism and free enterprise are widely recognised as two fundamental elements in the miracle of Japan's post-war recovery. As a consequence, there has been an understandable reluctance to unnecessarily fetter economic buoyancy and the further generation of affluence by what might be seen, in the short-term at least, as repressive intervention in the spatial expression of the economic system. The persistence of such an attitude may go some way to explain the distinctly mediocre performance of regional planning in the specific context of controlling the distribution of employment and economic growth; as implied earlier, the whole exercise may well have lacked a basic sense of conviction. However, now that the post-war recovery and Japan's status in the international community have been successfully consolidated, motivation and sacrifice of a patriotic complexion are beginning to give way to individual aspirations which focus on rather different priorities, such as access to decent housing, environmental quality, leisure time and the whole ethos of the good life. The 1976 plan is symptomatic of this fundamental change. The record of progress within the field of housing and in the abatement of environmental pollution suggests that there are aspects of national life in which it can be unquestionably demonstrated that planning is not only desirable, but that its benefits can be reaped on an impressive scale in a remarkably short time-span. Such accomplishments begin to compare with the effective fusion of technology and planning which the Japanese have achieved in transportation and which has been the linchpin of the National Capital Region's economic progress. In the immediate future, it is imperative that this transport expertise and enterprise continue to serve the centripetal forces endemic to Tokyo's growth, but looking rather further ahead perhaps it might be applied to bring about the integration of the Kanto, Chubu and Kinki regional growth centres into Tange's vision of 'an organically unified megalopolis' stretching from Tokyo to Osaka (Japan Centre for Area Development Research 1967). In Tokaido Megalopolis the problematic centripetal structures of four major cities would gradually be replaced by a much more efficient axial circulatory system. The attainment of such a goal will inevitably rest upon the adoption of a more macro-scale and comprehensive mode of planning than has been practised hitherto. The embryonic administrative framework is already in existence in the form of the Megalopolitan Region Reorganisation

Bureau, which seeks to co-ordinate the planning of the Kanto, Chubu and Kinki regions. It now remains for Japanese society to support the crucial transformation from an essentially retrospective, remedial regional planning undertaken in 10-year instalments to a much more progressive planning motivated by longer-term and national objectives.

References

Allen, G.C. (1965) *Japan's Economic Recovery*, OUP, London
Association of Japanese Geographers, (1970) *Japanese Cities: a Geographical Approach*, Association of Japanese Geographers Special Publication, Tokyo
Bell, G. (1972) *Human Identity and the Urban Environment*, Pelican, London
Berry, B.J.L. (1973) *The Human Consequences of Urbanisation*, Macmillan, London
Broadbridge, S. (1966) *Industrial Dualism in Japan*, Aldine, Chicago
Bureau of Statistics, (1977) *Japan Statistical Yearbook*, Office of the Prime Minister, Tokyo
—— (1976) *Population Census, 1975*, Office of the Prime Minister, Tokyo
Dempster, P. (1968) *Japan Advances*, Methuen, London
Environmental Agency, (1978) *Quality of the Environment in Japan*, Office of the Prime Minister, Tokyo
Fisher, C.A. and J. Sargent (1975) 'Japan's ecological crisis', *Geographical Journal, 141/2*, 165-76
Hall, P. (1974) *Urban and Regional Planning*, Pelican, London
—— (1977) *The World Cities*, Weidenfeld and Nicolson, London, pp. 219-39
Japan Centre for Area Development Research, (1967) *The International Symposium on Regional Development*, JCADR, Tokyo
—— (1972) *The Fourth International Symposium on Regional Development*, JCADR, Tokyo
Jones, R. (ed.) (1975) *Essays on World Urbanisation*, Philip, London, pp. 175-85
Kornhauser, D.H. (1976) *Urban Japan: its Foundations and Growth*, Longman, London
—— (1979) *A Selected List of Writings on Japan Pertinent to Geography in Western Languages*, University of Hiroshima, Hiroshima
Megalopolis Region Reorganisation Bureau, (1976) *Basic Plan for the National Capital Region*, National Land Agency, Tokyo
Nagashima, C. (1967) 'Megalopolis in Japan', *Ekistics, 24*, 6-14
—— (1968) 'Japan Megalopolis', *Ekistics, 26*, 83-95
National Capital Region Development Commission, (1958) *Master Plan for the National Capital Region*, Office of the Prime Minister, Tokyo
—— (1968) *Master Plan for the National Capital Region*, Office of the Prime Minister, Tokyo
—— (1969) *Outline of National Capital Region Development*, Office of the Prime Minister, Tokyo
Thomson, J.M. (1978) *Great Cities and their Traffic*, Peregrine, London, pp. 177-92
Tokyo Metropolitan Government, (1972) *Tokyo's Housing Problem*, Tokyo Metropolitan Government, Tokyo
—— (1975) *Traffic in Tokyo*, Tokyo Metropolitan Government, Tokyo
—— (1977) *Tokyo Fights Pollution*, Tokyo Metropolitan Government, Tokyo
—— (1978) *City Planning in Tokyo*, Tokyo Metropolitan Government, Tokyo
—— *Tokyo Municipal News* (a monthly journal of the Tokyo Metropolitan

Government)

Witherick, M.E. (1971) 'Sodegaura: a Japanese housing project', *Housing & Planning Review, 27/4*, 6-8

—— (1972a) 'Master Plan for the Japanese Capital Region', *Geography, 57/1*, 43-7

—— (1972b) 'The Japan Housing Corporation', *Town & Country Planning, 40/11*, 521-5

Yamamura, K. (1967) *Economic Policy in Postwar Japan*, University of California, Berkeley

4 THE JOHANNESBURG METROPOLITAN AREA

T.J.D. Fair and J.G. Muller

Any analysis of South African metropolitan areas necessitates an appreciation of the country's complex racial structure and the role that this structure plays in determining the governmental and the planning processes at present. For more than 100 years political and economic dominance has been maintained by a ruling White minority of European origin over a more numerous Black population comprising the indigenous African and Coloured (mixed) peoples and the immigrant Asian, mainly Indian, group (Table 4.1). In 1970 Whites accounted for only 32 per cent of South Africa's urban population and Blacks for the remainder. Similarly, of those in non-agricultural, mainly urban employment only 27 per cent were White. Yet in 1970, 65 per cent of those employed in white-collar occupations and 79 per cent of those with a Standard 8 education and beyond were White. In the major sectors of the economy incomes of Whites are three to five times greater than those of Blacks (1978).

Public policy and the planning of metropolitan areas display an ambivalence marked by less constraint in the economic and spatial systems as a whole and to the White sub-system in particular, and by severe constraint as they apply to the life and work of Blacks, especially Africans. This ambivalence is manifested in contrasting planning styles which, as a reflection of social progress, give rise to spatial forms that provide sharp contrasts not only within South African metropolitan areas but between these areas and metropolitan regions elsewhere in the developed and the developing world.

The city of Johannesburg lies within a wider metropolitan area which includes a number of smaller municipalities tributary to it. This Johannesburg Metropolitan Area (JMA) is, in turn, the hub of a larger economic region, the Witwatersrand, originally determined by the extent of gold mining. The Witwatersrand, in turn, forms the major component of a larger urban region comprising the three closely integrated metropolitan regions of Pretoria, Witwatersrand and Vereeniging, together termed the PWV region or the Southern Transvaal (Figure 4.1).

The Johannesburg Metropolitan Area which forms the subject of this chapter faces most of the challenges associated with the present

Table 4.1: Population Structure, 1970

	White	Coloured	Asian	African	Total
South Africa	3,751,328	2,018,453	620,436	15,057,952	21,448,169
PWV urban region[a]	1,377,354	126,861	65,243	2,055,157	3,624,615
Witwatersrand	949,751	113,387	53,279	1,520,437	2,636,854
Johannesburg MA[b]	611,019	86,243	40,476	883,979	1,621,717

Notes: a. Pretoria-Witwatersrand-Vaal triangle. b. Metropolitan area — Projections for the JMA for the year 2000 are: Whites—1,046,100, Blacks—1,649,800, total—2,695,900 (Johannesburg 1979).
Source: Census.

metropolitan age. However, it has been and still is confronted by three unique problems, one economic, one physical and one social. The first stems from the rapid transformation of its economy from one that only 25 years ago was heavily dependent upon gold mining to one whose base now lies in industry and especially the services. The second problem, consequent upon the first, is the need to plan a new physical structure to meet the requirements of a changing economic base and to incorporate vast areas of abandoned mining land into the new metropolitan landscape. The third is the social challenge of a multi-racial urban society in which a ruling White elite seek to accommodate, politically, socially and economically, a growing Black majority upon whose labour the future of the metropolitan economy increasingly depends.

South Africa's economic heart is the PWV region. It is an almost continuous area of urban and peri-urban settlement 13,707 km^2 in extent, covering only 1.1 per cent of the total surface area of South Africa. However, the economic significance of the PWV region lies in the fact that, in terms of gross geographic product (ggp), its earning capacity has increased from 38.4 per cent of the South African total in 1954 to 46.4 per cent in 1972 (South Africa 1977). This high degree of polarisation (Fair 1976) is reflected also in its employment structure, for here is found 38.6 per cent of the nation's work force in the secondary (manufacturing) sector and 31.7 per cent in the tertiary (services) sector. The region accounts for 16.9 per cent of the total South African population (1970) and for 35.3 per cent of the total urban population. Of South Africa's highly urbanised White population of mainly European origin, no less than 36.7 per cent were resident in the PWV region alone in 1970. Of the nationally more numerous African, Coloured and Asian

Figure 4.1: The Johannesburg Metropolitan Area and Regional Relationships

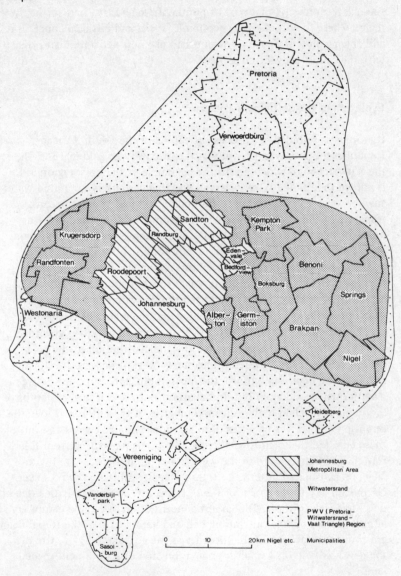

population, 19.7 per cent are found in the PWV region.

The JMA derives its economic strength and dominance from its location as the core of the PWV region. The JMA accounts for 45 per

cent of the PWV's ggp and for 45 per cent of its population accommodated within a radius of 10 to 30 km of the Johannesburg city centre.
As such it represents that part of South Africa and that part of the PWV
region where the problems of economic, social and physical concentration
and change present South African urban planners and administrators
with their most pressing challenges.

Evolution of the Settlement Pattern

Pretoria was founded in 1855 as the capital of the South African
Republic (the Transvaal) but it was the discovery of gold in 1886 on
the Witwatersrand which marks the beginning of the PWV region as it
is known today. The Witwatersrand was then a sparsely inhabited watershed between rivers draining to the Indian and the Atlantic oceans,
respectively. The ridges of the Witwatersrand are composed of hard
quartzite and rise to an altitude of 2,000 m above sea level. Poor soils
and treeless grassland were suitable only for extensive grazing. Early
maps show that few tracks covered this region and that it was simply
labelled 'sources of the Limpopo'. Main routes joining the towns of the
Transvaal with Pretoria mostly skirted the Witwatersrand. Its isolation
then bore little relation to the nodality that the region possesses today.

The settlement pattern (Figure 4.2) that was to arise was governed in
the first instance by the occurrence and the distribution of the gold-
bearing reefs, first discovered immediately west of present-day Johannesburg. The Main Reef group, the most important, crops out between
Randfontein and Benoni but dips sharply to the south so that depths of
3,000 m are reached within seven kilometres of the outcrop. Along the
outcrop there grew up a series of independent mining camps and out of
these emerged the main towns strung like beads on a string from Randfontein and Krugersdorp in the west to Benoni in the east, and with
Nigel on an isolated outcrop to the south-east. All these towns, except
Germiston, lay to the north of the outcrop with mining activities steadily
developing southwards. The largest concentration of mining camps lay
almost mid-way along the mining belt and here, in 1886, the Republican
government established Johannesburg as the administrative centre of
the new goldfield on a small triangular portion of government-owned
land.

In 1914 rich pay-shoots were discovered beneath the covering of
younger rocks on the Far East Rand (see sub-outcrop Figure 4.2) and
gold mining now encompassed the whole Witwatersrand, some 90 km

Figure 4.2: The Southern Transvaal or PWV Region, 1896

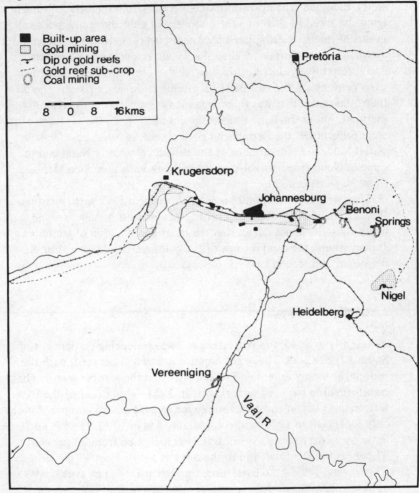

in length, and including the additional towns of Brakpan and Springs.
Survival of the gold-mining industry, however, necessitated early
solutions to a number of problems, among them the reorganisation of
many small fragmented mining operations into larger more viable groups,
the recovery of gold from the ore by the invention of the MacArthur-
Forrest cyanide process, the avoidance of flooding of deep-level mines
by the cementation process, and in 1903 the establishment of the Rand
Water Board to supply this watershed region from the Vaal River 60 km
to the south.

By the 1920s the east-west mining belt and its associated towns were well established. The north-south connection from Pretoria to Vereeniging also owed its origin to the discovery of gold and to the political events of the time. Stimulated by the discovery, railway lines from Cape Town and from Durban reached the Witwatersrand in 1892 and in 1895, respectively. In addition, the railway crossing at the Vaal River gave Vereeniging, then a small coal mining town, an importance as an industrial centre that was to emerge many years later as the region matured. About the same time as the connections to the southern ports were being made, the Republican government, in its desire to have an outlet to the sea independent of the British colonies of Natal and the Cape of Good Hope, established the rail link with Lourenço Marques (now Maputo) in 1894.

Thus were laid the foundations of the present PWV settlement pattern. It was a cruciform pattern comprising an east-west mining axis and a north-south road and rail axis, at the heart and junction of which was Johannesburg, the capital town of the goldfields, and Germiston, its neighbour and second town of the region.

Economic Transformation

As recently as 1945, the Witwatersrand was producing 96 per cent of South Africa's gold. Today the amount is barely 3 per cent, with the regional economy dominated by industry and the services sector. The transformation has been remarkable. In 1951, 34 per cent of the Witwatersrand's labour force was employed in gold mining compared with only 9 per cent in 1970, and considerably less in 1980. The labour force in the secondary sector, by contrast, has increased from 23 per cent to 37 per cent of the total, and in the services sector from 44 per cent to 53 per cent (Table 4.2). Even more important is the fact that the loss of nearly 200,000 workers in mining over this period was more than offset by an increase of 475,000 workers in the secondary and tertiary sectors, thus giving a net gain of 285,000 in the size of the region's labour force (Fair 1977). The region has clearly moved from a primary industrial phase into a fully-fledged secondary industrial phase. While this has been happening new gold mining areas have been developing in other parts of the Transvaal and in the Orange Free State. Predictions, however, that industry would move from the Witwatersrand to the new goldfields have proved unfounded and the industrial dominance of the Witwatersrand has been maintained. Its original economic and

Table 4.2: Witwatersrand: Employment, 1951 and 1970

	Primary sector				Secondary sector				Tertiary sector				All sectors			
	1951		1970		1951		1970		1951		1970		1951		1970	
	No.	%	No.	%	No.	%	No.	%	No.	%	No.	%	No.	%	No.	%
Inner zone (JMA)	87,408	18	35,958	5	131,131	27	230,466	34	272,368	55	422,029	61	490,907	100	688,453	100
Outer zone	212,804	53	74,172	15	74,301	18	210,816	43	119,071	29	208,486	42	406,176	100	493,474	100
Witwatersrand	300,212	33	110,130	9	205,432	23	441,282	37	391,439	44	630,515	54	897,083	100	1,181,927	100

Source: Census

geographical foundations are too powerful to be easily challenged.

Two sets of processes have governed the spatial structure of the Witwatersrand. Gold mining very early generated the linear pattern of zones of work and residence extending from west to east over a distance of some 100 km. Later, as mining declined and the manufacturing and services functions increased, a core-dominated metropolitan region with associated sub-centres has arisen (Figure 4.3). As a result it is possible

Figure 4.3: The Southern Transvaal or PWV Region, 1975

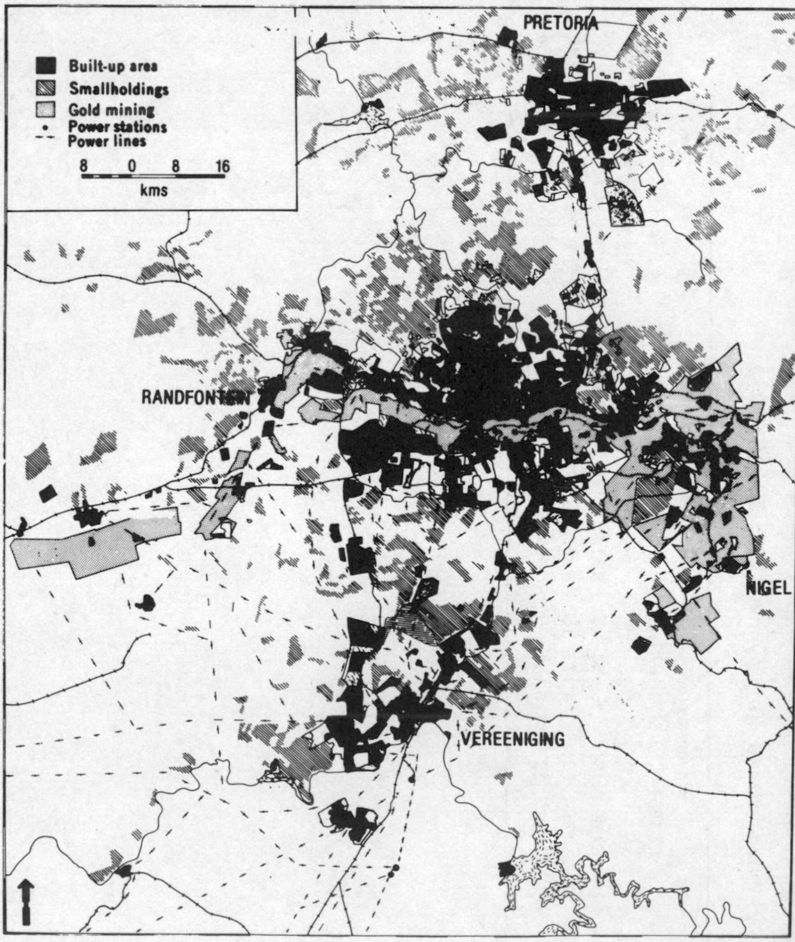

now to recognise an inner Witwatersrand metropolitan zone (the JMA) closely tied to the Johannesburg downtown core and an outer zone with weaker connections to that core (Figure 4.4).

The Johannesburg Metropolitan Area (JMA)

The JMA encompasses five peripheral towns (Roodepoort, Randburg, Sandton, Edenvale and Bedfordview) which contribute 50 per cent and more of their resident White workers to daily employment in the municipal area of Johannesburg, and the Black township of Soweto, the Asian township of Lenasia and numerous small Coloured townships all of whose residents work mainly in Johannesburg.

The economic transformation of the JMA has been even more dramatic than that of the Witwatersrand as a whole. Within a comparatively short period its economy has passed through the primary and secondary industrial phases and into the tertiary phase. In 1950 what is now the JMA produced about one-quarter of South Africa's gold. Today the proportion is minimal. Despite a loss of nearly 52,000 mine workers between 1951 and 1970, the overall work force increased by nearly 200,000 over that period. By 1972 70 per cent of the JMA's ggp was derived from the tertiary sector and 29.5 per cent from the secondary sector.

The JMA's regional and national dominance is overwhelming. Ninety per cent of all office space in the Witwatersrand region is found there, and 63 per cent of the major 130 companies in South Africa have their headquarters there (Rogerson 1974a). It has now joined the ranks of the corporate city. Decisions in the business world are being taken by the heads of fewer but much larger economic units as the earlier mining companies and groups have grown and merged into ever larger and diversifying conglomerates. The JMA manifests the early phase of a post-industrial stage in South Africa. As such it is the innovative heart from which social and economic impulses are generated and diffused throughout the region and the nation.

Moreover, the continuing industrial strength of the JMA has been maintained in the face of intensive government attempts to encourage industry to move to rural locations and to African reserves or 'homelands' from South Africa's major metropolitan areas. Rogerson (1974b) found that between 1960 and 1972 a total of 251 firms moved all or part of their manufacturing operations out of the city of Johannesburg, mainly for lack of space for expansion. Of this total movement to all parts of South Africa, 72 per cent moved to other parts of the Witwatersrand and no less than 60 per cent to towns immediately adjacent

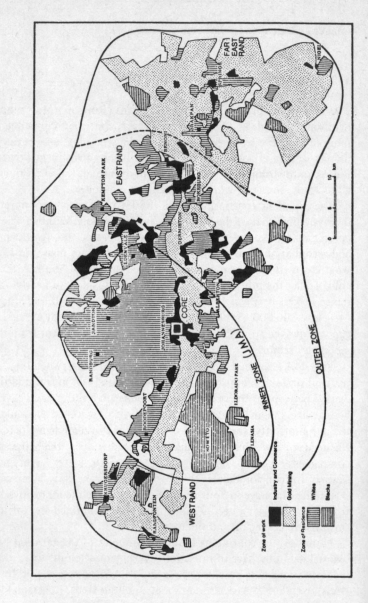

Figure 4.4: The Witwatersrand 1975, comprising the Johannesburg Metropolitan Area (JMA) or Inner Zone, and the Outer Zone

to Johannesburg itself, i.e. into the outer parts of the JMA and its neighbouring municipalities. Migrant firms retain a strong desire to remain accessible to the parent city for their inputs, labour, markets and major urban services. Between 1970 and 2000 the total population of the JMA will increase by 66 per cent or by more than 1 million to nearly 2.7 million people, of whom 61 per cent will be Black (Table 4.1).

The Planning Problems

Both the nature and the pace of economic change have brought their problems largely because of the time-lag that has arisen between the structural transformations in the economic system and the complementary reorganisation of the spatial system. The problems include increasing difficulty of access to, and congestion within, the centre, increasing social costs for Whites and particularly for poorer Blacks as greater and greater distances separate residence and work place, and increasing competition for different land uses. Pressure on the centre is manifested in the sixfold increase in road traffic entering Johannesburg over the past twenty years. Some consider conventional planning measures inadequate to meet expected traffic demands in the central area and that only the installation of mass transit facilities, busways and an underground railway will be sufficient to meet this demand (Jackson 1973).

Accompanying the growth of jobs at the centre has been the outward sprawl of residential townships, so much so that the White population of Johannesburg's fringe municipalities doubled to 177,000 between 1960 and 1970. Before 1960 the average length of the journey-to-work from suburb to city centre was 7-8 km. In 1980 it is 15-16 km.

However, it is the social changes, and particularly those affecting the Black population, that have been crucial to the success of the urban economic transformation. Blacks outnumber Whites by 5 to 2 in the JMA. Between 1951 and 1970 White employment in the JMA has increased by 83,000 and Black by 114,000. It is, however, the growing number of skilled Blacks that is important as the office function in Johannesburg comes to depend more and more on them. In 1950 there were about six White office workers to one Black. By 1970 this had been reduced to three to one and it is approaching two to one. This changing employment trend of Blacks towards more skilled jobs as the economy matures means greater incomes—Black wages have been rising at a faster rate than White in recent years—and a greater dependence of the metropolitan economy upon Black purchasing power. Additional housing and land for residential purposes, improvement in the quality of urban life and greater levels of education and training become ever more urgent as Black numbers grow, expectations rise and the viability of the urban economy comes increasingly to depend upon their labour.

The overriding goal of planning in the JMA is the need to sustain a high level of economic growth in the interest of national development and to promote those physical and social structures which will help do so. But the pressures to adapt to growth in such centres of advanced activity are relentless (Friedmann 1966), for the political structures, too, must be sufficiently flexible to encourage and guide the adaptations necessary. It is to the planning response to the more significant of these problems that the remainder of this chapter is directed.

The Economic Generator and the Planning Response

It is the economic generator of development that mainly fashions the processes and patterns of urbanisation in capitalist societies as Richardson (1973) and others testify. Since the discovery of gold in 1886 'exploitive opportunity-seeking' (Berry 1973) has been the dominant approach to the region's growth and development. This was the natural response on the part of private enterprise to the high risks but potentially large profits that accompanied the development of large-scale gold mining. Almost from the inception of mining, governmental policy and legislation was aimed at protecting and assisting the mining companies in their activities and quest for wealth. Thus mining ground, once proclaimed, is protected from too rapid deproclamation by stringent regulations applied by the Government Mining Engineer, while government acquiescence in, and encouragement of, the migrant labour system has ensured a regular supply of Black workers from all parts of South Africa. Having taken firm root, the capitalist system developed and flourished as the nation and the region moved into its subsequent stages of economic development.

Other than in their role as employers of Black labour, entrepreneurs, representative mainly of the White ruling elite, generally enjoy a freedom of economic operation less constrained than in the mixed economies of some Western European countries and no more constrained than their American counterparts with none of the controls exerted by powerful labour unionisation and the United States government's concern for anti-trust legislation. Despite the fact that the South African government has entered the economic field through the establishment of a number of parastatal financial and industrial profit-making concerns 'the ownership of the means of production has remained largely in private hands, and the economic generator has enjoyed a relative autonomy which . . . is unlikely to be seriously breached in the foreseeable future' (Urban and Regional Research Unit 1974).

The political system, however, has been ambivalent in its response to developments in the economic and social systems. On the one hand, the response has been rapid where changes have involved the role of Blacks in metropolitan areas and on the other, tardy where changes have called for an imaginative, bold and large-scale approach to the physical planning of the region commensurate with the pace and scale of its economic development.

Thus, over the past 40 to 50 years physical planning at national, provincial and local levels has been implemented on a city-by-city basis; only very recently has effective machinery, commensurate with the metropolitan scale of the problems of the Witwatersrand and the JMA, been introduced, and then only for purposes of transportation planning. Moreover, the planning machinery has been evolved to *control* the development of land use in fine and meticulous detail so that urban planning in the region has been viewed 'rather as a negative regulator of physical development than as a positive generator of growth and change in human society' (Urban and Regional Research Unit 1974). Consequently, much urban planning in the region has been of the 'ameliorative problem-solving' type (Berry 1973)—adaptive and *ad hoc*, essentially short term, focusing on presently-recognised problems, and past- rather than future-oriented in outlook.

The first attempt to establish a wider than city-by-city approach to the region's physical development was the establishment of the Witwatersrand Joint Town Planning Committee but it did not long survive. Since the late 1940s, to its credit, the Johannesburg City Council has attempted to take a metropolitan approach to the enlarging area that the city's economic activities were spawning but over which it had inadequate statutory control. In the 1960s it sought to incorporate adjacent local authorities, successfully on its southern, but unsuccessfully on its northern, borders.

Official reports by both national (South Africa 1957) and local (Johannesburg 1957) bodies in the 1950s had advocated the need for a metropolitan approach to the planning of the PWV, the Witwatersrand and the Johannesburg area. Nothing was done, however, until the government was prompted to respond to the speculative property boom of the late 1960s which produced a suburban sprawl of township land of unprecedented proportions, most of it undeveloped, around Johannesburg (Fair 1978). Guide-plan committees for the Witwatersrand were established (South Africa 1970) representative of national, provincial and local bodies. As purely advisory bodies, however, they proved inadequate and ineffective.

About the same time Johannesburg and its neighbouring municipalities established Metrocom, a voluntary consultative group of planning officials, but its infrequent meetings were confined to minor services involving more than one municipality and to non-contentious matters. Metrocom did, however, commission a major report on the planning needs of the JMA and the Witwatersrand (Urban and Regional Research Unit 1973). This, in turn, was followed by the publication of a guide plan for the PWV region prepared by the Department of Planning and the Environment, a central government agency (South Africa 1974a) and by a freeway grid plan prepared by a consortium sponsored by the Transvaal Provincial Administration (Transvaal 1974). There seemed little attempt at effective co-ordination, however, and while the former very general plan emphasised the need to channel the region's built-up area into the inherited cruciform pattern, the latter provided the base for a more dispersed pattern of urban development. However, although both plans lacked statutory backing for their implementation at the time, they were the cause of considerable public concern over the constraints they placed upon residential and other development by private entrepreneurs and over the environmental implications of so extensive a freeway network. Neither plan in any way however sought to address the problems of physical development in the JMA, the region's core.

Transportation Planning in the JMA

Mounting concern over the problems of transportation in the inner cities of South Africa's metropolitan areas led to the appointment by the central government of a Committee of Inquiry into Urban Transport Facilities in the Republic, commonly known as the Driessen Committee (South Africa 1974b). From the work of this committee has flowed, for the first time, the hope of an adequate and effective attack upon some of the physical problems of the JMA arising from the economic and social changes it has experienced over the past 30 years.

The terms of reference required the committee to report and make

recommendations on the problems affecting the planning and provision
of adequate urban and metropolitan transport facilities in the country
and the manner in which expenditure on the provision of such facilities
should be financed. Although the committee drew upon the Buchanan
Report (Buchanan 1963) and other publications emphasising the correlation between land use and transport planning, its findings and
recommendations were – as dictated by the terms of reference – directed
largely toward issues relating to metropolitan transportation. Certain
proposals, most notably those pertaining to development and controls in
the CBDs of major cities, evoked considerable private sector response
and led to the establishment of CBD associations in Johannesburg and
Durban.

The report of the committee, which was published in June 1974,
made reference to international and local trends concerning the urbanisation of population, low density residential spread, high employment
densities in city centres, increases in private car ownership and poor
patronage of public transport services, as well as features peculiar to
the South African metropolitan situation. Included in the latter is the
disparity between Black and White population groups in respect of
urban travel patterns. The report included, for example, estimates for
the early 1970s which indicated that the private car accounted for 80
per cent of the volume of urban travel by Whites in the seven major
urban areas, while the corresponding figure for Blacks was only 13 per
cent. Conversely, during the decade 1960 to 1970 subsidised bus
services for Whites suffered net losses while those serving Blacks showed
a 65 per cent increase in passenger journeys and consequential net
surpluses. These data illustrate the reliance of the Black low income
sector upon public transport in order to gain access to employment
centres generally located some distance from the outlying designated
Black residential zones. This spatial separation is clearly a most significant structural feature of South African metropolitan areas and the
recommendation was made in the Driessen report that

In the planning of Non-White residential areas and working areas,
attention should be given to the reduction, as far as practicable, of
the relatively long distances and time involved in the daily transportation of Non-Whites, as such reduction would entail savings on
transport costs and promote productivity as well as contentment of
the labour force. (South Africa 1974b)

However, there is to date little evidence of positive action undertaken to resolve the basic social and economic problems attaching to the segregated form of metropolitan areas.

While the recommendations of the committee can, in physical terms, be construed as concentrating on the three traditional elements of metropolitan form and transportation—place of residence, place of work and travel between the two—the residential component was accorded least attention. The major proposal in this regard was the promotion of higher residential densities in suburban areas in order to contain urban sprawl, a proposal which has been pursued in the planning study for the JMA. With regard to place of work, the committee proposed, in the interests of alleviating congestion in metropolitan CBDs and for purposes of gaining funds for the improvement of urban transport facilities, that existing maximum bulk factors (floor area ratios) in city centres be frozen until adequate transport arrangements are made; that additional levies be imposed on central city properties; that taxes on parking space and charges for loading zones be instituted, and a levy or permit system be introduced to control the number of cars entering congested areas or 'restricted zones' to better relate road capacity to traffic volume. With reference to intra-urban travel, the major thrust of the committee's recommendations lay in the promotion of public bus transport services as an effective alternative to the private car. To this end, bus lanes, peak hour road restrictions, contraflow systems and other devices were suggested, as well as the retention of government subsidies for bus services. The Driessen report offered less support for metropolitan underground rail systems such as that proposed previously in an urban transport plan for Johannesburg (Johannesburg 1970).

In order to implement the foregoing and numerous other recommendations contained in the report, the committee proposed the establishment of a Metropolitan Transport Advisory Council for each metropolitan area in the country. These councils, comprising representatives of central, provincial and local government, the railways and private trade and industry, were to operate under the aegis of the provincial administration and report to the National Transport Commission which, as part of the government Department of Transport, would retain final responsibility for urban and metropolitan transport policies in the Republic and hence the right of approval of transport plans for metropolitan areas. The metropolitan areas were to centre on 'core cities', the major local authority area of the region, which was to be responsible for the preparation of transport studies and plans.

The implications of the above recommendations were at the time of the publication of the Driessen report, and remain today, obvious. The guidance and control of metropolitan development in the country would be the concern of the national transportation authorities and all metropolitan planning would in consequence be required to be framed around transportation criteria. This basic procedure has, in fact, now been accepted and formalised in the Urban Transport Act of 1977.

The Act put into legislative effect many of the recommendations of the Driessen Committee, including the establishment of metropolitan transport areas around designated core cities and the creation of Metropolitan Transport Advisory Boards (MTAB) for such areas. The Act empowers the National Transport Commission to approve metropolitan transport plans and to administer an Urban Transport Fund established to provide, *inter alia*, financial support for approved transport studies and implementation programmes. The Act enables local authorities to impose levies as visualised in the Driessen report, the moneys from which are to be paid into a consolidated Metropolitan Transport Fund, and to exercise control over vehicle entry, parking, loading and off-loading in specific portions of the metropolitan area.

The Driessen Committee report and subsequent Urban Transport Act provide the frame of reference for metropolitan planning studies at present in the course of preparation, including that of the JMA.

Johannesburg Metropolitan Transportation Study

Johannesburg has, in accordance with the provisions of the Urban Transport Act, been appointed the core city of a metropolitan transport area comprising Alberton, Bedfordview, Edenvale, Elsburg, Germiston, Johannesburg, Randburg, Roodepoort, Sandton and certain Black residential townships administered by the East and West Rand Administration Boards. This complex of towns and cities is referred to as the Jomet area and is slightly larger than the JMA. As the core city, Johannesburg is responsible for the preparation of a transport study for the area and in mid-1979 produced a report on an investigation of alternative land use and transportation strategies for the metropolitan region (Johannesburg 1979). The strategies, which are seen as the first stage of a comprehensive and detailed planning study, comprise

... general concepts, policies and statements covering land use and transport such as the likely distribution of population and work places, the degree of emphasis given to public and private transport and an indication of some of the more important facilities that appear to be necessary. (Johannesburg 1979)

The land use component is therefore an integral part of the study, although the strategies which have been developed are expressed in terms of the journey-to-work in the metropolitan area.

At this stage, ten possible strategies based on defined long-term transport and land-use objectives have been developed and have been the subject of discussion at a series of public meetings. The meetings warrant mention as the first conscious move toward structured public participation in the planning process in the JMA, and indeed in the country as a whole. The fact that no public meeting was held with the residents of Soweto must however tend to compromise the value of the participatory exercise.

The ten broad strategies are made up of three alternative land-use strategies within which a number of alternative transport systems are contained. The point of departure for land-use policy was provided by the Driessen report: a land use pattern supportive of public transport; the accelerated growth of work places with good accessibility to Black residential areas; the freezing of existing statutory bulk in CBDs; the encouragement of higher density residential development initially adjacent to growth nodes of employment. The strategies accept and reflect the maintenance of the government policy of segregation of residential areas for different race groups.

The development of the alternative strategies moves from an analysis of the existing structure of the Jomet area. This analysis indicates that 72 per cent of all present work opportunities are located within a belt of development extending from Roodepoort in the west through Johannesburg to Germiston in the east. Industrial activity is concentrated mainly in the east of the area while the central sector containing the Johannesburg CBD comprises predominantly office functions with warehouse and industrial support. High and medium density residential areas are situated mainly in and immediately north-east of Johannesburg's city centre, beyond which low density housing spreads outwards. The main Black residential concentrations occur at Soweto in the south-west and at Katlehong and Tokoza in the south-east.

Against this physical background and based on projections for the year 2000, the study team has generated three alternative strategies; viz. trend, corridor and nodal. As the name implies, the Trend Strategy accepts and emphasises the concentration of work places in or adjacent to the existing east-west employment belt. Only limited expansion of centres beyond the belt will occur. The present trend toward smaller residential sites and apartment block living is promoted in locations convenient to employment areas, notably the Johannesburg central complex. The Corridor Strategy is derived from the railway line network, the major existing routes of which run east-west from Roodepoort to Germiston and south from Germiston to Alberton. The strategy envisages the introduction of new rail links from Johannesburg to the south (Lenasia) and to the north (Sandton), and proposes that residential and employment growth be concentrated along these corridors of movement. The final land-use strategy, the Nodal, places emphasis on the strengthening of existing minor employment nodes in the CBDs of Roodepoort, Randburg, and Germiston, and in Soweto, while accepting the Johannesburg CBD's role as the primary node of the metropolitan area. Higher density residential development is to occur around all nodes.

The travel demands relating to the different land-use strategies are incorporated in a further series of transportation strategies. The strategies are the Do-minimum, the Public Transport Maximum, the Private Transport Maximum and three variations on a Balanced Strategy. The titles of the transportation strategies are largely self-explanatory: the Do-minimum, which is applied to all three of the land use strategies, envisages a minimum of capital expenditure on highway improvements and the provision of public transport by bus and train services; the Public Transport Maximum seeks to encourage support of public transport by means of maximum investment in services such as a comprehensive bus network combined with a rail rapid-transit system, and is applied to the Trend Land Use Strategy only. The converse strategy is the Private Transport Maximum which suggests an extension of the existing motorway system by the introduction of a grid of north-south and east-west motorways around the central area connecting with the proposed regional freeway system. This strategy is applied to the Trend Land Use Strategy. The Balanced Transportation strategy has three variations, each of which envisages the use of both private and public transport but with a rapid rail bias in one case, a bussing emphasis in another and an integrated fare structure for public transport nodes in the third. The latter two strategies are applied to the Corridor Land Use Strategy only.

The study concludes with an evaluation based on land-use objectives, transport goals and objectives and economic performance. The three alternative land-use strategies are assessed against 19 stated objectives that are weighted in terms of relative importance. The objective of providing a land-use pattern which complements and supports a public transport system is, for example and in the judgement of the study team, ranked as most important. Measured against the weighted objectives, the Corridor Strategy emerges with the highest score. With reference to transportation, the objective of reducing 'the need to travel' followed by a reduction in the consumption of scarce energy resources are considered to be of most importance. The preferred combined land-use and transport strategies are tested across a range of possible future scenarios to measure their flexibility and robustness. In the final analysis, the Corridor Strategy is seen as most acceptable from a land-use viewpoint and the balanced transport strategy as providing the most acceptable transportation solution.

While the study proposes further detailed investigation and development of the preferred strategy, it emphasises that the study is, in essence, a discussion document to be modified in the light of public response.

Any planning criticism of the Jomet study stems almost inevitably from the restrictive nature of an approach based largely on transport criteria. Although the study incorporates land use and takes into consideration such issues as population growth, residential distribution, employment and unemployment, the transport focus is dominant throughout. Accepting that the form and nature of the study were predetermined by the provisions of the Urban Transport Act, the ultimate value and credibility of a planning investigation which precludes consideration of the social and environmental components must be open to question. As indicated previously, the goal of planning in the JMA must, above all, be one of ongoing economic growth accompanied by the provision of physical, social and political structures required to sustain that growth. Any response at this time must and should be primarily a response in terms of social process, and indeed social progress. In its present state of development, the Jomet study is deficient in this regard and unless the major objectives are restructured, it must be construed as incomplete.

The socio-economic circumstances attaching to the Black population of the JMA must be regarded as an area of major planning concern and one requiring sensitive and innovative action. The Jomet strategies provide broad indications of possible employment zones and new residential areas on the periphery of Soweto but the dysfunctional spatial separation between it and Johannesburg remains. As described elsewhere, the potential of the intervening mining land as an 'inter-city' development zone, and as a medium for drawing Soweto into the spatial mainstream of the JMA, is by and large overlooked in the proposed strategies

The study does not at this stage cover the environmental consequences of the proposed transportation strategies. To the extent that environmental impact analysis is today correctly considered to be a prerequisite in assessing the effect of proposed developments on existing environments, it is necessary that such analyses be undertaken for all strategies before a final decision is made.

An assessment of the land-use strategies leads to the conclusion that there is little significant difference between the three and that they represent variations on a single approach rather than meaningful alternatives. The expansion of employment opportunities, the encouragement of high density residential development and the utilisation of the existing transportation infrastructure are basically similar in location and intention in all three strategies, which are essentially consolidations of trends.

This limitation in range may be partly due to the fact that the study has had perforce to work within the provisions of the Urban Transport Act. The point can however be made that the study is as yet still in the formative stage and that it does exhibit elements of innovation which, with further sensitive planning attention, could be so developed as to provide a much improved physical framework for the JMA.

Mining Land in the JMA

The decline in mining activity over the past 25 years has brought about a unique situation where large areas of land situated in close proximity to the CBD of Johannesburg have now become available for types of development suited to the area's new economic base.

The major mining groups concerned owned some 5,500 ha in the JMA and have established a property arm in order to dispose of this land which is being used for new motorways, container terminals and produce markets, for factories, offices, warehouses and distribution depots. However, the cost of creating new building sites is comparatively high since waste sand dumps and slime dams of very considerable proportions, which give the Witwatersrand its very distinctive landscape, have in some instances to be removed. Certain derelict land may be irreclaimable, but the transformation is likely to be speeded up by the treatment (and removal) of sand dumps for traces of gold which they still contain.

However, such is the rigidity of the law relating to mining land that although much of the land will not again be used for mining purposes since it is worked out, it remains proclaimed mining land held under the jurisdiction of the government Department of Mines. No township development on this land is permitted without the consent of the Mining Commissioner who considers each application for township establishment on its individual merits. The JMA can accordingly be broadly seen as comprising two land elements: that which falls under the control of the provincial and local authorities who administer the provisions of the provincial planning ordinance and the town planning schemes, and that which is retained and controlled by the Department of Mines. The total extent of land held by the latter has, notably over the last 10 years, been regularly reduced by permitted township establishment. The urban fabric is therefore progressively intruding into available mine areas.

The most significant event leading to the opening up of the mining land for city related activities must be regarded as the construction of the urban motorway system in the 1960s and 1970s. The north-south M1 and east-west M2 motorways in Johannesburg, being partially situated on mining land, have created exceptionally good accessibility to large areas, the potential of which for industrial purposes was not previously appreciated. Recent years have witnessed the introduction of new land uses and activities in the vicinity of the motorways, particularly in positions convenient to points of motorway entry and egress. Although retailing and residential uses have found homes on the mining land, the dominant uses are of a light industrial and distributive nature which is compatible with the previously established industrial character of the land.

The process of township establishment as prescribed by the Ordinance on Town Planning and Townships of Transvaal, 1965, is lengthy. The provisions of the Ordinance are such that if permission for establishment is granted by the Mining Commissioner, the period between application and proclamation is typically 2 to 3 years. As the townships are generally established by private enterprise in response to market demand, they tend not to be large in area. Once demand has been shown to exist, further extensions of limited scale follow. The major consequence is that growth at present is largely incremental and occurs in parcels rather than in an integrated and continuous pattern.

The belt of mining land in the JMA represents a unique resource and opportunity. Few metropolitan areas in the world have vast tracts of undeveloped land within minutes of their CBDs and although some constraints on development are occasioned by shallowly undermined ground, the development potential of the land is considerable. The

Johannesburg City Council has from time to time prepared studies on
the mining area with a view to creating a comprehensive physical plan
to co-ordinate and guide development. This, and their proposals to
create an integrated open space system across the mine dumps, now
vegetated in compliance with legislation on atmospheric and water
pollution, have so far met with little success.

The Atmospheric Pollution Prevention Act of 1965 and the Water
Act of 1956 require that mines undertake measures against air and
water pollution emanating from waste dumps and dams before a closure
certificate is issued by the Government Mining Engineer. Although the
inorganic pollution of rivers by the mining industry is declining, it has
been pointed out that the leaching out of salts from slime dams and
sand dumps will continue and remain a source of pollution for many
years (Laburn 1972). Impressive work has, however, been carried out
on mine dump vegetation since the early 1950s in pursuance of pollution
control. Extensive experimentation by the Chamber of Mines Vegetation
Unit has resulted in a sophisticated process whereby vegetative cover
is established on waste dumps which, together with the provision of
evaporation paddocks, serves to control water run-off pollution. A
further and significant consequence of the grassing of mine dumps and
slime dams has been the positive effect it has made on the general
environmental quality of the JMA.

In general, however, it appears that the physical, and indeed social
and economic, potential of the mining land is in danger of being overlooked. Soweto is bordered on the east and north by land owned by
mining companies and the Jomet study appears to ignore the opportunities presented by this largely undeveloped area. The possibility of
consolidating the functional relationship between Soweto and Johannesburg by promoting the physical coalescence of the two across the
gap of mining land has not, at this stage, been pursued so that the full
potential of the mining land remains untapped.

The Planning Response in the Black Social System

If the planning response has been tardy to economic change generally,
it has been remarkably sensitive to the effects of that change upon the
social system as it relates to Blacks, and in particular, to Africans. As
indicated earlier, planning in South Africa emerges as a comparatively
mildly constraining process in the White social system and as a highly
constraining process in the Black social system.

Since the 1920s and especially since the 1940s, as industrialisation gathered pace in the metropolitan areas, the White ruling elite viewed with concern the effects of a growing Black, especially African, flow of workers and their families from rural to urban areas. In order not to threaten the security of White urban society it sought to contain the potentially massive flow of African migrants through influx control measures (Fair and Davies 1976), to constrain the geographic and social mobility of Blacks generally in towns and to segregate them residentially from Whites.

The place of the Black, and particularly the African, in the cities of South Africa must be viewed within the framework of the broader goals of *apartheid* ideology espoused by the present White government since 1948. Its grand design is based on the assumption that South Africa is a multi-national as well as a multi-racial country, that Africans and Whites can find peaceful co-existence in geographically separate, politically independent states, and that Coloureds, Asians and Whites can find it in a federal-type arrangement of racial parliaments. Ascribed political rights only in their mainly rural 'homelands', Africans, until recently, have not been accorded official recognition as an integral part of the urban scene, for all the major cities of South Africa occur in the White state. Ministerial statements are very clear on this point: 'the Africans in the White area, whether they were born here or whether they are allowed to come here under our control laws are here for the labour they are being allowed to perform' (van der Merwe 1972). Only those Africans with comparatively long terms of residence and employment are permitted to reside permanently in the urban areas of the White state. All others are migrants shuttling back and forth between rural homeland and urban work place and their flow is strictly monitored to meet employment needs.

The physical constraint upon the entry of Africans to urban areas has thus been matched also by economic and social constraints upon their becoming urbanised in a cultural sense. They have been made to perceive South African cities as largely the White man's creation and domain. Politically voiceless in White South Africa, they are excluded from national and municipal government. They have been denied the power of collective trade union bargaining over jobs and conditions of work. Training for skilled occupations has concentrated mainly on Whites. Blacks have been denied the range and choice of amenities and services enjoyed by Whites (Pirie 1976) and the migrant labour system has contributed to the disruption of family life for a great many (Smith 1976; Fair and Davies 1976; Fair and Browett 1979). Emphasis in this chapter is laid upon Johannesburg's residential pattern since it illustrates most clearly the nature of the planning process as it relates to the Black sub-system and manifests most visibly attempts by government to maximise the physical and social distance between Whites and Blacks and to accommodate a multi-racial population according to the tenets of separation rather than integration.

Residential separation is enforced through the Group Areas and other Acts. Buffer strips of open land for non-residential use separate areas occupied by the four major race groups. Where possible, direct access by road and/or rail between residence and work place is sought to avoid one group traversing the areas of other groups, and 'hinterlands' are reserved in order to meet the future space requirements of each group's residential area.

On the Witwatersrand the early fragmented pattern of mining towns had led to the establishment of a host of small Black townships which became engulfed by expanding White residential and other land uses and inadequate to accommodate the growing Black population. Since the 1950s the government has disestablished most of the old townships and has created fewer but much larger Black residential areas mainly to the south of the mining belt, in contrast to White development which has tended to expand mainly northwards (Figure 4.4). In Johannesburg alone the Native Resettlement Act of 1954 empowered the transfer of 10,000 African families to the new and consolidated township of Soweto. Here in 1970 were accommodated nearly 600,000 persons or at least 66 per cent of the JMA's African population. It is estimated that the population of Soweto in 1980 is more than 1 million. The remainder of Johannesburg's African population is housed in industrial and municipal compounds, in Alexandra, a small African township serving the northern municipalities of the JMA, or as domestic servants in White residential areas. Asians and Coloureds reside mainly in two large 'group areas', Lenasia and Eldorado Park, respectively, located south of Soweto. Together these three Black areas comprise a massive block of high density residence in strong contrast to the more expansive, lower density White areas to the north.

Gross density in White residential areas in the JMA is 24 persons per hectare compared with 100 in Soweto. Denied the freehold tenure enjoyed by Whites, Africans in Soweto rent houses provided by the government. Moreover, densities are increasing since the government, until recently, discouraged the building of family houses in favour of large hostels designed to accommodate single migrant workers on one-year contracts from their rural areas. Only 2,734 family houses were built by the government in Soweto between 1973 and 1979 (*The Star* 16 November 1979). Consequently, overcrowding—as high as 10 persons per house—and the shortage of family houses is serious (Boaden 1979). In 1979 some 15,000 Soweto families were on the official waiting list for houses but the actual demand is considered to be much higher. The Urban Foundation, a private organisation, estimates that 32,000 new houses need to be added immediately to Soweto's present housing stock of 100,000 units in order to meet current demand (*The Star* 16 November 1979).

Although transport by road and rail is subsidised the social costs of long and expensive journeys to work are high. Added to the unattractive physical living conditions of most Africans in Soweto are many symptoms of deprivation, high rates of crime and social pressures and anxiety.

Disturbances and rioting in 1976 were in large measure the outcome of these conditions and the imposition over the years of a normative goal-oriented planning style (Berry 1973) aimed at rigidly regulating the lives of the city's African inhabitants in the interests of *apartheid* ideology. Fortunately, the disturbances have led the government to a radical reappraisal of the conditions of life and work of Africans (and other Black groups) in the metropolitan areas of South Africa. The findings of commissions of inquiry into labour legislation and the utilisation of Black manpower (South Africa 1979), calls by government for greater co-operation with the private sector, the appointment of a government-sponsored committee to oversee all development projects in Soweto and the establishment of the Urban Foundation in 1977 by concerned businessmen, are making new and meaningful commitments to improving the quality of life of urban Blacks and widening their opportunities for social and economic advancement.

It is increasingly accepted by the ruling elite that South Africa's economic progress and the ordered development of its metropolitan areas, as the country moves into a more advanced and sophisticated stage of economic development, can be achieved only by providing more stable and acceptable living conditions and by developing the skills of those who constitute the majority of the work force.

The recommendations of the official reports on labour reform (South Africa 1979), accepted by the government, are that, among others, all Black workers, excluding for the present temporary migrant workers, be entitled to full trade union rights; that reservation of particular classes of employment for Whites be abolished; that the training and retraining of Black workers be improved and rapidly increased; and that any measures which are designed to curb the creation of job opportunities and prevent Blacks from working in areas where they are lawfully residing and housed be dispensed with. The reports emphasise that discrimination based on colour in labour legislation and employment is unrealistic and indefensible. Influx control is to be severely curtailed and retained only in modified form to prevent unreasonable levels of housing demand and unemployment arising from unchecked rural-urban migration.

Whereas in the PWV region 79 per cent of African housing has been available only on a monthly basis and 21 per cent on 30-year leaseholds (Boaden 1979), home ownership on a 99-year leasehold has now been introduced by the government. The transition from renting homes to owning them will be a slow process for people the majority of whose incomes are extremely modest, but access to finance is being facilitated through employer-employee assistance and generous interest rates. One view is that the 99-year leasehold scheme is beyond the pockets of 60 per cent of prospective home owners in the African townships (*Star* 16 November 1979). However, in the long term the social change towards greater stability, engendered by the security that pride of ownership brings, should help transform Soweto into a community mainly of permanent urban residents rather than one of migrants and temporary sojourners. Perhaps of even greater immediate significance are the plans being discussed by the South African Building Industries Federation and the government to undertake a massive home-building programme in Soweto and other African townships to eliminate the Black housing shortage in South African cities as soon as possible.

The extension of trading rights to Africans in their townships and the opening of the CBDs and industrial areas of South Africa's cities to entrepreneurs of all races are further reversals of policy which now recognises the cultural significance of the urbanisation process going on among the Black population of the country and the legitimacy of their aspirations as urban dwellers.

Combined with these changes has been the work of the Urban Foundation, the Ecoplan consortium and other private groups in improving the quality of life of the urban Black through housing, education, health services and community facilities generally. Commensurate with these activities is the government's improvement of internal and external communications and transportation facilities in Soweto and its decision to supply electricity throughout the township. Eighty-two per cent of transportation between Soweto and places of work in the JMA is by public bus and train (460,000 trips per day). The South African Railways at present transports 250,000 passengers per day to and fróm Soweto and this volume will rise to 440,000 by 1990 (Lloyd 1976). Black commuter rail traffic is growing rapidly while White is almost static. Similarly, Black car ownership is rising more steeply than White, in Johannesburg from 50 per 1,000 persons in 1978 (300 per 1,000 for Whites) to an estimated 180 by the year 2000. Soweto's physical connections with the JMA are thus receiving increased attention by government and city planners.

Within the framework permitted by government ideology, the changing administrative control of a large African urban township such as Soweto, contained wholly within a White-run Johannesburg, illustrates that recognition is now being given to Africans in South African cities in a sense far more profound than simply the recognition of their physical presence. Until 1971 a Black urban township such as Soweto was administered by the White-run municipality within which it was located. In that year, however, the Black Affairs Administration Act replaced the Johannesburg City Council's control of Soweto by the government-controlled West Rand Administration Board (WRAB). African participation in managing the affairs of Soweto was confined to an advisory committee established in terms of the Black (Urban Areas) Consolidation Act of 1945. In 1961 an African Urban Council was established but still with advisory powers only.

In 1977 the Community Councils Act enabled African urban communities to administer the affairs of their townships more effectively. Three councils have been established by the election of officers for Soweto as a whole with limited powers over certain aspects of the township's welfare, for example, the administration of housing, control over the unlawful occupation of land and buildings, and the allocation and administration of sites for church, school or trading purposes (de Wet 1979). These councils fall under the jurisdiction of WRAB which, however, now has the responsibility of assisting them 'to develop into independent, self-supporting councils with the ultimate aim of becoming independent municipalities' (de Wet 1979).

Recent statements by government (*The Rand Daily Mail* 20 November 1979) indicate that new legislation is to be passed in 1980 to repeal the Community Councils Act and to create a new, fully-autonomous and independent municipality for Soweto with powers identical to the White City Council of Johannesburg and those of the other municipalities constituting the Johannesburg Metropolitan Area. Some 2,000 new posts for Africans in the new municipality will be created and enlarged training programmes for Africans in public administration and other relevant fields have been commenced.

While such developments are of considerable importance compared with the subordinate role thus far played by Africans in matters closely affecting them, all Blacks (including Asians and Coloureds) will continue to be barred from sharing power in the White-run City Council of Johannesburg and the other municipalities of the JMA. The dual nature of the administration of so large an economically integrated region as the JMA will thus persist. Whites will run one part, the major part, and Blacks will run another. Residential segregation of Whites, Africans, Coloureds and Asians will remain an essential structural feature of the JMA and some control over the movement of Africans into and out of the area will continue.

Moreover, Africans will continue to realise their full political rights and aspirations only in the 'homeland' states. While Soweto has thus become a municipality on its own the boundaries between Black Johannesburg and White Johannesburg in an administrative sense remain as sharp as ever. Also, until Soweto obtains large industrial and commercial areas of its own, its economic base as a separate municipality will remain weak, and its inhabitants will be obliged to continue to seek work and to do most of their shopping in the White-controlled areas of the JMA. Thus the current recommendations and plans regarding administrative changes and improvements in the quality of life view Soweto primarily as a residential area, a dormitory to White Johannesburg. While this status continues, its full integration into the social, economic and political life of the JMA will be incomplete.

However, the recognition given to Africans through the new arrangements, through labour reforms and through changing White attitudes towards them as urban dwellers indicates the extent of the transformation that is taking place towards according Africans, and Blacks generally, a fuller and more meaningful role in South African cities. The ruling elite now stress that the planning of Black townships is proceeding in full association with the people themselves. Ultimately, the full integration of Blacks and Whites into the administration, life and work of a single Johannesburg Metropolitan Area seems inevitable.

Conclusion

One is today witnessing changes of immediate significance to both the economic and social organisation of the JMA and its physical morphology. As Davies (1976) has pointed out 'the form of the South African city has been identified as essentially that of the segmented, disunited colonial city' – first the segregated city and more recently the *apartheid* city.

> Problems of social, economic and spatial injustice inherent in the structure of cities moulded in a colonial idiom are very strongly present in the South African city. If society is to be subject to change, pressures for the functional and spatial restructuring of the city will be an inevitable consequence.

Urban research and planning must take cognisance now of the transition processes that have been set in train first through the forces of metropolitan economic expansion and latterly through changes in urban social policy that the government has embarked upon. Planning today must anticipate the deep structural changes that South African cities are likely to follow in the next 20 years.

For the JMA, the heart of South Africa's urban system, a vital threshold stage has been reached where the strains engendered by economic development are forcing adaptations in the political, social and spatial systems. For this reason the planning challenge is socio-political rather than purely physical. For example, pleas are made by prominent citizens (Mandy 1979) for a single metropolitan government for the inner Witwatersrand zone where not only is a co-ordinated approach to the provision of transport, health, housing, sewerage, water and electricity services desirable, but where consensus among equally autonomous White and Black municipalities to deal with matters of common interest is essential. Moreover, structural changes are needed which would permit Coloureds and Asians, and in time Africans, to occupy certain of the inner suburbs of Johannesburg rather than the peripheral areas in which they are now obliged to live 30 and 40 km from the city centre; and the facilities of CBD and industrial areas should be increasingly opened to people of all races.

The conclusion is inescapable. The relentless pressures of an expanding urban economic system can no longer be met by the rigidities of *apartheid* planning and its emphasis on a race-class system maintained through the coercive organisation of a minority elite. Modern industrial-urbanisation demands a flexibility and a looseness in its class system and the inexorable integrative forces of a modernising economy should in time radically transform the constraining forces which have characterised the social structures of South Africa's metropolitan areas. Of equal importance, in a society which promotes the free enterprise system, the preservation of a capitalist-oriented economy by the White elite can be achieved only by permitting the Black peripheral population to compete and to share in it on an equal footing. Profound changes arising out of the trends and the attitudes of the metropolitan population, both rulers and ruled, can be anticipated in the economic, social and physical structures of the JMA, and of South African metropolitan areas generally, in the years ahead.

References

Berry, B.J.L. (1973) *The Human Consequences of Urbanisation*, Macmillan, London

Boaden, B.G. (1979) *A Laissez-Faire Approach to the Housing of Urban Blacks*, Paper delivered to the Economics Society of South Africa Conference, Cape Town

Buchanan, C. (1963) *Traffic in Towns*, Penguin, Harmondsworth

Davies, R.J. (1976) *Of Cities and Societies: A Geographer's Viewpoint*, Inaugural Lecture, New Series No. 38, University of Cape Town

de Wet, H.C. (1979) 'Councils for Black Urban Residential Areas', *Informa, 26 (8)*, 1-16; The Information Service of South Africa, Pretoria

Fair, T.J.D. (1976) 'Polarisation, Dispersion and Decentralisation in the South African Space Economy', *SA Geographical Journal, 58(1)*, 40-56

—— (1977) 'The Witwatersrand — Structure, Shape and Strategy', *SA Geographer, 5(5)*, 380-9

—— (1978) *Spatial Patterns and Determinants of White Residential Land Development on the Witwatersrand 1950-75*, Urban and Regional Research Unit, University of the Witwatersrand, Johannesburg

—— and R.J. Davies (1976) Constrained Urbanization: White South Africa and Black Africa Compared, in B.J.L. Berry (ed.) *Urbanization and Counterurbanization*, Sage, Beverly Hills and London

—— and J.G. Browett (1979) 'The Urbanization Process in South Africa', in D.T. Herbert and R.J. Johnston (eds.) *Geography and the Urban Environment*, Vol. 2, Wiley, Chichester

Friedmann, J. (1966) *Regional Development Policy*, MIT Press, Cambridge, Mass.

Jackson, R.I. (1973) 'Factors in Urban Transportation Planning', in *Focus on Metropolitan Areas*, Symposium, Rand Afrikaans University, Johannesburg

Johannesburg, (1957) *The Future Development of Johannesburg*, First and Second Interim Reports, City Council, Johannesburg

—— (1970) *Greater Johannesburg Area Transportation Study, Vol. 2, The Plan*, City Engineer's Dept, Johannesburg

—— (1979) *Johannesburg Metropolitan Transportation Study*, City Engineer's Dept, Johannesburg

Laburn, R.J. (3 Oct. 1972) *Some Aspects of Water Management in the PWV Metropolitan Region*, SA Institute of Civil Engineers, Symposium, Johannesburg

Lloyd, J.D. (1976) 'Planning of Railway Services to the City Centre', Seminar on Planning the Future of Johannesburg, City Council, Johannesburg

Mandy, N. (1979) Address to Johannesburg Rotary Club, *The Rand Daily Mail*, 16 Jan. 1980

Morris, P.M.R. (1980) *Soweto*, Urban Foundation, Johannesburg

Pirie, G.H. (1976) 'Apartheid, Health and Social Services in Greater Johannesburg', in D.M. Smith (ed.) *Separation in South Africa: Homelands and Cities*,

Occasional Paper No. 7, Department of Geography, Queen Mary College, London

The Rand Daily Mail, Johannesburg, daily

Richardson, H. (1973) 'Theory of the Distribution of City Sizes, Review and Prospects', *Regional Studies, 7(3)*, 239-51

Rogerson, C.M. (1974a) 'The Geography of Business Management in South Africa', *SA Geographical Journal, 56(1)*, 87-93

—— (1974b) 'Some Aspects of Industrial Movement from Johannesburg, 1960-1972', *SA Geographical Journal, 57(1)*, 3-16

Smith, D.M. (ed.) (1976) *Separation in South Africa: Homelands and Cities*, Occasional Paper No. 7, Dept of Geography, Queen Mary College, London

South Africa, (1957) *A Planning Survey of the Southern Transvaal*, Natural Resources Development Council, Government Printer, Pretoria

—— (1970) 'Commission of Inquiry into the Occurrence of High Selling Prices of Vacant Residential Sites and Unplanned Land being Acquired for Township Development', RP 74/1970, Government Printer, Pretoria

—— (1974a) *Proposals for a Guide Plan for the PWV Complex*, Dept of Planning and the Environment, Government Printer, Pretoria

—— (1974b) *Report of the Committee of Inquiry into Urban Transport Facilities in the Republic*, RP 60/74, Government Printer, Pretoria

—— (1977) *Gross Geographic Product at Factor Incomes by Magisterial District, 1972*, Report No. 09-14-03, Government Printer, Pretoria

—— (1979a) Report of the Commission of Inquiry into Labour Legislation, Part 1, Key Issues, RP 47/1979, Government Printer, Pretoria; (b) Report of the Commission of Inquiry into Legislation affecting the utilisation of Manpower, RP 32/1979, Government Printer, Pretoria

The Star, Johannesburg, daily

Transvaal, (1974) *PWV – Major Network Investigation, Interim Report*, Transvaal Provincial Administration, Pretoria

Urban and Regional Research Unit, (1973) *The Witwatersrand: Regional Setting, The Economy, Population and Land Use*, University of the Witwatersrand, Johannesburg

—— (1974) *The Witwatersrand: Implications for Strategy*, University of the Witwatersrand, Johannesburg

Van der Merwe, P.J. (1972) 'Manpower in South Africa', *Finance and Trade Review, 10*, 73-113

5 GLASGOW

Michael Pacione

Within Scotland the greatest concentration of people and housing is found in the Clydeside conurbation, at the heart of which is the city of Glasgow (1979 pop. 794,316). Since the reorganisation of local government in 1973 Glasgow has been a constituent district of the Strathclyde region which contains half of Scotland's population. The first regional report prepared in 1976 identified the high level of unemployment and the severity of urban deprivation as the two major problems facing Glasgow, and these key issues underlie the regional authority's strategies for development and resource allocation. A clear indication of the nature and severity of those problems can be gained by examining, at the level of individual enumeration districts, a range of census statistics covering the broad themes of housing, demography, employment and socio-economic structure.

The housing and employment statistics normally used in such analyses incorporate measures of the proportion of households without exclusive use of all basic amenities and of economically active males unemployed and so provide direct indicators of these aspects of urban deprivation. The group of demographic measures usually considered includes 'the proportion of the population aged 0-14' and 'pensioner households'. While these, in themselves, do not provide conclusive evidence for the presence of deprived families, when they occur in areas where incomes are low and housing conditions are bad, they represent factors that may aggravate conditions of deprivation. Similarly, the indicators based on housing tenure, levels of car ownership and socio-economic class provide useful supplementary information about areas of multiple deprivation.

The housing and employment indicators essentially define conditions that would be widely accepted as the minimum tolerable standard for an individual or household. This includes the exclusive use of all basic amenities; hot water, fixed bath or shower and inside toilet; the occupation of sufficient housing space for each household to live at less than 1.5 persons per room; and the opportunity for employment for all. The task of providing this level of life quality in the seriously deprived areas of Glasgow is an over-riding objective of regional policy.

Table 5.1 allows the problems of Clydeside to be placed within a

Table 5.1: Census Indicators: Conurbation Shares of the Worst 5 per cent of British Enumeration Districts for Eleven Indicators

Conurbation	Households sharing or lacking hot water	Households sharing or lacking bath	Households lacking inside WC	Households without exclusive use of all basic amenities	Households living at beyond 1.5 persons per room	Economically active males unemployed	Economically active females unemployed	Households with no car	Economically active and retired males in SEG 11	Population aged 0-14	Pensioner households	% share of EDs in Great Britain
Tyneside	2.7	3.1	6.0	4.2	1.3	6.7	2.9	7.2	4.4	1.9	1.4	2.0
London group A[a]	27.7[c]	28.2	7.0	21.7	21.8	2.9	6.3	12.9	9.9	3.5	4.3	8.6
London group B[b]	3.9	2.6	2.1	1.9	5.5	0.4	1.9	0.4	3.2	3.3	3.3	10.4
West Yorkshire	1.7	1.9	3.6	2.6	3.0	4.2	3.5	8.6	3.9	3.3	5.3	4.3
Merseyside	5.2	5.0	6.8	5.4	1.5	9.0	6.2	5.0	6.0	3.4	0.9	2.7
SE Lancashire	4.8	6.0	13.6	9.6	1.9	6.1	5.4	8.9	8.1	4.3	3.8	5.8
West Midlands	7.5	3.9	6.2	4.7	5.6	2.8	3.8	2.9	4.1	5.5	1.4	4.8
Clydeside	15.5	15.6	5.9	13.5	37.3	23.1	13.7	25.7	11.7	12.8	4.8	4.3
Scotland (excl. Clydeside)	6.9	11.9	2.6	8.3	16.3	11.4	11.7	10.2	10.2	13.4	12.2	6.8

Notes: a. Inner London Education Authority Boroughs (excluding Haringey and Newham) plus Greenwich.
b. Remainder of GLC Area.
c. Values underlined are highest for each indicator.
Source: Holtermann (1975).

national perspective by indicating each conurbation's share of the worst environmental conditions as measured by a set of eleven census indicators. The most striking feature is the fact that Clydeside has an excessive share of the worst 5 per cent of enumeration districts for nearly all kinds of deprivation. The conurbation recorded the largest proportion of the worst 5 per cent for six of the eleven indicators and the second largest proportion for three others. With particular reference to housing, Clydeside clearly has more than its 'fair' share of problems. In terms of severe overcrowding, for example, the conurbation accounts for 37.3 per cent of the worst 5 per cent of British enumeration districts, even although it contains only 4.3 per cent of all enumeration districts. Equally, in terms of both male unemployment (23.1 per cent) and female unemployment (13.7 per cent), the severity of the problem on Clydeside is far in excess of any other conurbation area in the country. Within Scotland the relatively low level of life quality in many parts of the Glasgow area is clearly demonstrated by reference to the four basic indicators of deprivation shown in Table 5.2. Employment

Table 5.2: Percentage of the Worst 5 per cent of Scottish Enumeration Districts Located in Strathclyde

Indicator	% in Strathclyde
Households without exclusive use of hot water	74
% of male workers who are unskilled	57
% of males who are unemployed	69
% of households living in overcrowded conditions	87

Source: 1971 Census.

opportunities for both adults and school-leavers are bleak with 87 per cent of all jobs lost in Scotland over the period 1964-73 disappearing from Strathclyde. Throughout this period regional unemployment ran at twice the United Kingdom average and was well above the average for the rest of Scotland. Between 1961 and 1971 the number of jobs in the city of Glasgow fell by 78,000 in sharp contrast to an overall UK increase; and the continuing erosion of the employment base is reflected in the high levels of out-migration. Between 1966 and 1976 for example the city of Glasgow lost 205,000 people (21 per cent) (Department of the Environment 1977), and the latest projection for 1981 is for an·urban population of not more than 750,000.

Further evidence of the scale of the problem facing Glasgow is provided in Table 5.3 which reveals the differing levels of deprivation in urban Scotland by examining the coincidence of the three major problems of overcrowding, lack of basic amenities and male unemployment. Just as the Clydeside conurbation topped the national deprivation league, so its major urban agglomeration, Glasgow, emerged head and shoulders above the other Scottish towns, with almost one person in five being affected by some aspect of deprivation. In a national context the next most afflicted urban area was the inner London borough of Islington, with 11.3 per cent of its population living in severely deprived conditions, but one would have to aggregate the entire deprived populations of Birmingham, Manchester, Liverpool and Bradford in order to surpass the absolute level of the problem in Glasgow.

Table 5.3: Local Authorities with Ten or More Enumeration Districts in the Overlap of Worst 15 per cent on Overcrowding, Lacking Exclusive Use of all Basic Amenities, and Male Unemployment

Local Authority	No. of qualifying EDs	Population in qualifying EDs	Pop. in qualifying EDs as % of total LA population
Dundee	70	12,904	7.3
Edinburgh	101	24,810	5.8
Glasgow	578	165,422	18.9
Clydebank	10	2,467	6.2
Rutherglen	10	2,493	10.1
Paisley	35	9,319	10.0

Source: Holtermann (1975).

Figures which have become available since the 1971 Census do little to alter this position. In May 1973 Glasgow's Chief Sanitary Inspector estimated that of the 292,500 houses in the city, 69,500 were below the tolerable standard as defined in the Housing (Scotland) Act 1969. As a result of a redefinition of tolerable standards in the Housing (Scotland) Act 1974, this total was increased by the addition of 5,000 houses which lacked an inside toilet. In 1976, despite strenuous government efforts since the war, Glasgow still contained 77 per cent of the region's sub-tolerable housing. The poor quality of living conditions in the worst parts of the city identified by the census indicators is confirmed by high rates of truancy, vandalism, crime and alcoholism. Locally unsatisfactory standards of education provision and shortages of social workers serve to compound the problems. As Holtermann (1975) concluded, when viewed from the perspective of conditions in small areas the problems of the Scottish cities, especially Glasgow, stand out most starkly.

Housing and Employment in the Pre-war Era

The economic fortunes of Glasgow have been closely linked with heavy engineering, and much of the engineering industry is dependent directly or indirectly on shipbuilding. Between 1870 and 1913 the annual tonnage of Clydebuilt shipping rose from 200,000 to 757,000 and in the first decade of the present century some forty firms employing 60,000 men produced one-third of British shipping. The prosperity of these years stands out in marked contrast to the prolonged depression that overtook the industry between the two world wars. A short-lived boom period after World War I extended the illusion of a soundly based economy. But the naval work that had occupied many of the Clyde yards soon disappeared, and mercantile construction never regained its pre-war proportions as foreign owners increasingly turned to their domestic shipyards. The great slump after 1929 brought one yard after another to a standstill and by 1933 output had fallen to only 60,000 tons. Two-thirds of the men normally engaged in shipbuilding lost their jobs and unemployment in the engineering industries was often over 30 per cent and rarely below 20 per cent for much of the inter-war period. The amount of new industrial development in the area was negligible. The decline in the traditional economic base of the city was at the root of the city's social problems. The situation could only be improved by a large scale programme of restructuring sponsored and largely financed by central government. Such a step was inconceivable in practice, both to the independently-minded businessmen who had created the industrial basis of the city, and to a government lacking any experience of such a major intervention in the economy. Even when an active policy of attracting new industry to depressed areas by the provision of industrial estates was commenced in the late 1930s Glasgow did not benefit directly as the city was at that time excluded from the designated Special Area. Glasgow also failed to benefit from the expansion of lighter industrial activities in this period, not least because of the shortage of suitable skills and the city's reputation for labour unrest. Combined with the fact that the nucleus of many of the new electronics industries already existed in the Midlands and South of England, close to the important domestic market, a depressed area with heavy unemployment offered little attraction for a 'foot-loose' industrialist.

The advent of World War II solved the unemployment problem in Glasgow and regenerated the heavy industrial base of the city, but did little to promote the much needed diversification and rationalisation. In economic terms Glasgow had been in a state of inertia since the turn of the century. The two world wars simply compounded the situation by artificially prolonging the life of the city's heavy industry base. The collapse of the economy was thus more real than apparent (Johnston 1976).

The other half of Glasgow's dual problem lay with its most important physical component—housing. The rapid growth of the city in the nineteenth century was marked by a shortage of suitable building land, partly due to the surrounding collar of hills and moorland. This led to the creation of much of the bad housing and slums. Glasgow became a working city with little or no working class suburbia (Checkland 1964). By 1914 there were no less than 700,000 people resident within 3 square miles of Glasgow Cross, creating the most densely populated central area in Europe. Within this intense form of urbanism there operated a particular family budgetary pattern in which a proportion of income, lower than in any other major British city, was spent on housing (Checkland 1976). In the years before 1914 Glasgow had empty houses that were better than some occupied ones. Incomes of workers in Glasgow were not conspicuously inferior to those of other cities, yet there was only a slight move to better accommodation at higher cost. In part this budgetary pattern was due to the fact that in many trades wage levels were highly unstable so that 'canny' Scots workers tended to rent houses that were affordable in the bad times, to treat the surplus of good times as a windfall and seldom to aspire to home ownership. The Scottish tradition of building the four- or five-storey terraced tenement was ideally suited to a pattern of minimal spending on rents, for the very high densities (450-700 people per acre) provided little in the way of extra amenities. In the early period of city development (1841-61) these high densities, together with considerable overcrowding, created appalling living conditions. Until the inter-war period the provision of houses was almost entirely a matter of private investment and rents were the outcome of the interplay of market forces. As a consequence the housing supply for persons of low or unstable incomes was minimal. By the end of the nineteenth century some official action to halt the deterioration in the standards of tenements was urgently required. In 1891 more than two-thirds of Glasgow's population lived in overcrowded conditions of two or more persons per room, with the problem particularly acute in parts of the Gorbals and the inner city areas of Townhead, Bridgeton, Tradeston and Anderston (Figure 5.1). Legislation such as the Police (Amendment) Act 1890 and the Consolidating (Housing of the Working Classes) Act of the same year defined more stringent minimum standards for many aspects of tenement living. Still in 1917 the Royal Commission on Housing in Scotland reported conditions in which there were more than four persons per room in 10.9 per cent of Glasgow houses, more than three persons in 27.9 per cent, and more than two in 55.7 per cent; percentages for corresponding English cities were 0.8, 1.5 and 9.4.

The city corporation turned to a programme of subsidised housing, with financial aid from the central government. The Housing Acts of 1919, 1923 and 1924 initiated housing estates on the periphery of the city (the largest being Mosspark and Knightswood), as well as building on several sites within the built-up area. These housing estates, however, were not created for the most needy households. The theoretical basis of the policy formulated by a Conservative administration was the filtering process; houses vacated by people moving to the new estates then became available to those who could not afford the higher rents. These inter-war estates uncharacteristically consisted of cottages and flats provided with garden space. Knightswood (1923-9), the largest, with its libraries, social centre and shopping parades, was intended to be a model of its kind. The area still retains its respectability. In other parts of the city, however, the policy followed was quite different. Blackhill, where 980 new houses were built in the 1930s, exemplifies the problem. The site was close to the city centre and adjacent to gas works, industry and railway lines. The development was planned at minimum cost in order to have low rents, but serious deterioration soon occurred. With a population of low-income tenants and a disproportionate element of anti-social families, the character of the area became self-confirming as persons seeking betterment moved out to be replaced, over time, by problem families. Blackhill has been a social problem area almost since its construction. Part of the blame lies with the city corporation's failure to provide a range of community facilities, an omission which the present district authority is attempting to remedy at a cost of £12 million.

The major policy innovation until World War II was the growing

Figure 5.1: Glasgow: Residential Areas

GLASGOW : RESIDENTIAL LAND USE

0   1
miles

Corporation
Post-war
Private
Post-war
Corporation
Pre-war
Private
Pre-war
Comprehensive
Development Area

① Easterhouse
② Drumchapel
③ Pollok
④ Castlemilk
⑤ Mosspark
⑥ Knightswood
⑦ Blackhill
⑧ Gorbals
⑨ Townhead
⑩ Bridgeton
⑪ Anderston
⑫ Tradeston

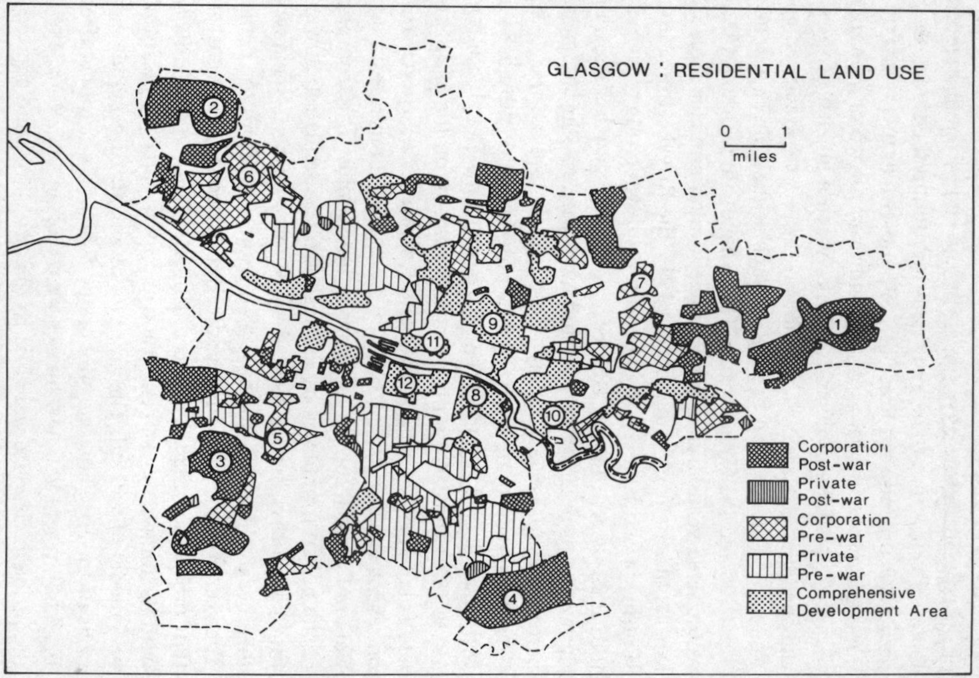

public intervention in the provision of housing and employment in the city. Of the 73,630 houses authorised to be built in Glasgow between 1919 and 1939 only 9,106 were for the private market, and by the end of this period the balance of Glasgow housing had swung violently in the direction of public ownership. Housing had become a subsidised social service by 1945 and the corporation had acquired the power through the house letting system to determine the social composition of large areas. Progress towards a more balanced and modern economic base for the city was less apparent, but the public commitment to both objectives was now irreversible.

The Post-war Period

Housing in Glasgow continued down to the 1960s to reflect the legacy of the past. Eighty-five per cent of dwellings were soot-stained tenements. These classic nineteenth century four-storey structures, with a doorless entry from the street and common stone staircase, dominated the housing stock. The tenure pattern had changed since 1914; in 1965 private landlords owned 38 per cent of houses, owner occupiers 19 per cent, and the corporation 43 per cent (Cullingworth 1968). The amount of private house building since 1945 has been negligible; Miller (1970) estimated that only 75 houses per year have been built for sale, and anyone who wants to own a house must, in effect, move from Glasgow. Until recently the corporation's insistence that it retains building sites for subsidised housing had driven private contractors outside the city boundaries. Since 1977 vacant inner city sites and land within the peripheral council estates has been offered to private builders but the scale of development remains low.

Policy disputes in the post-war period began over the recommendations in the Clyde Valley Plan of 1946 (Abercrombie and Matthew 1949). Its essence was that in the interests of the city and the region as a whole there should be a planned decentralisation of both population and industry from Glasgow. The report also expressed concern about the tendency towards urban sprawl and recommended that a green belt policy should be adopted to limit urban growth and to preserve agricultural land and recreational space. The Scottish Office accepted the report's recommendation that a substantial proportion of Glasgow's population should be transferred to new towns and that overspill agreements should be concluded with existing towns. The corporation of Glasgow disagreed strongly, and argued against any loss of land within the city's boundaries for the proposed green belt. In 1947 the Secretary of State designated East Kilbride a new town site, and prevented the corporation from building on a large section of land at Castlemilk, less than five miles from the new town. East Kilbride was in easy commuting distance of Glasgow and clearly represented a new and rival source of jobs and houses.

Faced with a desperate post-war need for housing, estimated in the early 1950s between 80,000 and 90,000 families, the corporation responded by planning and by building large housing estates on green field sites around the perimeter of the city with higher densities than previously considered acceptable for such projects. Some of the schemes still contained a significant proportion of cottages, as in the inter-war estates, but the trend was to rows of three- and four-storey walk-up flats. Peripheral largely working class dormitory suburbs such as Drumchapel (8,660 houses), Easterhouse (8,720), Castlemilk (8,902), Pollok and Priesthill (8,600) were founded and absorbed approximately 10 per cent of Glasgow's population (Figure 5.1). In spite of the experience in Blackhill, there was minimal provision of amenities and community facilities. Preoccupied with the construction of houses, the corporation was ill organised to provide shops and entertainment; private enterprise was generally dubious about participating in the schemes on economic grounds; and there was a long standing corporation resolution dating from 1890 that public houses (bars) should not be provided on Corporation property. Not until 1971 with the development of Easterhouse Township Centre were these difficulties overcome. Today in many post-war estates, distant from the traditional centre of Glasgow life, the resurgence of social problems and the demand for housing transfers (Table 5.4) are strong reminders that the provision of houses is not sufficient to create a humane environment.

In the 1950s the dispute between the Scottish Office and Glasgow Corporation ameliorated, and the concept of an overspill policy was accepted by the city. The corporation agreed to operate a voluntary scheme that would allow people and firms to leave Glasgow. The out-movement of industry was not positively advocated by the corporation, the decision to relocate being based on individual firms' judgement of their needs. The corporation did undertake to buy the land and buildings of firms that wanted to relocate under the scheme. The corporation estimated in 1960 that approximately 200,000 people would move from Glasgow by 1980 with the probability of more later. The figure was challenged with the argument that between 400,000 and 500,000 people would have to be rehoused outside Glasgow in new or expanded

Table 5.4: Requests for Transfers out of Council Housing Areas, 1977

Area	Total no. of houses	No. of transfer requests to other areas	Transfer requests as % of total households
Anniesland	16,171	784	4.84
Bardowie Street	15,093	2,245	14.87
Castlemilk	9,735	2,754	28.28
City centre	11,804	1,241	10.51
Drumchapel	10,339	3,361	32.50
Easterhouse	15,040	4,731	31.45
Gallowgate	12,700	1,602	12.61
Mid-east	11,075	1,421	12.83
North-east	16,685	3,183	19.07
Pollok	11,595	3,542	30.54
South	12,633	877	6.94
South-west	14,279	662	4.63

Source: Glasgow District Council (1978).

towns (Forbes and MacBain 1967).

The Overspill Policy

The redistribution of economic activity within metropolitan areas and in particular the increase in manufacturing activity on the periphery at the expense of the inner city has been noted in several cities, especially ones that grew rapidly in the nineteenth century and early twentieth century. This tendency for firms to move out from the inner city areas has frequently been used as an argument for planning objectives to decrease urban congestion. In Glasgow, with its surfeit of old dilapidated industrial and commercial properties, industrial overspill has been considered an essential policy because it is not enough to provide houses in the reception areas. Jobs must be made available for the people who move to them (Farmer and Smith 1975). In 1959 the corporation considered that many of these jobs could be provided by Glasgow firms, either by complete relocation or by the establishment of offices and factory extensions in the reception area. A basic assumption behind the overspill policy was that there would be a sufficient volume of industry both able and willing to move out of Glasgow to the designated reception areas, although neither the Clyde Valley Regional Plan (1946) nor Glasgow Corporation (1959) had actual figures. Henderson (1974), based on a study of manufacturing establishments which moved from Glasgow over the period 1958-68, found that at the time of moving the firms employed a total of 5,486 people (3,744 males). Subsequent closures and rationalisation reduced the employment loss to the city to 4,978 jobs (3,142 males). It is doubtful whether the relocation of 107 manufacturing plants in eleven years reflects the anticipated scale of movement. Furthermore the majority of establishments deciding to relocate preferred to remain in Glasgow. Between 1958 and 1968, 79.5 per cent of all transfers that originated in the city remained within the urban area, defined to include places adjacent to the city that are an integral part of its labour market. Even if places such as Barrhead, Johnston and Linwood are excluded, only 12.8 per cent of all transfers originating in the city actually moved away from the city's travel to work area. Over the period, closures accounted for almost four times (79.6 per cent) as many firms lost to the city as did outmigration (20.4 per cent). The volume of industry that would be prepared to leave the city seems, in retrospect, to have been overestimated. A second assumption also proved by subsequent events to have been overstated was that redevelopment would act as a major stimulus to outmigration. Although redevelopment caused 27.8 per cent of the moves it was not the principal push factor, being overshadowed by the firms' need to expand. In addition only 18.1 per cent (27 firms) of all moves originating in the city as a direct result of redevelopment had destinations outside Glasgow, which suggests that the greatest demand was for alternative premises within the city. Furthermore, although the comprehensive development areas were expected to be major contributors to overspill, establishments located in these areas showed no greater desire to move out of the city than firms from other parts of Glasgow. Finally there was no evidence to support assertions that redevelopment, by forcing some firms to move, disrupted them so severely that they were subsequently forced to close. None of the 26 concerns which moved from the eight comprehensive development areas had closed by the end of 1968, whereas 12.1 per cent of all transfers from the city had closed by this date. A third assumption was that Glasgow would benefit from the industrial overspill policy because the creation of employment opportunities in the reception areas would entice Glaswegians from the city and thereby would increase the rate of urban renewal. In practice firms seem to have transferred their skilled rather than semi-skilled or unskilled workers, and the skilled:

unskilled ratios of 2.9:1 in Glasgow and 14.6:1 in East Kilbride indicate
a gross imbalance in favour of the new town. The overspill policy
contributed to the depletion of Glasgow's skilled labour force, and as
Cameron and Johnson (1969) have stated 'the objective of any policy
which causes the dilution of the skilled content of the Glasgow labour
force without compensatory programmes of skill creation must be
seriously questioned'. The empirical evidence suggests that many of
the assumptions underlying the industrial overspill policy are open to
question, because despite a number of theoretical attractions the policy
has not worked effectively in practice. The policy incorporated a
potential conflict between the physical and economic planning needs
of the city. As Henderson (1974) observed a policy of encouraging
industrial overspill to pursue physical planning objectives may conflict
with the need to create new employment opportunities in order to
reduce the continually high levels of unemployment in the city itself.
It was assumed that population overspill would decrease the supply of
labour in the city and enable Glasgow to export industry, but despite
the loss of 160,000 people between 1961 and 1971, unemployment
rates have remained above the Scottish average (Table 5.5). As Table
5.6 shows the greatest decline in employment opportunities has
occurred in manufacturing where every SIC order suffered a reduction.
Approximately 65 per cent of the decline in this sector was concentrated
in only four orders, namely metal manufacture, engineering and electrical
goods, shipbuilding and marine engineering, and vehicles. Table 5.7
which compares Glasgow's main industries with their Scottish counterparts highlights the fact that the rate of industrial decline in Glasgow
over the period 1966-71 was twice the Scottish rate. Glasgow needs
to generate employment opportunities, not to export its established
industries and skilled workers.

Table 5.5: Comparative Rates of Unemployment

	Unemployment rates (Jan. 1973)		
	Male	Female	Total
Glasgow	11.4	3.0	8.0
Scotland	7.8	3.4	6.1
GB	4.6	1.6	3.5

The population encouraged to leave Glasgow was directed to new
towns developed on the few remaining buildable sites in the area, and

Table 5.6: Total Employment in Glasgow, 1961-71, by Standard Industrial Classification (SIC) Order

SIC Order (1958)	1961	%	1971	%	Change
Agric., forestry & fishing	846	0.16	381	0.09	-465
Mining & quarrying	1,279	0.27	1,811	0.41	+532
Primary	2,125	0.43	2,192	0.5	+67
Food, drink & tobacco	31,648	6.1	28,476	6.5	-3,172
Chemicals & allied industries	6,629	1.3	3,684	0.8	-2,945
Metal manufacturing	13,152	2.5	6,994	1.6	-6,158
Engineering & electrical goods	46,955	9.1	32,788	7.4	-14,167
Shipbuilding & marine engineering	26,013	5.0	14,261	3.2	-11,752
Vehicles	19,326	3.7	11,814	2.7	-7,512
Metal goods—not elsewhere specified	7,274	1.4	5,870	1.3	-1,404
Textiles	10,496	2.0	6,112	1.4	-4,384
Leather, leather goods & fur	2,017	0.4	961	0.2	-1,056
Clothing & footwear	17,532	3.4	14,531	3.3	-3,001
Bricks, pottery, glass, cement, etc.	4,463	0.9	3,272	0.7	-1,191
Timber, furniture, etc.	7,739	1.5	6,729	1.5	-1,010
Paper, printing & publishing	18,566	3.6	16,561	3.8	-1,705
Other manufacturing industries	3,846	0.7	2,425	0.6	-1,421
Manufacturing	215,656	41.6	154,778	35.0	-60,878
Construction	40,201	7.8	38,503	8.7	-1,698
Gas, electricity & water	6,435	1.2	6,310	1.4	-125
Transport & communication	42,737	8.2	29,932	6.8	-12,805
Distributive trades	85,128	16.4	67,952	15.4	-17,176
Insurance, banking & finance	13,529	2.6	19,165	4.3	+5,636
Professional & scientific services	60,406	11.6	68,571	15.6	+8,165
Miscellaneous services	39,854	7.7	36,142	8.2	-3,712
Public administration & defence	12,542	2.4	17,171	3.8	+4,629
Construction & services	300,832	57.9	283,746	64.2	-17,086
Total	518,613		440,716		-77,897

Note: The above figures refer to those firms employing five or more persons only.

to existing towns with which agreements had been concluded under the Town Development Act 1952. The authors of the Clyde Valley Plan thought that the new towns should be near Glasgow if decentralisation of population and industry was to be popular. In this they were probably affected by the criticism levelled at the first garden city,

Table 5.7: Comparative Performance of Selected Industries in Glasgow and Scotland, 1966-71

Industry SIC 1968	Glasgow % decline/increase of employment 1966-71	Scotland % decline/increase of employment 1966-71
Mechanical engineering	-22.7%	-16.7%
Food, drink and tobacco	-10.3%	+0.6%
Shipbuilding	-11.9%	-9.2%
Paper, printing	-9.3%	-9.0%
Clothing	-13.4%	+0.3%
Textiles	-34.6%	-21.7%
Timber, furniture	-27.0%	-9.8%
Vehicles	-7.7%	-10.2%
Total manufacturing industry	-16.7%	-8.0%

Letchworth, which at 35 miles from London was said to be too distant to attract industry from the capital. In the event, the planners could find only three sites that were large enough to accommodate a self-contained town of 50,000, and where physical separation from the existing conurbation could be maintained. These were at East Kilbride, Cumbernauld and Bishopton. Only the first two were selected, and East Kilbride was designated to serve as an outlet for the surplus population of the Clyde Valley. In one sense this objective has been fulfilled. In March 1963, 57 per cent of all tenants had been drawn from the city of Glasgow and 34 per cent from other centres in the county of Lanark. The estimated population was then 36,500 or 73 per cent of the original projection of 50,000. In another sense, however, East Kilbride has not fulfilled its intended function. Its construction has had little effect on the population pressures of Greater Glasgow, and the new town has not provided an escape for the families most urgently in need of new housing. At first the housing allocation policy in East Kilbride gave preference to the employees of its industries, but they were not necessarily the Glaswegians who were homeless or living in overcrowded or sub-standard dwellings. This policy was relaxed in 1959. In order to speed the movement of population from the redevelopment areas in the city, the East Kilbride Development Corporation agreed to allocate houses to people from Glasgow irrespective of employment in the new town. The proximity of Glasgow makes commuting to work in the new town easy

and as early as 1959 it was estimated that 50 per cent of the labour
force lived outside East Kilbride. The comparatively high rents and
rates meant that some people found it cheaper to travel to work from
south and east Glasgow rather than move to East Kilbride. There has
also been very little relocation of industry from Glasgow to East
Kilbride. The major industries have been drawn from further afield,
a major attraction being the town's location in a development
area. East Kilbride has become more of an industrial growth point in
an economically depressed area than an instrument for the redevelopment of Glasgow (Smith 1967).

A second new town, Cumbernauld, was designated in 1956 as a
result of the continuing urgency of Glasgow's housing problems. The
city's needs in 1955 were no less than they were ten years earlier despite
the construction of 40,000 new dwellings. The immediate need for
houses for homeless families, for new families and for occupants of
condemned properties was estimated at 100,000 units. That figure
included no allowance for the population that would be displaced by
the plans to redevelop the congested inner quarters of the city. In an
attempt to avoid repetition of the indecisive outcome of East Kilbride's
housing allocation mechanism it was decided from the outset that at
least 80 per cent of Cumbernauld's houses would go to Glasgow residents
approved by the city corporation as persons in need of accommodation.
In most other respects, however, the progress of Cumbernauld has
been similar to its predecessor; the initial target population of 50,000
was later raised to 70,000. Commuting meant that the ideal of a self-
contained town physically and economically distinct from the
conurbation has only partly been realised and there has been almost
no industrial relocation from Glasgow. Another new town not formally
envisaged as part of the overspill policy became linked with Glasgow's
housing problem. Under the terms of the Housing and Town Development (Scotland) Act 1957 new financial incentives were offered to
towns willing to accept migrants from Glasgow. The Glenrothes
Development Corporation, stimulated by the slow growth rate of the
town, entered into an overspill agreement with the city of Glasgow, and
by 1960 Glenrothes had virtually become a third new town for Glasgow.
The need for a fourth new town was created by the final acceptance of
plans to redevelop Glasgow's worst housing areas. The reasoning behind
this was contained in the draft designation order for Livingston new
town.

Over the next twenty years a massive redevelopment programme will be undertaken by Glasgow Corporation in twenty-nine separate areas. Some 100,000 families at present living in bad housing conditions will be displaced by the entire operation, and although the redeveloped sites will include residential accommodation to the greatest densities acceptable by modern standards, it will not be possible to rehouse more than about 40,000 of the original 100,000 families. (Department of Health for Scotland 1962)

Further overspill pressure from Greater Glasgow led to the designation of Irvine in 1967 and of Stonehouse in 1972 as new towns, although the latter was abandoned in 1976 due to a government decision to devote more direct attention to the problem of multiple deprivation in the east end of Glasgow.

Comprehensive Redevelopment

When the large housing schemes began to exhaust the available open sites near the periphery of the city, the corporation, faced with a housing shortage, a waiting list which stood at 100,000 by the mid-1950s and a lack of developable land, turned its attention to the redevelopment of decayed areas nearer the centre. Not only was most of the housing there intolerable but the industrial premises, built mostly for heavy industry, were unsuitable for modern industries and, being in a poor state of repair, were unattractive to new ventures. A report to the Housing and Planning Committees of the corporation proposed the comprehensive redevelopment of three inner-city areas as early as 1953. By 1957 the magnitude of the redevelopment problem was apparent and the City Architect and Planning Officer submitted a report suggesting that 29 comprehensive development areas (CDAs) should be established in order to achieve a realistic clearance and redevelopment programme. These covered a total area of 5 square miles (8 per cent of the city). The sizes varied from 25 acres to 270 acres, and populations ranged from 4,000 to 40,000. Approximately 2,500 industrial concerns were within the CDA limits. The comprehensive redevelopment programme set out in the report depended on the city pursuing an overspill policy:

it cannot be too strongly emphasised that the provision outwith the city of accommodation for the reception of Glasgow's overspill is the governing factor in all proposals made in this report. Without this provision little or no redevelopment can be undertaken.

From its inception the comprehensive development area programme had far reaching implications for city planning beyond the clearance of slum housing and the creation of modern residential areas (Hart 1967). Each CDA was planned to be reasonably self sufficient in terms of support facilities for the new population. Areas were thus zoned for commercial development, education, open space and industry. The planners hoped that these new developments would assist in city-wide rationalisation and modernisation of commercial activities, especially shopping, in the release of land for new industrial development and in the development of an improved highway network. Although 29 CDAs were identified in the 1957 report, initiation has not been uniform. The time scale for the physical redevelopment can be spread in phases over a period of up to 20 years, but plan preparation and implementation for a single CDA, together with the legal difficulties associated with compulsory purchase and compensation, stretched to the limits the resources of the corporation. Thus there have been long intervals between the approval of one CDA and of another. Of the nine CDAs that have been approved, the first was accepted in 1957 and the most recent in 1973. The original goal to complete a considerable portion of the redevelopment programme by 1980 could not be realised. There is no doubt, however, that the comprehensive redevelopment programme has brought about massive changes in the physical and social environment in the city. It is instructive to consider the example of the Gorbals CDA.

The Gorbals: Historical Background

The area known today as the Gorbals is situated on the south bank of the river Clyde less than a quarter of a mile from Glasgow Cross, the traditional centre of the city. Until the end of the eighteenth century the area consisted of approximately 47 acres of open fields, together with the two small villages of Bridgend (or Gorbals) and Little Govan. Towards the end of the eighteenth century there was a major westwards expansion of the city centre on the north bank of the Clyde as the rising merchant classes strove to avoid the mass of working class housing and industry which had grown up in the east-end areas of Bridgeton and Calton. The first major development south of the river took place in the Gorbals area. Undertaken by James and David Laurie, it was conceived as a high quality residential quarter to rival Craig's new town in Edinburgh. The advantage of the site was that it was to the windward

of the old city centre and was separated from it by the river. Unfortunately
for the Lauries the scheme, begun in 1804, proved a disaster. The main
reason was that they did not own all the land south of the river, and
the south bank did not come within the jurisdiction of the corporation
until 1846. As a result their residential development was surrounded
by industries, brickworks and mine workings. Further deterioration of
the residential environment followed. In 1834 William Dixon, an iron
master with a works in the south-east of the area, drove a service rail
line across the Gorbals streets to a quay on the river Clyde. The further
intrusion of railway tracks in the early 1840s hastened the decline of
the area and the middle class moved out to the pleasanter suburbs in the
west-end of the city. Large houses left by the wealthy were divided
internally to form single rooms that were often let to entire families.
The decaying residential area attracted backyard industries and service
trades searching for cheap accommodation near the city centre. The
period 1850-70 saw the growth of densely-packed tenement buildings
and behind rather impressive sandstone facades lay appalling housing
conditions. Nearly 90 per cent of the tenements built in the Gorbals had
either one room (the single end) or two rooms (room and kitchen), and
toilet accommodation was generally restricted to a shared WC on a
common stair landing. It was not uncommon to find families of eight
or nine sharing a single end with a floorspace of about 100 sq. feet, i.e.
approximately the size of a modern double bedroom. In the Gorbals
almost one-third of the houses were built back-to-back with no through
ventilation. These overcrowded and insanitary conditions were made
worse with the development of backland tenements. When the shortage
of building land became acute the back courts of some tenement blocks
were used by developers to erect a single line of tenements that were
permanently cut off from sunlight and fresh air. In these tenements
conditions were wretched.

   The physical decay of the area did not come about because the
tenements were badly built. Part of the reason lay in the intensive use
of the buildings, but the main reason was a lack of maintenance by the
building owners, particularly in the war years and in the depression of
the 1930s. A radical improvement of these conditions did not occur
until the 1950s when the redevelopment programme began. One of the
first areas to be tackled was the Hutchesontown-Gorbals Comprehensive
Development Area (Figure 5.2). A corporation report of 1953 defined
the area for action. The 342 acre site, comprising most of the Gorbals
district, contained 16,271 dwellings and had a total population of
55,284, which was slightly more than the population of a large Scottish

Figure 5.2: The Gorbals Comprehensive Development Area

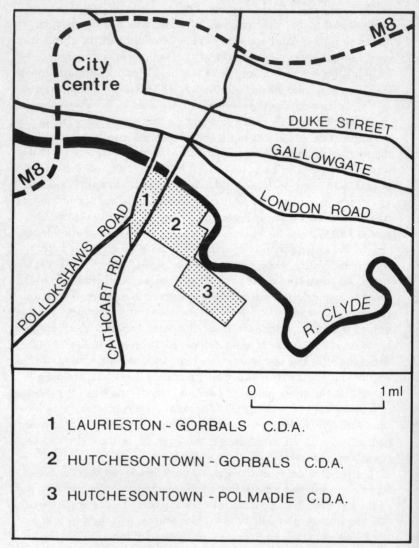

1 LAURIESTON - GORBALS C.D.A.

2 HUTCHESONTOWN - GORBALS C.D.A.

3 HUTCHESONTOWN - POLMADIE C.D.A.

town such as Kilmarnock or Kirkcaldy. One of the main considerations was the question of housing density and overspill. If modern standards of development were to be adopted and the overspill of population kept to a minimum, the population density in the new housing was crucial. The existing net residential density was around 450 ppa and the gross density around 162 ppa. The report calculated that if multi-storey development was undertaken the gross density would be 78 ppa. If development up to five storeys only was considered then the gross density would be around 44 ppa. This would mean a difference in over-spill of 11,000 people. If the corporation's policy of reducing overspill was to be maintained, a considerable amount of multi-storey development would have to be undertaken.

The size of the area was an obstacle to developing the district as a single integrated unit. Consequently it was divided into three more manageable units within the overall planning framework. These neighbourhood units, east, central and west, were designated the Hutchesontown-Polmadie CDA; the Hutchesontown-Gorbals CDA; and the Laurieston-Gorbals CDA (Figure 5.2). The central unit was to be developed first and this area would contain the principal shopping and service facilities for the district as a whole. The redevelopment process also benefited areas beyond the Gorbals by improving traffic access to and from the city centre, and by reducing atmospheric pollution by introducing a smokeless zone policy which eliminated 20,000 domestic flues from the Gorbals.

The Hutchesontown-Gorbals CDA

The planning process for this central neighbourhood unit began in the summer of 1954. In September 1955 the formal plan documents were approved by the corporation who submitted them to the Secretary of State in April 1956. The public inquiry took place in September/October, and final approval was given by the government in February 1957. The total cost of development was estimated at that time to be approximately £13 million. The CDA boundary enclosed 111 acres. The population was 26,860 and the total number of families was 7,790. With a net residential area of 58.6 acres the average net residential density was 459 ppa. This high density was reflected in the average number of persons per room (Table 5.8). The high level of overcrowding was matched by the condition of the houses (Table 5.9), most of which were between 60 and 100 years old.

The area was not important industrially, with only 12 firms out of a total of 105 having floor areas greater than 10,000 sq. ft. The majority

of businesses were either service trades or performed functions ancillary to the retail trade, such as hosiery manufacture, and food and
drink processing. Commercial activity included 444 shops and 48
public houses. The high number of buildings set aside for community
use (6 church halls and 15 other meeting rooms) was striking, particularly in light of the criticisms directed at more modern local
authority schemes.

Table 5.8: Average Number of Persons per Room in Major British
Cities, 1954

City	Occupancy rate	City	Occupancy rate
Glasgow	1.27	Birmingham	0.77
Edinburgh	0.93	Manchester	0.74
Newcastle	0.88	Bristol	0.72
Liverpool	0.83	Hutchesontown-Gorbals	1.89
Greater London	0.77		

Source: Johnston (1976).

Table 5.9: Condition of the Housing Stock in the Hutchesontown-
Gorbals Comprehensive Development Area (CDA)

Total no. of dwellings	7605
One/two apartment houses	87%
Back-to-back houses	33%
Houses with baths	3%
Houses with shared WC	78% (average: 4 families per WC)
Houses unacceptable sanitarily	91%
Houses unacceptable structurally	95%

Source: Johnston (1976).

The redevelopment plan revealed a residential area of 62 acres to
accommodate 3,502 dwellings housing a population of 10,179, at a net
residential density of 164 ppa. It was proposed that low rise (up to four-
storey) development would constitute 48.7 per cent and multi-storey
housing 51.3 per cent. This meant that 16,681 people had to be rehoused
outside the CDA. During the initial stages of development, in order to
demolish and rebuild, it was necessary to decant 500 families per year.

Of these, 40 per cent could be relocated within the CDA. Apart from a small industrial zone in the north-east of the area almost all other industry (whether by virtue of size, function or the type of process) was considered to be incompatible with a residential area. It was proposed that 72 firms be relocated in various sites on the periphery of the city on land already owned by the corporation and zoned for industrial use. The 444 shops dispersed throughout the area were to be replaced by 57 units located in one main and three subsidiary shopping centres. The 48 pubs were reduced to a maximum of 9 to be located in the shopping areas, while support services such as banks, post offices and surgeries would be provided as required. Sites for a cinema and community centre were provided and it was proposed that the existing library, police station and 9 churches would be retained.

The programming of the redevelopment was based on four 5-year stages. In addition to the residential component, the first phase included the main shopping centre. The second and third stages would incorporate the community centre and the completion of local shopping centres. The bulk of the housing in the second and third phases of development was carried out by the Scottish Special Housing Association (SSHA), a government agency set up to supplement the programme of local authorities with severe housing shortages.

The rebuilding of the Gorbals has taken place according to the programme, although plans have been amended during the 20 year period. For example, because of changing entertainment habits the site for a new cinema has not been developed, and a district health centre has removed the need for doctors' surgeries. Alterations to the road pattern have followed changes in the city-wide highway planning policy. The final sector of the Hutchesontown-Gorbals CDA to be developed is currently under construction in the east of the area, although indecision on the line of the southern section of the city's inner ring road has caused delay.

It is difficult to evaluate the success of a programme of environmental rehabilitation such as the redevelopment of the Gorbals. The master plan drawn up 20 years ago is almost complete, and 27,000 people living in slum conditions have been rehoused in new dwellings. An attempt has been made to create a new community by providing a wide range of facilities not found in many large housing schemes, and by developing a physical environment of a high design standard and layout. Yet the Gorbals in parts still resembles a vast building site. Teenagers have spent their whole lives surrounded by 'temporary' arrangements for community facilities, pedestrian access and transport. Despite this, or perhaps because of it, local community groups, particularly the tenants' associations, are strong and in 1967 the area produced the first community newspaper in Britain. Because of such feelings Hutchesontown-Gorbals was a 'natural area' for one of the new urban community councils established under the terms of the Local Government (Scotland) Act 1973.

Of the remaining comprehensive development areas on which work is proceeding the majority are located within the inner city (Townhead, Cowcaddens, Woodside and Anderston) and work in these areas will continue well into the 1980s.

The High-rise Solution

In spite of the comprehensive development areas and the overspill policy, Glasgow's housing problem in the mid-1960s was still severe. Earlier housing construction was hopelessly inadequate to keep ahead of the rate of decay in the old tenements. The problem was exacerbated by the scarcity of building land in the city. With increasing scarcity of sites, and possibly because of contemporary architectural fashions, Glasgow Corporation began to erect multi-storey housing. This move was a revolutionary step for the city since it meant altering the whole meaning of urban living for many people. Although some planners expressed misgivings the policy was implemented on the argument that high-rise buildings would increase the number of housing units more rapidly than other programmes. From the late 1950s the corporation was committed to the new high-rise formula. A major change in the city's skyline occurred during the 1960s. By 1968 there were six multi-storey housing units being built to every low-rise, and by the following year 163 tower blocks were occupied. By 1969 the Housing Management Department had 15,000 high-rise units and 121,500 low-rise homes on its books. The new form of building reached its extreme at Red Road, a 22-acre complex of 31-storey blocks designed to house 4,000 people at a density of 180 ppa. Many tenants appreciated the modern facilities that were so different from their previous living conditions but with use several major disadvantages soon appeared in the form of lift breakdowns; maintenance of stairs, communal areas and landscaped surrounding; isolation of the elderly; and lack of space for families with young children. Although high-rise buildings put a large population in a small area in a short period of time, the land economies have been less than anticipated. Moreover, the cost of constructing high-rise flats has

often proved expensive, sometimes as much as £7,000 per dwelling
(Miller 1970). The high-rise of today may be the slums of tomorrow.
Partly in response to the doubts about the programme, Glasgow has
retreated from its policy of multi-storey building and has returned to
the familiar four-storey and five-storey structures (Pacione 1979).

A Change of Philosophy

The beginning of the 1970s was an opportune time to assess the city's
progress. There had been a major improvement in the quality of Glasgow
life in the 30 years since the war. The high residential densities had all
but disappeared and the crowded core of the city, inherited from the
nineteenth century, had been remade. More than 100,000 municipal
houses had been built since 1945 and during the same period 200,000
of the city's population dispersed. The percentage of households with
exclusive use of hot and cold water, a fixed bath and an inside toilet,
though lower than the steadily rising British average, improved between
1961 and 1971 from 58.9 per cent to 75.2 per cent. The percentage of
the urban population living at more than 1.5 ppa fell from 46.9 per
cent in 1951 to 26.0 per cent in 1971. Partly because of judicious
amendments to the boundaries of the inner city CDAs, a new urban
motorway had been inserted in the highway system to ease traffic
congestion in the centre and speed cross-city movement (Pacione 1977).
Despite these achievements planning in Glasgow continued to be dominated by the two major issues of housing and unemployment.
Development plans in the early 1970s rested on the dual strategies of
overspill and redevelopment. The comprehensive development programme continued, and in 1972 a sixth new town was designated at
Stonehouse, 17 miles from Glasgow, to provide 30,000 new jobs and
accommodate 70,000 people. The CDA programme had not been
completely effective, and of the 29 CDAs proposed in 1957 only 9 had
been approved by 1973. Doubts were expressed on the efficiency of
large scale redevelopments that create prolonged disruptions of
community life. The land use zonings of the 1947 Town and Country
Planning Act were used rigidly as prime controls in the redevelopment
programme so that the boundaries of the CDAs were tightly drawn and
virtually unalterable once approved. The results were inflexible and
slow responses to changing ideas on the restructuring of urban areas.
Such criticisms may be levelled at the redevelopment of the Gorbals. The
original report on the area proposed that development should take place

in three sections but to date only the central unit (Hutchesontown-Gorbals) is nearing completion. The plans for the western unit (Laurieston-Gorbals) were only finally approved in 1966, almost a decade after the development of the whole area had begun, and this section will not be completed until the mid-1980s. The third sector (Hutchesontown-Polmadie CDA) has been dropped from the comprehensive redevelopment programme.

Changes occurring in the planning profession affected urban redevelopment schemes. In the immediate post-war period architects, engineers and surveyors who dominated the planning process saw planning problems mainly in terms of the physical environment. By the 1960s the profession included geographers, economists and sociologists. The change to an interdisciplinary approach shifted the focus from physical land uses to the consideration of socio-economic problems. Two government reports were commissioned in the mid-1960s and became instruments of the change toward a more flexible planning (Planning Advisory Group 1965; Skeffington Committee 1969). The first report recommended that the range of planning activity should be widened in economic and social terms to provide an integrated planning framework from regional to local levels, and that the CDA procedure should be discontinued and replaced with a less rigid and less time-consuming system. The second report dealt with public participation and outlined in detail a mechanism for public consultation at each stage of the planning process. The government incorporated the principal recommendations of both reports in major planning and housing legislation of 1968 and 1969, especially the Town and Country Planning Act 1968, in which the planning process was divided into a two-tier system of structure planning and local planning. Under this new system the CDA approach to urban renewal has been replaced by a process that identifies 'action areas'. These areas may be defined in a local plan for either improvement or redevelopment. They are generally expected to be much smaller than the CDAs and all development is required to be completed within a ten-year period. For the older areas of Glasgow the decision to include improvement of existing stock or rehabilitation along with redevelopment is most important, because one of the major disadvantages of the CDA programme was that it often removed fit houses along with the unfit and efficient businesses along with the inefficient in order to comply with the overall master plan. In practice, progress with rehabilitation of existing dwelling houses was slow, despite the fact that improvement grants have been available since 1949. Between 1960 and 1972 the grants approved by the corporation

were insignificant for the scale of the problems of obsolescence and
insanitary conditions (Glasgow Corporation 1974). By 1975 rehabilitation had been accepted as a major policy. The social motives behind
this change were supported by figures from the corporation on the
relative costs of rehabilitation and redevelopment. From the limited
information available on costs, long term rehabilitation proves to be
cheaper than new construction in comprehensive development areas,
'but the difference is not sufficiently great to recommend one method
at the expense of the other' (Glasgow Corporation 1974). The strongest
argument in favour of rehabilitation is the effect that demolition can
have on long established residential areas, such as Partickhill, Hillhead,
East Pollokshields and Dennistoun. A total commitment to
rehabilitation would be impractical because a large proportion of the
city's 31,000 sub-tolerable houses is beyond repair. The city has thus
embraced a dual programme involving both rehabilitation and redevelopment. In view of the sensitive structure of local economies and
communities, wherever and whenever possible the emphasis is placed
on improvement rather than redevelopment.

Glasgow Eastern Area Renewal

The new planning philosophy has been applied in the east-end of
Glasgow, where the various symptoms of urban deprivation are seen at
their most virulent (Figure 5.3). Glasgow's east-end is one of the
bleakest urban areas in Britain – 3,500 acres of wasteland from which
population and industry have consistently retreated since 1961. Partly
as a result of the city's overspill policy of the 1950s and 1960s and
partly by choice, 85,000 people have left the area in the last 20 years.
More than half of the remaining population of 55,000 live in single
rooms or room and kitchen dwellings. Unemployment rates are well
above the city average, reaching 36 per cent in places, and vast areas of
derelict land blight the landscape.

In order to cure what had almost become a terminal case of urban
decay, drastic measures were called for. To this end the most ambitious
urban renewal programme in Britain is being undertaken jointly by
Glasgow District Council, Strathclyde Regional Council, and SSHA
under the general direction of the Scottish Development Agency. The
aim of the Glasgow Eastern Area Renewal Project (GEAR), for which
an initial sum of £120 million over eight years has been assigned, is to
revitalise the area by halting the drift of population, re-establishing

Figure 5.3: Glasgow Eastern Areas Renewal (GEAR) Project Area, and Cambuslang Recovery Area

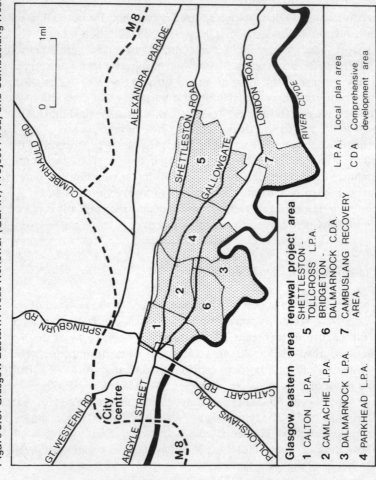

Glasgow eastern area renewal project area

1 CALTON L.P.A.
2 CAMLACHIE L.P.A.
3 DALMARNOCK L.P.A.
4 PARKHEAD L.P.A.

5 SHETTLESTON –
   TOLLCROSS L.P.A.
6 BRIDGETON –
   DALMARNOCK C.D.A.
7 CAMBUSLANG RECOVERY
   AREA

L.P.A.   Local plan area

C.D.A.   Comprehensive
          development area

industries, and improving the quality of the general environment. The GEAR project, announced on 21 May 1976, was primarily a response to the 1971 Census statistics. Supported by this evidence the local authorities argued that the development of Stonehouse new town as a rival source of housing and employment would only serve to increase Glasgow's problems. Amid growing pressure the government decided to abandon the new town project and concentrate resources on regenerating the inner areas of Glasgow. First thoughts were to place the problem in the hands of an experienced new town development corporation (such as that no longer required at Stonehouse), but in the interests of maintaining harmony with existing authorities this idea was dropped and the work was entrusted to a multi-agency group which included the district and regional authorities.

The GEAR project area comprises the five local plan areas which have been designated in the east-end, together with the existing Bridgeton-Dalmarnock comprehensive development area and the Cambuslang recovery area (Figure 5.3). Public perception of the problems and priorities for the area varied. In Camlachie the main concern was with atmospheric pollution from a local chemical works, while in Dalmarnock attention focused on the lack of local shopping. Generally however the major issues were seen as crime and vandalism, the physical environment, shopping needs, employment, leisure and recreation, public transport, and uncertainty about the future of the area.

Insight into the problems and prospects for the east-end as a whole can be obtained by examining the situation in the Camlachie local plan area (Figure 5.4). Here the main problems include the poor quality of the environment including housing, the lack of social and community facilities, industrial pollution, and the presence of obsolescent and physically run-down property which is unattractive to both industrialists and workers. In this area the closure and demolition of houses in poor sanitary and structural condition has proceeded steadily since the early 1960s and the population has fallen considerably, as has the number of shops and range of community facilities. Many of the industrial firms have closed down as a result of clearance, poor structural condition, or simply because of the inadequacy of the premises for modern industry. The considerable time-lag between demolition and redevelopment has resulted in a marked deterioration of the physical and social environment in which derelict buildings, unkempt vacant sites, closed up tenements and shops, and scrap yards dominate the scene.

In Camlachie there are two distinct areas of residential land use. In

Figure 5.4: Camlachie Local Plan Area: Existing and Proposed Land Use

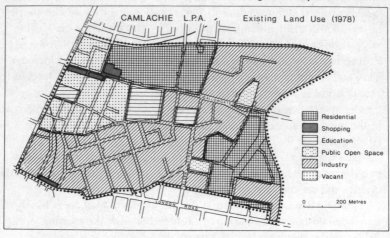

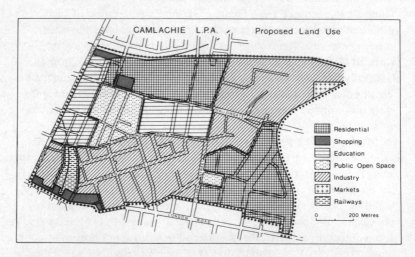

the south-east the Barrowfield council housing scheme, consisting of 590 three-storey and four-storey post-war tenements, has recently been modernised by the District Council; while to the north of the Gallowgate old property has been cleared and a new housing development is under-way. Gallowgate A was completed in the early 1970s when the area was designated for comprehensive redevelopment. Phase B, to provide 272 houses for 1,216 persons, was completed in November 1979, while the smaller Gallowgate phase C (43 houses) was due to be completed in 1980. Nearby, on the main road, is an area of commercial development part of which, together with an adjacent area of vacant land, is zoned for a replacement primary school. Prior to construction however this site will be temporarily landscaped as part of the Scottish Development Agency's improvement programme.

Environmental improvement has formed a major element of the Early Action Projects identified by the governing committee of GEAR partly because it is an activity which generates obvious physical benefits in the short term, but also because new industrial development is hampered by the unwillingness of employers and workers to move into the area. There are concentrations of industrially-zoned land in the north-east (Camlachie Industrial Area) and south-west (Broad Street). The former area comprises two large scrap yards and a variety of industries including a chemical works. Part of the latter zone is being developed by the SDA to provide a number of small (50-100 m^2) industrial workshops. The demand for these premises has exceeded the number of available units and, encouragingly, seven of the sixteen companies installed by September 1978 were new creations. In terms of the overall development of the area it is expected that demolition, rehabilitation, and new building will produce 1,542 houses by 1981. Based on an average occupancy rate of 2.44 persons per dwelling (as opposed to 2.53 at present) and a vacancy rate of 4 per cent (5.3 per cent at present) the 1981 population of the Camlachie area will be 3,611, and it is on the basis of these calculations that the level of service provision has been planned.

An ambitious housing programme is underway in each of the five local plan areas within the east-end (Table 5.10) with the emphasis now on renovation and rehabilitation where possible rather than clearance. This should help to prevent the break-up of existing communities, and reduce the acreage of derelict wastelands which discourages developers and despoils the townscape. Although the physical problems of the east-end can be resolved to a large extent by redevelopment, the social problems engendered by such an impoverished environment and manifested in high tenancy turnover, abscondences, eviction and vandalism are less tractable to physical planning in the short term. The modernisation of the Barrowfield housing area in Camlachie, for example, has eliminated some of the environmental factors which underlie anti-social behaviour, but a major problem remains in the high level of unemployment throughout the east-end. Job opportunities are divided between traditional small-scale manufacturing in which more than half of the firms employ less than ten persons and service industries with low growth prospects. The attraction of new employment opportunities

Table 5.10: Population and Housing Changes in East-end Local Plan
Areas, 1971-81

	Camlachie	Calton	Dalmarnock	Shettleston-Tollcross	Parkhead	Total
Population 1971	9,374	6,437	9,000	21,839	20,030	66,680
Population 1981	3,611	3,100	4,558	16,702	9,545	37,516
% change	-62	-52	-49	-24	-52	-44
Housing stock 1971	1,437	2,656	1,983	7,831	7,805	21,712
Loss due to clearance and rehabilitation	206	1,902	300	381	846	3,635
New built additions	315	470	69	160	250	1,264
Housing stock 1981	1,542	1,224	1,742	7,610	7,209	19,327
% change	+7.3	-53.9	-12.2	-2.8	-7.6	-11.0

suited to the characteristics of the local labour force is of paramount
importance for the success of the GEAR project.

One of the most important factors in bringing new industry into any
inner city area is the availability of suitable vacant industrially-zoned
land. Within the GEAR area there exists a good supply of sites of less
than 5 acres as well as a number of larger sites, including the 155-acre
Cambuslang recovery area. Numerically there is sufficient land to meet
all industrial needs, yet development has been disappointingly slow.
New industrial developments have taken place in the SDA sponsored
Broad Street Industrial Action Area and on the site of the abandoned
Clyde Iron Works at Cambuslang. On part of this partially cleared site
the British Steel Corporation have retained ancillary buildings such as
office blocks and workshops for lease to local firms requiring specialised
facilities or additional space. This area, now known as the Tollcross
industrial village, has attracted firms engaged in a range of activities
including precision engineering, litho printing, a taxi service, a television
repair workshop, and a cooperage; the 15-acre site will eventually
employ 450 people. The SDA are also engaged in a programme of
advance factory building as part of the GEAR project and a range of
regional, national and EEC incentives has been assembled to attract
potential employers into the area (Pacione 1980).

The partnership of agencies is committed to the difficult task of bringing about the economic revival of the area at a time when throughout Britain the forecast is for increased levels of unemployment as a result of economic and technical change. The GEAR management has been criticised for not paying sufficient attention to the wishes of the local people, and friction among the constituent agencies has been suggested to explain the slow rate of progress. Whether the present management structure is retained or replaced by an urban development corporation similar to that proposed for the London docklands and the Merseyside dock area, the problem is immense.

Analysis of the 1981 census will provide some indication of how far Glasgow's rehabilitation has progressed in the last decade. It will have been a major achievement if the city's place at the top of the national deprivation league is found to be in danger.

References

Abercrombie, P. and R.H. Matthew (1949) *The Clyde Valley Regional Plan* (HMSO)

Cameron, G.C. and K.M. Johnson (1969) 'Comprehensive Urban Renewal and Industrial Location – the Glasgow Case', in J.B. Cullingworth and S.C. Orr (eds.) *Regional and Urban Studies*, Allen and Unwin, pp. 242-80

Checkland, S.G. (1964) 'The British Industrial City as History: The Glasgow Case', *Urban Studies, 1*, 34-54

―― (1976) *The Upas Tree* (University of Glasgow Press)

Cullingworth, J.B. (1968) *A Profile of Glasgow Housing 1965*, University of Glasgow Social and Economic Studies Occasional Papers No. 8, Oliver and Boyd

Department of Health for Scotland, (1962) *Draft New Town (Livingstone) Designation Order*, HMSO, Edinburgh

Department of the Environment, (1977) *Policy for Inner Cities*, Cmnd 6845, HMSO, London

Farmer, E. and R. Smith (1975) 'Overspill Theory: a metropolitan case study (Glasgow)', *Urban Studies, 12*, 151-68

Forbes, J. and J. MacBain (eds.) (1967) *The Springburn Study*, Glasgow

Glasgow Corporation, (1974) *Planning Policy Report: Housing*, Glasgow

Glasgow District Council, (1978) *Implications of Population Changes to 1983*, Planning Dept. Policy Report Appendix 1, Glasgow

Hart, T. (1967) *The Comprehensive Development Area*, University of Glasgow Occasional Paper No. 9, Oliver and Boyd

Henderson, R.A. (1974) 'Industrial Overspill from Glasgow: 1958-1968', *Urban Studies, 11*, 61-79

Holtermann, S. (1975) *Areas of Urban Deprivation in Great Britain*, Social Trends No. 6, HMSO

Johnston, N. (1976) 'Reclamation of the Urban Environment', in J. Lenihan and W.W. Fletcher (eds.) *Reclamation*, Blackie, pp. 129-67

Miller, R. (1970) 'The New Face of Glasgow', *Scot. Geog. Mag., 86(1)*, 5-15

Pacione, M. (1977) 'The revivification of the transition zone in Glasgow', *Norsk Geog. Tidsk, 31*, 137-41
—— (1979) 'Housing Policies in Glasgow since 1880', *Geog. Rev., 69* (4), 395-412
—— (1980) 'New Patterns for Deprived Clydeside', *Geog. Mag.*, August, 756-62
Planning Advisory Group, (1965) *The Future of Development Plans*, HMSO, London
Report by the Skeffington Committee, (1969) *Peoples and Planning*, HMSO, London
Smith, P.J. (1967) 'Changing objectives in Scottish New Town policy', *Ekistics, 23*, 26-33
Strathclyde Regional Council, (1976) *Regional Report*, Glasgow

6 BARCELONA

John Naylon

The Stabilisation Plan of 1959 marked the beginnings of Spain's belated transformation from a rural-agrarian to an urban-industrial society. Her economic growth rate during the 1960s was the third highest in the world after Brazil and Japan; between 1960 and 1972 — the years of the Spanish 'economic miracle' — gross industrial output increased thirteen times, a rate surpassed only by Japan among the OECD nations. By 1973 Spain had become the fifth industrial power in Europe and the twelfth country in the world in the value of her gross national product.

This transformation, however, has taken place under special political circumstances and in the absence of effective or committed regional planning. Accordingly, the pressures and conflicts to be seen in Spain's regions and cities are not simply those which are likely to emerge in any nation experiencing very rapid industrialisation and socio-economic change. The classic features of centre-periphery, cumulative causation and metropolitan dominance have been exaggerated by the short space of time over which economic growth has taken place and by the authoritarian nature of the regime in power between the end of the Spanish Civil War in 1939 and the death of General Franco in 1975 — a regime closely allied to big business, domestic and foreign, and able to ignore protests from the peripheral regions and from other sectors (migrants, the working class) adversely affected by the growth process. In the open Spanish economy, with free rein given to market forces, funds have flowed from the periphery to a handful of already-established dynamic centres, particularly Madrid, Barcelona and Bilbao. The advice of the World Bank in 1963 — that Spain should forgo the goal of greater regional equality and seek instead that of maximum national economic growth — found echo in the philosophy and allegiances of the regime, whose prestige was enhanced in terms of industrial achievement; it also suited Spain's seven big banks, which handle over 70 per cent of all financial credit and directly control 50 per cent of Spanish industry.

Well-intentioned but inadequate regional development programmes, based on irrigation, land settlement, land consolidation and growth poles, have failed to diminish spatial disparities, especially between the countryside and the town. Consequently, the populations of Spain's

223

cities have exploded in parallel with industrialisation. Over half the rural population has become urbanised; between 1960 and 1970 three million Spaniards left their homes to live and work either abroad or in Madrid, Barcelona or Bilbao; one in every four Spaniards now lives in Madrid or Barcelona. These three cities are the nerve centres of Spanish economic growth; they contain the nation's three stock exchanges; 75 out of the 100 biggest Spanish industrial firms have their headquarters here; here reside Spain's financial oligarchy and industrial bourgeoisie; here the decisions are taken about investment and expansion.

The advantages of this kind of 'development' are national, favouring the country as a whole; the burdens are regional and local, yet the regions often lack the means — politico-administrative and financial — to bear the weight. The modern expansion of Barcelona and its planning experience reflect the political climate of Franco Spain between 1939 and 1975. Spatial planning takes place in the context of conflicts between political groups, social classes and vested interests. From this particular political climate have stemmed several conflicts which have enormously increased the social costs ordinarily to be expected from metropolitan growth: conflicts between the forces of urban agglomeration and regional planning; between technocrats and planners on the one hand, and political and other interest groups on the other; between a highly-centralised government and local preoccupations; between a non-democratic regime and popular aspirations; between powerful associationist groups (landowners, property developers, building companies, banks, finance houses, local politicians) and an urban proletariat trying to defend and improve its position. Barcelona is an example of what can happen when urban growth is left to the uncontrolled play of market forces, with private entrepreneurs amassing profits without regard to social effects. In this and other senses it occupies an intermediate position between the great cities of the fully-industrialised countries and those of the Third World.

Centre and Periphery in Catalonia

The relative affluence and economic dominance of Catalonia over the rest of Spain have been reinforced during the 1960s and 1970s. With only 6.3 per cent of Spain's national territory, Catalonia contains 15 per cent of the Spanish population and enjoys nearly a quarter of the national income; it accounts for over 25 per cent of Spain's net industrial output and provides 22 per cent of all exports. Catalan-based banks hold more than 19 per cent of all Spain's bank deposits and 23 per cent of industrial bank deposits. This prosperity is a powerful attraction for workers from less-developed parts of Spain such as Murcia and Andalusia; between 1950 and 1974 the population of Catalonia rose from 2 millions to 5.5 millions, largely as the result of immigration.

These generalities, however, conceal the fact that in common with the rest of Spain, two-thirds of Catalonia is losing population (Figure 6.1). Catalonia has become an extreme case of hydrocephaly: a shrivelled body with a bloated head. The province—and more specifically the Metropolitan Area—of Barcelona has attracted by far the greater part of economic and demographic growth while the rest of the region, apart from Gerona, the small Tarragona-Reus axis and the fruit-growing area of Lérida, has remained out of play. In 1974 the province of Barcelona contained 4.25 millions out of Catalona's 5.5 million population. The Barcelona Chamber of Commerce, Industry and Shipping groups 120,000 companies, representing 20 per cent of Spanish national industrial output by value. Over 3.5 million people—70 per cent of the population of Catalonia and one in every ten Spaniards—live in the city of Barcelona or within 30 kilometres of its centre. They include 71.49 per cent of all Catalonia's industrial workers and enjoy 73.65 per cent of the region's disposable income.

At least since the initiation of the industrial revolution at the end of the eighteenth century, Barcelona has been the major centre of economic innovation in Spain. As its traditional industries, such as textiles, have stagnated or declined, new activities have grown up in their place; the multiplicity of interests of the city facilitates constant renewal, as Myrdal suggests, compared with the narrow and inflexible economic base of the periphery. Psychological criteria, too, appear to be partly behind the strong element of risk aversion shown by Catalan entrepreneurs: in the economic boom period 1964-73 over 70 per cent of the industrial investment in Catalonia was placed in the sub-regions of the Barcelonés, Maresme, Baix Llobregat, Vallès Occidental and Vallès Oriental, whose centre is Barcelona—as though the mere fact of locating not more than 25-30 kilometres from the city centre were a guarantee of business success. While 75 per cent of all new Catalan industrial employment in this period was created in and around Barcelona, 28 out of the remaining Catalan sub-regions received only 7.3 per cent of total industrial investment and 10.4 per cent of new industrial jobs. In some parts of the Catalan periphery industrial employment hardly exists; thus, the Cerdanya has only 0.11

Figure 6.1: Catalonia: Population Density by Sub-region (comarca), 1975

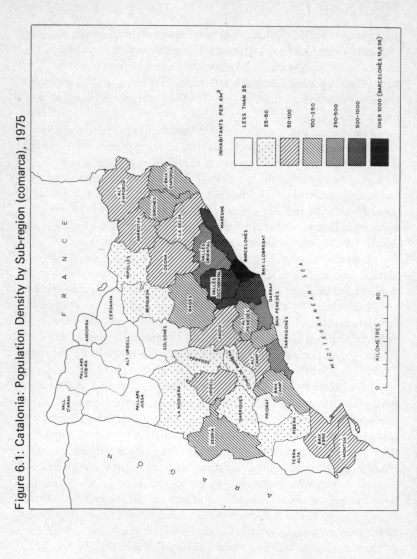

per cent of Catalonia's industrial workers, the Garrigues 0.08 per cent, the Solsonès 0.06 per cent, the Priorat 0.05 per cent and the Terra Alta 0.03 per cent. The reverse side of the gigantism of Barcelona has been the debilitation and impoverishment of most other towns and villages in Catalonia, and indeed of many elsewhere in Spain.

Immigration and Urban Sprawl

The growth of Barcelona is the product of industrialisation and in-migration since the mid-nineteenth century. In-migration was an absolute necessity for the Catalan industrial revolution, given the low growth rate of the indigenous population: from an annual increase of some 11,500 around 1860 the growth of the native Catalan population in 1900 was only 2,000. No amount of modern machinery could compensate for this lack of a local labour force. The new urban-industrial opportunities attracted first of all the surplus rural population of Catalonia, but before long the catchment area spread further afield— first to Aragón, then to Murcia, and finally, in the twentieth century, to Andalusia and Extremadura. Barcelona is now the second province in Spain, after Madrid, as an attraction to migrants.

The 1970 Spanish census revealed that of the population of the Barcelona municipality 53.73 per cent were born either in the city itself (49.00 per cent) or in Barcelona province (4.73 per cent), while 43.84 per cent were first-generation immigrants from the rest of Spain, including the other three Catalan provinces. In-migration on this scale brings with it certain advantages to the entrepreneur: markets rapidly expand as successive demand thresholds are crossed; and the *naïveté* and malleableness of immigrant labour, its lack of union organisation and solidarity, confers an advantage on the employer. But over three-quarters of the immigrants are unskilled labourers, mainly of rural origin and of low social status; the private benefits which they represent are accompanied by high public costs.

After remaining stable for centuries, the population of Barcelona and its region shows a marked exponential growth from the mid-nineteenth century onwards. From the first modern Spanish census of 1857 to that of 1970 the population of the city proper rose from 183,787 (representing 11.1 per cent of the total population of Catalonia) to 1,745,142 (34.8 per cent). Population estimates for the Metropolitan Area are 4.4 millions in 1980 and 6.5 millions in 2010 (although projections range between 7 and 11 millions by the end of the twentieth

century). This growth has taken place at the expense of the rest of
Catalonia and of more distant regions. Over the period 1842-1970
Barcelona city increased its population by 849 per cent, while the rest
of Catalonia grew by only 130 per cent. Large areas of the rural
periphery have been depopulated, for instance, the Pallars Sobirà, which
in 1950 had only 59.4 per cent of its 1857 population. By 1970 eight
of the ten largest cities of Catalonia belonged to greater Barcelona and
contained 94 per cent of the inhabitants. Some parts of the Metropolitan Area have arrived at the almost complete saturation of living
and working space; the population density in the Barcelonès is
14,746.00 persons per square kilometre while the average density for
Catalonia as a whole is only 32.30, falling in some parts of the periphery
as low as 10.57 (Pallars Jussà) and 4.30 (Pallars Sobirà).

Up to 1920, approximately, when it had a population of 710,335,
the city of Barcelona managed to absorb population, industry and
tertiary functions within its own confines. Since then, the influx of
migrants, the exhaustion of building space and the consequent
prohibitive price of land, have produced an outward spread of
population and industry to a ring of adjacent municipalities which
includes L'Hospitalet, Prat de Llobregat, Cornellà, Espluges, Sant Just
Desvern, Santa Coloma de Gramanet, Sant Adrià de Besòs and
Badalona. While maintaining its power of attraction, Barcelona has
lost its power of absorption, and has compensated by becoming more
selective through the mechanisms of rents and land values. First of all
the city expelled its poorer residents to neighbouring dormitory settlements; secondly, diseconomies of agglomeration forced industry to
follow suit; and as selection continues, the latest phase is a tendency
for the city to become a focus of tertiary activities and high-class
residence. The corollary of this selection process is the extraordinary
growth of the immediately adjacent urban ring, as illustrated by the
figures in Table 6.1.

L'Hospitalet is now Catalonia's second most populous municipality
after Barcelona, and Badalona the fourth. Put another way, while
Barcelona increased its population six times between 1860 and 1965,
Sant Adrià de Besòs increased 68 times, L'Hospitalet 54 times and Santa
Coloma de Gramanet 43 times.

Under such pressure it has not been possible to plan metropolitan
growth properly. The ring of municipalities around Barcelona has been
ill-prepared, physically and humanly, to become the receptacle for
immigrants and industries seeking cheap accommodation. Many have
become no more than working-class dormitories, and their proletarian-

isation has often meant that their budgets have declined in proportion to their growth. Public penury and private speculation have produced a degraded urban sprawl between the Llobregat and the Besòs, spilling over into the Vallès (Figure 6.2). Some of these municipalities are now themselves saturated and there is every indication that if the metropolis continues to grow in the same uncontrolled way the conurbation will extend to a radius of 50 kilometres around Barcelona.

Table 6.1: Population Growth in Municipalities Adjacent to Barcelona, 1920-75

	1920	1970	1975
L'Hospitalet de Llobregat	25,000	241,978	282,141
Badalona	29,361	162,888	203,719
Sabadell	37,529	159,408	182,926
Terrassa	30,532	138,697	161,049
Santa Coloma de Gramanet	2,728	106,711	138,091

The Planning Response

Up to the mid-nineteenth century Barcelona coped with economic and demographic growth by increasing its population density to the point of asphyxia within the confines of its fourteenth-century walls. In 1859 the density per hectare was 859, rising to 1,724 in *barrio* 10 of the Second District; these densities compare with Paris, 356 inhabitants per hectare, and London 86 (in 1858). Not surprisingly, mortal epidemics were frequent. Laureano de Figuerola, in his *Estadística de Barcelona en 1849* (Barcelona, 1849; republished by the Instituto de Estudios Fiscales, Madrid, 1968), provides the life-expectancy figures for the period 1837-47 (Table 6.2).

Table 6.2: Life Expectancy in Barcelona, 1837-47

	Rich	Tradespeople	Working class
Men	38.83	25.44	19.68
Women	34.11	24.90	27.43

Figure 6.2: Barcelona and its Urban-industrial Satellites

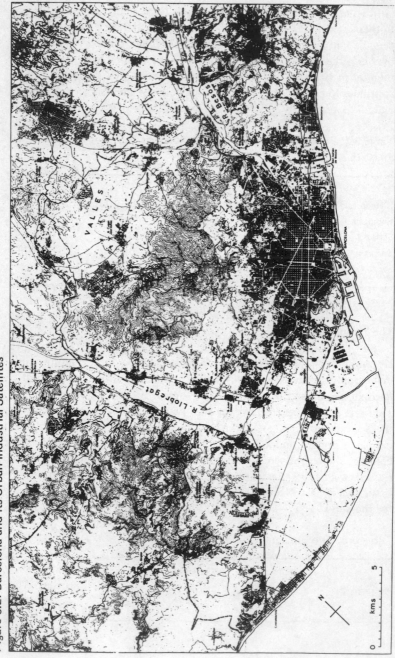

The average for all classes and both sexes was 25.71 years; this fell to 24.82 years in the period 1862-64.

To relieve these pressures, the medieval walls began to be demolished in 1854 and in 1860 a project by Ildefonso Cerdà was adopted as the development plan for the expansion (*ensanche*) of Barcelona. Any map of the city reflects graphically the contrast in urban morphology between the tortuous alleys of the *casco antiguo*, the grid pattern of the Ensanche and the haphazard growths of the contemporary periphery (Figure 6.3). The Cerdà Plan was a vision of an egalitarian city. Communal service elements (markets, social centres, open spaces) were to be evenly distributed throughout the chessboard (*damero*) of octagonally-shaped blocks. The typical block was to be built up on only two sides, leaving large open spaces in the interior.

The Ensanche was effectively completed by the 1920s and by that time its degradation by population pressure and speculative response was already under way. Building along the third and fourth sides of the blocks had taken place almost from the beginning, followed in the twentieth century by the addition of extra storeys and the conversion of the interior open spaces into enclosed yards, used in the majority of cases for warehousing or workshops. By the 1940s and 1950s most of the communal service areas had been eliminated, so that today's block has a building density four to five times greater than that intended by Cerdà. An up-dated version of the Cerdà Plan—the Macià Plan—was formulated in 1932 but was overtaken by the Civil War of 1936-9; as a result, the Cerdà Plan—albeit only a bastardised version of what its author had intended—was still the official development plan for Barcelona until well into the 1950s.

There was an imaginative effort in the 1920s and 1930s to plan the future growth of Barcelona within the context of Catalonia as a whole. The idea, clearly inspired by Ebenezer Howard, was first proposed in 1920 by the Societat Cívica La Ciutat Jardí. During the 1920s the Mancomunitat de Catalunya drew a zonal scheme for Catalonia, based on regional resources and ignoring the conventional provincial divisions of 1833; but action had to wait until the Second Spanish Republic was established in 1931 and conferred a degree of autonomy on the Catalans. In 1932 the newly-constituted Generalitat de Catalunya (the autonomous government) published the Pla de Distribució en Zones del Territori Català, promulgated as a decree on the 'Territorial Division of Catalonia' in 1936; and in 1937 a conference was held on the 'industrial exploitation of the natural resources of Catalonia'. The tenor of these projects was a strong emphasis on assessing the resources of the whole

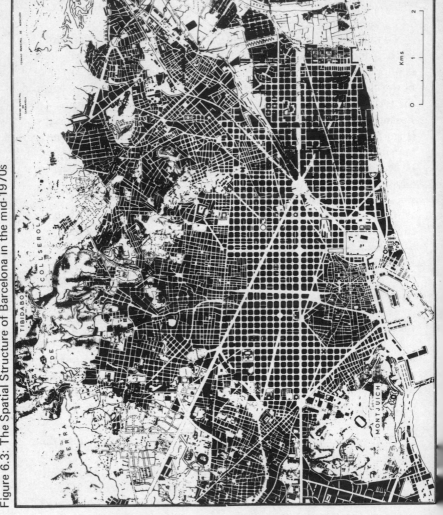

Figure 6.3: The Spatial Structure of Barcelona in the mid-1970s

of the region. The particular problems of Barcelona were recognised, but always with a view to preventing the excessive growth of the city, and thinking in terms of an evolutionary 'Catalonia City' (Catalunya Ciutat) involving the planning of Catalonia as a single unit.

The Civil War abruptly truncated this line of thought. The Generalitat was abolished; Catalonia lost its autonomy; academic and professional institutions, such as the Societat Catalana de Geografia and the Institut d'Investigacions Econòmiques de Catalunya were closed down or survived only clandestinely; 'regional planning' criteria were forgotten and there was a return to the provincial division and administration of the country, better suited in the eyes of the new regime in Madrid to the purposes of centralised control and repression of autonomist ideas. From this time onwards, planning for the growth of Barcelona would always be subordinated to the interests of the Madrid government and of its political and business allies.

In the aftermath of the Civil War these interests were concentrated upon the targets of industrial development and economic autarchy, as a reaction against Spain's backward agrarian condition and 'colonial' dependency status. There was no national urban planning policy and hardly any urban planning institutions. The Dirección General de Arquitectura, set up in 1939, was the only body with any competence in the urban planning field until 1949, when the Jefatura Central de Urbanismo was created, while the strong centralist structure of the administration frustrated any efforts at local level. The 1940s house-building programme of the central government largely ignored 'republican' Barcelona which struggled, unaided, to absorb, house and employ the rising tide of immigrants from Spain's rural areas. It was not until the 1950s that the central government reluctantly relinquished its negative attitudes towards migration and city growth. The arrival of the first United States aid ended Spain's long post-war ostracism and isolation, and brought with it brighter economic prospects, improved transport facilities and greatly increased migratory movements—which faced, however, an alarming lack of housing in the great cities.

Belatedly, from the mid-1950s onwards, the Madrid government created an institutional and legal superstructure of urban planning, and a series of national housing policies and programmes, which under a more democratically-responsible regime might beneficially have influenced the growth of Barcelona and other large Spanish cities during the following two decades. The most important of these was the 1956 Ley de Régimen del Suelo y Ordenación Urbana (Land and Urban Planning Act), which is a good illustration of what was to become a familiar situation of legislation being excellent in its stated objectives but of negligible practical application. The Act introduced a five-level planning system of local plans, municipal development plans, sub-regional plans, provincial plans and national plans, and set out the procedural steps for plan approval. At the same time, it proposed the creation in each municipality of a 'patrimony' of publicly-owned land for development purposes. In practice, although the Act formed the basis of Spanish urban planning up to the late 1970s (it was reformed in 1976), like other public sector measures during the Franco period its impact was derisory and it proved completely unable to stop the major problem of speculation. Outside a few main urban areas, very few plans were actually drawn up, although it was obligatory under the Act for every municipality to present its development plan. The majority of town councils proved incapable of producing plans because of their lack of initiative, experience and technical ability; a concerted land-use policy in metropolitan agglomerations such as Barcelona, where independent municipalities often had conflicting interests, proved particularly elusive. The Act was aborted by the lack of technical teams and of specialised administrative organisations, the lack of adequate finance, an absence of inter-ministerial coordination, lack of action on the part of those institutions which did exist, and by the break-down of communication between the technocrats and the executive—the former stating objectives which turned out to be unrealistic or politically inconvenient in the eyes of the latter. Few procedural steps were adhered to during the Franco era; and at all stages urban planning considerations were subordinated to those of economic growth.

In the case of Barcelona, from 1953 onwards five different plans were formulated to regulate the expansion of the metropolis; sometimes these were co-existent, often they were deliberately contradictory, and all were largely failures.

Apeing the plans for Greater Paris (1939), Greater London (1940) and Greater Madrid (1946), in 1953 the Plan de Ordenación de Barcelona y su Zona de Influencia defined a 'Greater Barcelona' within which urban development would be regulated (Figure 6.4). Commonly known as the Plan Comarcal or Sub-regional Plan, the scheme embraced 27 neighbouring municipalities and was to be managed by a Planning Commission (Comisión de Urbanismo y Servicios Comunes de Barcelona y Otros Municipios). The duration of the plan was to be almost 50 years, up to the year 2000. It contained, on paper, the usual admirable provisions. Affirming the need for urban development legislation to avoid speculation, to prevent Barcelona becoming one immense sprawl,

Figure 6.4: Municipalities of the 1953 Sub-regional Plan

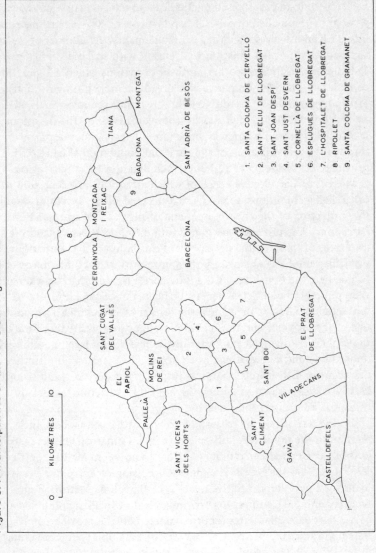

KILOMETRES

0   10

1. SANTA COLOMA DE CERVELLÓ
2. SANT FELIU DE LLOBREGAT
3. SANT JOAN DESPÍ
4. SANT JUST DESVERN
5. CORNELLÀ DE LLOBREGAT
6. ESPLUGUES DE LLOBREGAT
7. L'HOSPITALET DE LLOBREGAT
8. RIPOLLET
9. SANTA COLOMA DE GRAMANET

MONTGAT
TIANA
BADALONA
SANT ADRIÀ DE BESÒS
MONTCADA I REIXAC
CERDANYOLA
BARCELONA
SANT CUGAT DEL VALLÈS
EL PAPIOL
MOLINS DE REI
PALLEJÀ
SANT VICENS DELS HORTS
SANT BOI
SANT CLIMENT
GAVÀ
VILADECANS
CASTELLDEFELS
EL PRAT DE LLOBREGAT

and to permit an orderly and methodical growth, industry and housing were to be channelled to other urban nuclei. The Sub-region was zoned into 37 land-use classes and in each municipality the number of hecatres to be allotted to each function was set out, with specific stipulations as to building densities and other norms. For reasons which will presently be reviewed, the Plan Comarcal was already demonstrating its inefficacy in 1960; nevertheless, it continued in force until the mid-1970s.

In 1959 the Plan Comarcal was 'complemented' by the Barcelona Provincial Plan whose aim was, once more, balanced development through the redistribution of industry and population (Figure 6.5). The province was divided into 11 zones, including the 1953 Sub-region (*comarca*) of Barcelona, in each of which attention was to be paid to urban living conditions, sociological aspects of urban development, and the protection of the environment and of the cultural and artistic patrimony. The province was zoned into different types of land use and into areas of 'preferential development' for industry and agriculture, and particular emphasis was placed upon intra-provincial communications. In practice, the objectives of the Provincial Plan and the Plan Comarcal were directly in conflict. Whereas the main aim of the latter was to 'potentialise' Greater Barcelona, the former placed emphasis upon the rest of the province and thus could not count on the collaboration of the city. The Provincial Plan was only indicative; it placed no obligations upon the public sector; it possessed no effective legal, administrative or executive institutions, resources or powers of decision; and accordingly, it was incapable of providing the basic infrastructure, especially transport, to channel industrial decentralisation.

By the late 1960s the pattern of growth of Barcelona bore little relation to the nominally still-operative Plan Comarcal. On the instructions of the General Directorate of Urban Planning in Madrid, between 1963 and 1966 the Urban Planning Commission of Barcelona drew up plans for a new administrative region, the Barcelona Metropolitan Area (Figure 6.6), comprising 162 municipalities with a combined area of 3,206 square kilometres (approximately half the province of Barcelona and 10.3 per cent of the area of Catalonia) and containing in 1970 3,579,316 people (69.8 per cent of the total Catalan population). This time, the Barcelona conurbation was to be decentralised by accommodating overspill population, industry and tertiary activities in inland growth centres. Considerable effort was put into the theoretical organisation of the Metropolitan Area; bureaucratic delays and conflicts, however, delayed the publication of the new plan until 1972, by which time it was once more evident that the Metropolitan Area could only

Figure 6.5: The 1959 Barcelona Provincial Plan: Sub-regions and Proposed Urban Planning Structure

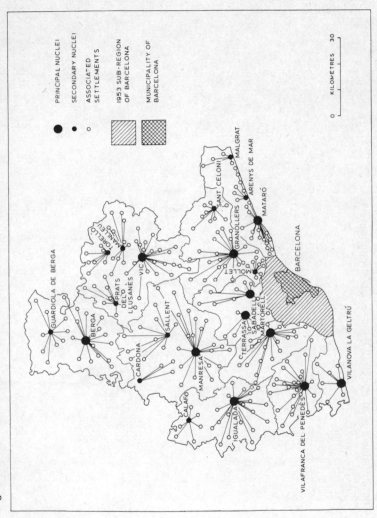

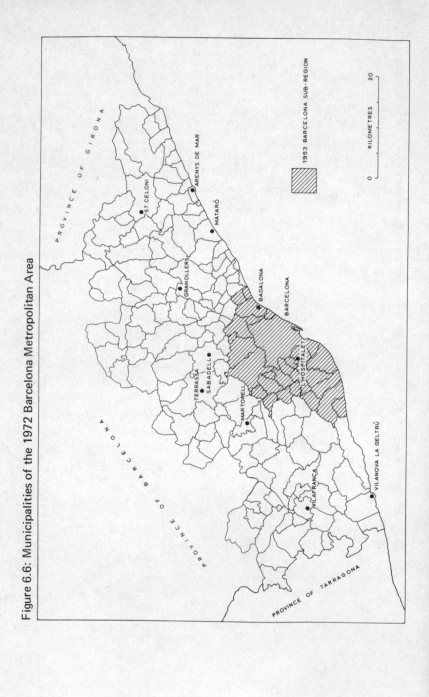

Figure 6.6: Municipalities of the 1972 Barcelona Metropolitan Area

PROVINCE OF GIRONA

PROVINCE OF BARCELONA

PROVINCE OF TARRAGONA

ST. CELONI
ARENYS DE MAR
MATARÓ
GRANOLLERS
BADALONA
BARCELONA
TERRASSA
SABADELL
L'HOSPITALET
MARTORELL
VILAFRANCA
VILANOVA LA GELTRÚ

1953 BARCELONA SUB-REGION

0   KILOMETRES   20

achieve decentralisation if it were endowed with authority on a par with other administrative organisations, and were given its own adequate resources and its own political organisation holding legislative and decision-making powers. These it did not have and could not hope to have under the Franco government, as events soon proved.

In August 1974, during the summer recess and without prior consultation, the central government's Council of Ministers created a new Metropolitan Corporation of Barcelona (Entitat Municipal Metropolitana de Barcelona) which, the following year, replaced the Metropolitan Area of Barcelona and put the planning clock back twenty years. Ostensibly, the Decree-Law 5/1975 created an effective and officially-recognised executive organisation which responded to the spreading popular demand for reform of the 1953 Sub-regional Plan. In fact, from the 162 municipalities of the Barcelona Metropolitan Area the planning area of the new Metropolitan Corporation was reduced to the 27 municipalities of the 1953 plan—an area totally inadequate to meet urban development needs. The true objective of Decree-Law 5/1975 was to forestall the setting up of an administrative unit such as the Barcelona Metropolitan Area which, by virtue of its size and socio-economic potential, might serve as a platform for the expression of Catalan regionalism. The Metropolitan Area would have overshadowed the national capital in population, economic power and wealth; to the Madrid of General Franco—and, so far, to his successors—the creation of such a power base outside the direct control of the political nerve centre was anathema. And thus, with the situation in the area of the 1953 Sub-regional Plan well-nigh insupportable, the Barcelona conurbation came to the end of the dictatorship and passed into the democratic transition and the world economic depression.

A Critique of Barcelona's Planning Experience: the Mechanics of Urban Sprawl

After the Civil War, planning perspectives in Catalonia shifted from a view of the region as a planning unity to the view that the motor and beneficiary of urban and industrial expansion should be Barcelona. Given the attitude of the Franco government towards the potentially autonomist regions of Spain, to divorce planning for the Barcelona conurbation from that for Catalonia as a whole was a foreseeable tactic.

At the technical level, as Wynn observes, Spain in general and Barcelona in particular have kept abreast of developments in planning

theory. Spain's technocrats have produced large numbers of excellent
plans to solve the nation's spatial problems. The true lesson of Barcelona's
experience has been the irrelevance of sophisticated projects when local
authorities are not democratically representative and when they lack
the funds and the human resources to translate theory into practice.
The way in which the Barcelona conurbation has grown bears little
relation to the various plans formulated since 1953, and their
irrelevance is explained by the nature of the institutions responsible
for administering them. Between 1936 and June 1977 Spain held no
democratic central government elections, and it was not until April
1979 that the country held its first municipal elections since 1931. In
the authoritarian Francoist state, central government bodies held sway
in the Urban Planning Commissions; municipal mayors and presidents
of provincial councils were nominated by the Home Office (Ministerio
de Gobernación); town councillors were elected by a very limited
suffrage; and there was no popular participation in municipal affairs.
The principle of hierarchy and tutelage built into the centralised
Spanish politico-administrative system leaves local authorities with
only residual powers over those issues which concern them most, and
even here they may be overruled by state bodies. Some of the most
important elements in urban planning—for instance, the primary
transport network—are directly under the control of the central government and the provincial councils; as a consequence, notably less
attention has been paid to Barcelona's transport network than to that
of Madrid. Between the strong centralised control of public resources
and the essentially decentralised nature of local development, the system
breaks down. There is a conscious irony in the evident intention of the
Madrid government to continue to divide and rule the Barcelona conurbation by maintaining the fiction of the administrative and juridical
independence of the municipalities which compose it.

When population and industrial growth were concentrated mainly
in Barcelona city, the situation could be handled by the single municipal authority which, up to 1936, had in its hands powers of initiative,
control, administration and execution of urban planning; it was,
moreover, accustomed to coping with growth since the eighteenth
century and had had the experience of the Cerdà Plan. After the Civil
War, when growth began to spill over adjacent municipal boundaries,
control became extraordinarily complicated. Not only is responsibility
for urban planning fragmented between municipalities, with each
authority sovereign (albeit only in theory) in its own territory, the
plurality of bodies involved, and the disparity of their powers, turns

planning into a conflict of interests, a series of contradictions. Within
the Metropolitan Area of Barcelona, for example, functions were
divided between the Comisión de Urbanismo y Servicios Comunes de
Barcelona y Otros Municipios, responsible for the 27 municipalities of
the 1953 Sub-regional Plan, and the Comisión Provincial de Urbanismo,
embracing the rest of the municipalities of Barcelona province and also
those of the Metropolitan Area which were not included in the 1953
Plan; both these bodies had equal rank, but depended on the Dirección
General de Urbanismo in Madrid. Similarly, at the housing level, central
state organisations such as the Syndical Housing Authority (attached to
the Ministry of Labour) and the National Housing Institute (attached
to the Ministry of Housing) conduct their operations alongside the
local public housing authorities and private foundations.

The financial situation of Barcelona warrants special mention. In a
rational socio-political situation, local authorities invigilate and mediate
the quality of urban life; one of the major constraints upon the
Barcelona authorities performing this normal function is their state of
virtual bankruptcy. Financially, as in almost every other respect, Spain's
municipalities depend upon Madrid; yet as urban populations have
mushroomed and town councils have been called upon to provide an
ever-wider range of services, municipal budgets have dwindled. In 1930
Spanish local authorities accounted for 23.6 per cent of all central
government spending; by 1970 this proportion had shrunk to 18.3 per
cent and by 1979 to 9 per cent. The corresponding figure for Italy is
32 per cent and for the United States almost 45 per cent. Put another
way: in 1930 the combined budget of the Spanish municipalities
equalled only a modest 3.3 per cent of the country's GNP; by 1970 it
had dropped to 2.4 per cent (compared with 8.4 per cent in West
Germany). Any absolute increase in the cities' budgets is more than
swallowed up by population increase.

In the early 1970s the arrival of each new immigrant in Barcelona
was calculated to call for an investment of not less than 400,000
pesetas in adequate service provision; but in 1970 the city budget of
5,420 million pesetas worked out at only 3,111 pesetas per inhabitant
(little more than £20.00). Collectively, Spain's town halls reached the
end of 1979 with a combined debt of some 400 billion pesetas (£2.9
billions); Barcelona was the worst affected, with debts in excess of 60
billion pesetas (£437 millions). In these circumstances, authorities
cannot fulfil their normal responsibilities. They barely cope with roads,
paving, drainage, lighting and similar basic necessities, while anything
which is not absolutely urgent or within their most specific brief—

housing, education, health, social assistance—is relegated to second place and can only be covered by extraordinary budgets, by borrowings from the Banco de Crédito Local (whose funds are limited and which could not fully meet Barcelona's needs because this would leave nothing for the other municipalities), by public debt issues, by international loans—or by the private sector. During the Franco period the situation was not helped by the size of the municipal bureaucracy, its 36 years of unchecked graft and administrative incompetence, and the spending of scarce resources on the city centre, the better-off residential districts and costly projects such as the Tibidabo tunnels, costed at 27.3 billion pesetas (£202 millions) in 1967 and abandoned in the early 1970s.

The incoherence of Barcelona's urban growth is thus based upon the division of powers between many bodies and their lack of co-ordination, the weakness of local authority budgets, and a technical inability to tackle the often desperate situation in the suburbs. In these circumstances, town councils simply have to cede important functions to private initiative. The tide of immigrants arriving in the conurbation finds neither an infrastructure nor a housing programme calculated for its needs. The demand for dwellings is met by private improvisation— the sale of parcels of land, the construction of tower blocks—guided only by the desire for maximum returns in the shortest time. The private sector, often enjoying state house-building subsidies, has not only been given a free hand; little effort has been made to curb its illegal activities.

There were several loopholes in the 1956 Land and Urban Planning Act, the most serious being the absence of precise regulations about the modification, through the medium of local plans, of already-approved municipal and sub-regional plans. Local authority impotence, but more frequently corruption in the town councils and collusion with private economic interests, meant that this vehicle for re-classifying land could easily be exploited by speculators. Residential and industrial classifications were extended at the expense of green zones and collective amenity areas; local plans would alter sub-regional plan residential classifications to allow higher building densities. The majority of local plans, especially in the 1960s, were thus used to reclassify and re-value land which otherwise was not sufficiently profit-generating for the private entrepreneur. Local authorities, meanwhile, would vacillate between applying controls or ignoring the issue; commonly, they validated illegalities *a posteriori*. Through their passivity they failed to control the worst aspects of development—for instance, determining land prices or insisting that development companies should instal basic infrastructures before constructing dwellings, as the law demands. Frequently, local authorities have only intervened and provided services after many years of pressure and insistence from citizens.

In the sphere of housing, public sector institutions (Gerencia de Urbanización, Instituto Nacional de la Vivienda, Comisión de Urbanismo, Patronato Municipal de la Vivienda de Barcelona, Syndical Housing Authority) have done little more than fill the gaps left by private developers and have had little effect on the property market or on building standards. At the end of 1970 the housing deficit in the Metropolitan Area was 136,053. These state bodies have themselves contravened the planning regulations. Thus, in the housing estates of Verdun and Trinidad, built by the Syndical Housing Authority, building densities were respectively 3.7 and 3.9 times greater than those laid down in the Sub-regional Plan.

Industrial location is the key to population decentralisation and urban planning, but Greater Barcelona has not possessed a general plan for industrial estates. The Ministry of Housing, responsible for many of Spain's industrial estates, has been conspicuous by its absence in the nation's densest industrial region. Up to 1970 only one industrial estate 'La Torre' in Martorell, a mere 17 hectares in size) had been built by the Gerencia de Urbanización in the Metropolitan Area—a region in which 30 per cent of Spain's total population growth had taken place since 1960. Industrial location has been reduced to a proliferation of estates promoted by individual municipalities; these have often remained half-occupied because the communications network continues to focus upon Barcelona, and thus constitute burdens rather than assets to the town councils and local communities. Industrialists have been left to their own devices to improvise infrastructures such as roads, drainage, sewage and water supply, and they in turn have left the local authorities to struggle with the legacy. In the early 1970s, according to the Comisión de Urbanismo, 50 per cent of the land zoned for industry in the 1953 Sub-region had no services laid on; in the rest of Barcelona province the proportion rose to 80 per cent.

Within the general climate of instability created by constant changes in the major plans, the jungle of urban legislation at municipal level has been manipulated, or ignored, by economically powerful or politically influential groups. A weak official planning policy, coinciding with a great demand for building land and housing, could not help but produce a speculative fever in which working class housing—although officially subsidised and stated to have priority—suffered. The aggressiveness of the building and development companies, banks and finance houses has accumulated wealth in their hands while virtually pauperising large sections of the population. Planning policies have a clear social and political context, and spatial planning is just one of the policies imposed by the social class holding power; the form it has taken in Barcelona is a reflection of the social and political as well as economic conditions obtaining in Spain generally under Franco. This subordination of planning to economic growth and private gain leads in the long run to accumulating diseconomies and the need for unproductive investments to try to rectify the consequences of ignoring the social costs of growth, the degradation of the environment and the absence of any imaginative view of the future. A case in point is the state of Barcelona's road network, inadequate both quantitatively and qualitatively, and aggravated by the geographical location of Barcelona and its satellites in relation to international traffic, which mingles with local traffic. The efficiency of the Catalan economy is closely bound up with official spending on infrastructures of this kind, yet spending lags far behind the economic and urban growth of the region. One study (1975) estimates that Catalonia loses at least 3 billion pesetas per year through traffic holdups caused by the inadequate road network.

If one of the objectives of planning is to reduce inequalities, planning for Catalonia and Barcelona is an evident failure. Inter-regional differences continue to widen in terms of population movement, capital investment, industrial location and infrastructure provision; large areas of Catalonia are progressively abandoned in favour of others considered more profitable. These spatial inequalities are repeated in Barcelona itself and in its satellites. The *barriadas* of Greater Barcelona are social ghettoes, the products of discrimination, indiscriminate piles of housing and factories rather than ordered components of a true city; amidst increasing land prices, congestion and pollution, living conditions deteriorate until they are almost beyond reform.

Centre and Periphery in the City: Indices of Urban Poverty

The free operation of the market economy in Spain has brought about rapid national economic growth but at great social cost, not only to the peripheral provinces but to the dynamic urban-industrial centres as well. The social and economic disparities to be seen in Barcelona, between districts and between classes, between those who gain from and those who pay the price of growth, are reminiscent of conditions in Third

World cities. Indices of urban poverty are not necessarily incomes per head. When entire new districts are built without what is generally accepted in Europe to be the minimal provision of infrastructures and services, these may be used instead as valid indicators.

Squatter Settlements

The most obvious nuclei of urban poverty are the *barracas* which occupy the wasteland and the slopes of hills, and line the railway tracks and other public property, especially on the northern and eastern margins of the city. The present islands of *barraquismo* are the residue of a phenomenon which reached its peak in the 1950s and 1960s (in 1957 there were 52,377 people living in shanties on the slopes of the Montjuich hill alone); but the problem refuses to go away entirely. The figures of 4,041 shanties, containing some 22,000 people, in 1972 do not include the municipalities adjacent to Barcelona proper, nor the self-constructed, sub-standard dwellings which make up the greater part of housing in certain districts. Commonly, the *barracas* have neither electric light nor running water; an average unit of 30 square metres houses one or two families. It is a measure of the shortfall between housing demand and supply that shanty-dwellers are often ordinary workers or self-employed people who either cannot find, or cannot afford, a better dwelling. Often enough, the *barracas* have produced their own community organisations to exert pressure on the authorities for improved conditions, and in the post-Franco period have learnt how to enlist the aid of the communications media. The shanty settlements become more problematic when the original inhabitants improve their status and move on, to be replaced by gypsies and *marginats* (social outcasts).

Housing

The housing problem of Barcelona and its satellites goes beyond *barraquismo* and takes the form of what Candel has called '*barraques verticals*'—sub-standard housing in both the old centre of Barcelona and in the new working-class districts.

Over-crowding and squalor are widely evident in the historic heart of the city—the *casco antiguo*, the Barrio Gótico and the port area of the Barceloneta. The pre-Civil War Macià Plan proposed a remodelling by partial demolition and the planting of green spaces and communal services. However, to improve conditions in the old city would be a highly complex and costly operation in which neither the town council nor private enterprise has wished to get involved when there have been

so many other, and less complicated, pressures and opportunities on
the fringes of the city. The result is that a barely habitable 3 per cent
of the city's dwellings houses 9 per cent of Barcelona's total population,
at an Asiatic density of 531 persons per hectare.

The most lamentable feature of Barcelona's housing situation,
however, has been the anarchic peripheral growth arising from the
conflict between urban planning and speculative development. On the
northern and eastern fringes of the city the order and coherence of the
Ensanche come to an end and are succeeded by a confusion of high
tenement blocks, self-built houses, *barracas* and high-tension lines,
built without reference to any general development plan and often
without licence. In the process of land parcelisation from the 1950s
onwards, each landowner has decided what he would build on his
land. A common way for development companies to acquire parcels
of building land is by offering owners of small holdings or old houses
one or two apartments in the block which it is proposed to construct;
this explains the appearance of many high, narrow buildings with idio-
syncratic shapes. Houses, shops and businesses are constructed without
planning controls or services. Common problems are: irrational street
patterns; lack of paving; absence of 'bus routes or journeys of as much
as two kilometres to a 'bus stop (public transport services are most
deficient in the peripheral districts where private car ownership is least);
no running water, so that entire estates depend on public hydrants or
road tankers; irregular garbage collection, or none at all, so that
rubbish accumulates on waste land and building sites; inadequate
sanitation services, clinics, hospitals, schools, recreational space and
even shops. Building densities go well beyond acceptable limits, for
example, in the district of Montbau 508 people per hectare; Canaletes
527; southwest Besòs 612; La Mina 709.

This chaotic process has been repeated again and again, and not only
by the private developer. A notorious case is the Besòs district, developed
from 1960 onwards by the Patronato Municipal de la Vivienda de
Barcelona to house people displaced from the shanties of Montjuich and
elsewhere, and by public works schemes. Other developments have
accreted around this nucleus—the 'La Pau' estate built by the Obra
Sindical del Hogar; tenement blocks built by the COBASA company
and others along the Maresme highway—until the zone now houses
some 83,000 people. The development might have been a showpiece
for public housing policy; instead, it has been an arithmetical exercise in
accommodating the maximum number of inhabitants in the smallest
space, built without schools, hospitals or recreational spaces; in the

case of the 'La Pau' estate, 16-storey blocks of flats were constructed
without lifts. There is, in fact, often a close correlation between the
estates built by the Syndical Housing Authority (Obra Sindical del
Hogar) and the worst instances of poor building materials, bad work-
manship, inadequate services and premature deterioration. This is well
illustrated by the San Cosme housing estate in Prat de Llobregat, studied
by Wynn.

San Cosme: a Case Study

San Cosme was largely built between 1965 and 1967 as part of the state
housing programme to remove population from shanty towns in
Barcelona to adjacent municipalities. The urgency of the pressures was
such that the official housing organisations ignored legislation and by-
passed their own procedures. The choice of Prat de Llobregat to house
8,000 shanty dwellers from the slopes of Montjuich was opposed by
the local authority on the grounds of the high agricultural value of the
intensively-farmed delta site, and by the civil aviation authority because
the scheme encroached on land earmarked for the extension of Barcelona
airport; nevertheless, the site was expropriated, although it contravened
the land-use classification of the existing municipal and sub-regional
plans, as well as presenting worrying physical conditions: subsidence,
flooding, lack of gradient and pollution by industrial effluent because
the area was partly below sea level, plus a recent history of malaria
throughout the Llobregat marshes. It is not clear whether the dwellings
constructed were ever approved as up to standard by the technicians of
the Ministry of Housing, while both the Syndical Housing Authority
and the local authorities subsequently disclaimed responsibility for the
severe financial burden represented by the upkeep of roads, sewerage,
water supply, street lighting, drainage, gas supply, gardens and open
spaces.

The consequent rapid deterioration of the state is revealed in a letter
written on behalf of the inhabitants to the President of the central
government in 1973, by which time the Syndical Housing Authority
and the local authority were refusing to carry out repairs, and the
residents of San Cosme were refusing to pay their mortgages:

The Housing Area . . . is in a lamentable state. Its abandonment is
total; the zones officially destined for use as parks and gardens are
rough terrain, dirty and unkempt; there exists not one proper 'green'
area . . . A large number of the public street lights not only do not
work, but also constitute a constant danger to children who may be

electrocuted, as has already happened several times; only one of the two schools planned is in operation and instead the residents are using as temporary schools 14 buildings originally destined for use as shops. These shops are unhygienic with poor ventilation and lighting and fail to comply with any of the demands of the 'Law of Education'. There is no kindergarten and only one of the two planned day nurseries exists. Furthermore, the transport service is deficient.

As regards the houses, they are in a state of advanced disrepair. All the upper flats have leaks in the roof and there are transversal and longitudinal cracks in the walls. The walls are consistently damp and the flats, as a whole, are damp to the extent of being a health hazard. The floor tiles are coming up. The cellars are regularly flooded by waste water, producing bad smells, bringing dangers of infection and providing a breeding ground for rats and mice. The badly constructed foundations have been the cause of cracks in the upper storeys . . . having on various occasions collapsed to the great danger of the inhabitants. The outside walls, apart from the cracks, are badly finished, with materials of poor quality, that allow the passage of moisture. The interior is also badly finished, with the interior walls damp and covered with mould and flaking plaster.

A report on San Cosme by the Provincial Director of Health is even more telling:

the cellars were inundated with waste water which had escaped from the sewage system, filling the building with foul-smelling gases. In some houses . . . there were cesspools in the cellars, which had to be emptied every 15 days . . . patches of moss are beginning to appear on the roof of many houses . . . on the floor of these cellars there is a foul-smelling sludge of more than 5 centimetres depth. There is a serious danger of short circuits in the electrical system and a consequent risk of fire. People who enter the cellars are in danger of being electrocuted . . . The rat problem is reaching dramatic proportions; the residents use rat powder to try to keep down the numbers, but . . . in No. 65 . . . the ceiling is covered with yellow-brown stains with the characteristic smell of rat excreta coming from the unhabited (by humans) flat above. The school is very small . . . There is only one lavatory for all the children, and one wash basin and no drinking water, no playground and the same danger from rats. The inside of the classroom is very cold . . . The children have to play in the street and so run the risk of being knocked down, as happened some days ago when a child suffered serious abdominal injuries. In the whole Housing Area there is not one sign limiting traffic speeds, nor are there any traffic lights. In front of the school, children who do not attend the school often gather to insult, swear and throw stones at the pupils . . . I was pleasantly surprised by the civility and maturity of the Residents' leaders, given the desperate situation in which they find themselves . . . Nevertheless, the atmosphere is tense, approaching crisis point. The residents have not paid rents for two months and they express their reasoning in the following ways: 'We will always pay if it is fair and they treat us like human beings'.

Public Services

Logically, immigrants in search of industrial or commercial employment require not only jobs and housing but also education, health provision, transport and recreational opportunities; but with inadequate central and local government funds (the result of fiscal, banking and investment systems under which the fruits of economic growth and speculation have not gone to improve general living conditions but into further economic growth and speculation) the unsatisfied demand for services has to be met by the private sector. But large segments of the population—and precisely the neediest strata—cannot afford private services. The private sector, substituting for what would normally be public responsibilities, tends to mask the inadequacies of government; but it is utopian, of course, to imagine that the free market system, of its own volition, is going to satisfy all popular needs. The private sector seeks profit and provides only those services which are easiest to introduce and which offer the greatest returns, for example, schools and kindergartens; naturally, it shows no interest in other facilities which are no less desirable, such as parks and gardens, and it either avoids the poorer districts or appears there only in a cheap and shoddy way. Sometimes even basic services such as electricity supplies, water, drainage, road surfacing and flood control measures are laid on and paid for by despairing residents themselves.

The lack of open space and even open air, the level of traffic pollution, the deplorable state of drainage, sewerage and refuse disposal, the lack of supervision of food markets—all call for adequate health and sanitary provision. Yet Barcelona in 1970 had a deficit of 100,000 hospital beds; in some working-class districts there was only one dispensary for over

20,000 people; in the whole Metropolitan Area there were only two social security residences. The World Health Authority considers an adequate hospital provision to be 10 beds per 1,000 inhabitants; the index in Barcelona is 5, and in the satellite towns of Badalona and L'Hospitalet only 1.35 and 0.3. The high ratio of private medical provision in Barcelona (63 per cent of hospital beds) does not make up the deficiencies.

Even if viewed only from the economic standpoint, the failure of the authorities to build enough schools and the large numbers of children dropping out of the education system bode ill for the future competitive position of Barcelona face-to-face with new technology and greater commercial rivalries within the European Community. In 1970 there was a deficit of 170,964 school places in the city; in District II (the free port area) only 40 per cent of children in the obligatory school attendance age of 6 to 13 actually had school places. Seventy per cent of education in Barcelona is in private establishments, often deficient in both physical equipment and quality of staff; in L'Hospitalet, an immigrant receptor, the private sector embraces 82.8 per cent of the schools and 76.1 per cent of the pupils.

In 1859 Cerdà included 380 hectares of parks in his plan for the Ensanche; of these, the 1953 Sub-regional Plan retained 129 hectares; since 1969 2 hectares of Cerdà's parks have actually been created. Barcelona city has a theoretical ratio of 13.5 square metres of open space per inhabitant, considerably less than the majority of West European cities; and this limited area is very unevenly distributed. The highest ratio – as with most other indices of urban well-being – is to be found in the West Residential District, whereas the working-class area of Poble Nou has only 0.3 square metres per inhabitant. The same can be said of the satellite municipalities such as L'Hospitalet, Badalona and Santa Coloma de Gramanet; part of the cost of their rapid growth has been the impoverishment of the natural environment and the irreparable loss of recreational space. The Tres Turóns Local Plan illustrates the process at work. The 1953 Sub-regional Plan extended and combined into one large 'urban park' the two existing small Güell and Guinardo parks on the slopes of the Tres Turóns hills. However, not only did the hills become an area of shanty development in the 1950s and 1960s, but the Barcelona Council's Tres Turóns Local Plan of 1967 allowed landowners to build seven 11-storey residential blocks on their south-facing slopes. The new Pelada Urban Park, opened in 1978, thus contains 15,000 people in dwellings ranging from high-rise flats to squatters' huts.

Views to the Future

The contradictions and failures of the 1950s, 1960s and 1970s have produced a widespread scepticism about the ability of plans and planners to exert any effective control over the growth of Barcelona. At the same time there has been an upsurge of opposition to the mechanics of this growth. All the issues reviewed in this study have come into the open since the death of General Franco in 1975 and the subsequent democratisation of Spain's politics and administration.

Public campiagns against specific planning proposals and against the general state of the metropolis were formerly almost certain to be ignored. There were few community organisations to stand up for the working class and the immigrants, and the very gigantism of Barcelona made it difficult to cultivate a collective spirit. In the 1970s a major role in putting pressure on public and private interests to improve housing and general living conditions, especially in the poorer residential areas of the inner city and the periphery, has been played by the Residents' Associations (Asociaciones de Vecinos), which have become a force in local politics and planning. As the Residents' Associations have become aware of their strength, better organised and with greater access to the media, they have conducted increasingly successful campaigns against officialdom and powerful private interests. An example is the struggle of the inhabitants of the San Cosme housing estate in Prat de Llobregat against the Syndical Housing Authority for the rehabilitation of their homes. Another private body which has campaigned against the urban chaos of Barcelona, and especially that of the periphery, has been the Círculo de Economía, a group of academics, economists and industrialists which has drawn attention to the mismanagement of the city and its problems of congestion, lack of suitable land for industrial expansion, and property speculation.

In the new democratic climate the municipal authorities themselves, especially the Metropolitan Corporation of Barcelona, have rebelled against the financial burdens imposed by uncontrolled growth and by central government constraints. Under a fresh General Metropolitan Development Plan, published in 1976 and revising—yet again—the 1953 Sub-regional Plan, the corporation is making efforts to control peripheral sprawl and to make private developers adhere to planning procedures.

The post-1975 political and administrative changes in Spain are fundamental to an improved planning future. The key issue to be resolved is the conflict between public and private interest. The combination of Catalan regional autonomy and democratic municipal elections has raised hopes that public authorities will now have the political will effectively to direct Barcelona's growth, perhaps through increased public acquisition of land (the 'patrimony' proposed in the 1956 Land and Urban Planning Act), and that the populace and its elected representatives will be involved in the preparation and implementation of plans. In 1976 new state housing policies introduced fresh administrative and technical regulations, and a Land Law Reform Act (revising the 1956 Act) provided a new legal, administrative and planning framework, including 'Special Plans' for remodelling existing built-up areas through decongestion schemes, new urban and community services, and improved traffic circulation and environmental conditions. Under this legislation the central authorities (Ministry of Housing, Ministry of Public Works and Urban Affairs), the local authorities and the Residents' Associations are cooperating to remodel and re-equip housing estates (such as San Cosme) and shanty areas (such as Ramón Casellas). The active participation of the residents themselves in the planning process has shown that there is no lack of interest, energy and skills on their part. It was essentially the absence of democratic institutions and popular involvement which enabled private developers, in collusion with public authorities, to dominate and warp the growth of Barcelona during the Franco period.

Under the dictatorship Catalonia did not exist as a separate entity; its four provinces were administered from Madrid in the same way as the other 46 in Spain. Not surprisingly, post-Franco Catalan thinking sees the future development of the whole of Catalonia taking place through a regional framework of the Catalans' own devising, substituting the old provincial division favoured by the central government. The reconstitution in 1977 of the Generalitat (Catalonia's traditional form of autonomous government) and the restoration of autonomy in 1979 devolve substantial powers to the Catalans. They are to be responsible for their own economic development, including town and country planning, the regulation of agriculture, fisheries and industry, transport, energy and public works. It thus becomes realistic to think once more of planning Catalonia as a unit — a return to the idea of 'Catalunya ciutat' envisaged by Pau Vila in the 1920s, with Barcelona as the potentialising centre of a network of cities based on the resources of the different sub-regions. This concept finds favour among the new middle class of administrative, industrial and service sector cadres, and among students — especially among the ever-more numerous students from the peripheral areas of Catalonia. Such elements do not admit the division of Catalonia into privileged and neglected areas; this is seen as a threat to the newly-acknowledged unity of the region—a constitutional collectivity with its own historical traditions, economy and society.

A more effective regional division of Catalonia in accordance with its resources and potential implies a multi-disciplinary study of the structure of Catalan space and the publication of an inventory of resources—human, mineral, agricultural, industrial, ecological—in the form, for instance, of a National Atlas of Catalonia. Upon this basis a regional plan for Catalonia could be constructed which would define the urban hierarchy and assess the need at each level for public services and communications, decentralise industry in relation to each sub-region's potential, and indicate a rational land use related to agricultural possibilities and the need to protect the natural environment.

The 1979 Catalan Statute of Autonomy tacitly asserts the belief that the traditional European nation state is now too small for some purposes and too large for others. It may be regarded not only as a natural reaction against the extreme centralisation of power in Madrid between 1939 and 1975 but also as a step towards greater efficiency. Each regional entity, each level of administration in the 'Catalonia of the *comarcas*', ought to be equipped with the legal status, the decision-making apparatus and the economic means to face up to its own problems and to make sure that local interests are recognised. Because urban and regional planning imply previous economic planning, each sub-region ought to have its own organisation for the study of development possibilities, instead of leaving this to uncontrolled private initiative. This plurality of power, with executive control vested in local assemblies, is not incompatible with harmonious planning; the sub-regions might be grouped—for instance, for the sharing of certain services—into larger economic regions, as proposed in the Divisió Territorial de la Generalitat in 1936.

The Statute of Autonomy now empowers the Catalans to administer the social services, education, social security and cultural activities, and above all to collect and spend their own taxes and control local savings banks—above all, because none of these devolved powers would mean anything in practice unless they were accompanied by financial decentralisation. Central control of public finance and tax revenue has traditionally been extremely strong in Spain. In the last years of the Franco regime 92.6 per cent of tax income went to public spending whose destination was decided in Madrid; 49.1 per cent of town council resources and 67.0 per cent of provincial council resources were allotted by the central administration, which furthermore retained a degree of control over the way they were spent. Spain's fiscal system in general has remained anachronistic in comparison with the country's level of development. While the public spending sector of most advanced OECD countries equals 30 to 40 per cent of their GNP, in Spain in the early 1970s it amounted to only 20 per cent; and while progressive income tax and other flexible automatic taxes provide 40 per cent of government income in the United Kingdom, in Francoist Spain they provided less than one per cent. Spain has traditionally relied on indirect taxes and on taxes on production. If they are to exercise their own devolved powers, the local authorities will need to be able to impose local taxes, besides augmenting their budgets from central government subsidies and a greater share in the income raised by the central government; and this will call for continuing reforms in Spain's fiscal practices and in the Law of Local Administration.

The insertion of the Barcelona Metropolitan Area into a hierarchy of sub-regional and regional plans for the whole of Catalonia would help to avoid some of the conflicts described in this study and would create a planning framework large enough to admit imaginative options. Besides the new democratic climate which raises hopes of more effective urban and regional planning, Barcelona is experiencing something of a breathing space as economic recession diminishes the flow of migrants from the countryside. Nevertheless, several basic questions remain to be asked. Will not agglomeration pressures reassert themselves when the economy picks up again? Although Barcelona is becoming less and less industrial and more and more a tertiary centre, will this process really persuade industry to decentralise over an area of such size and with such difficulties of terrain and communications as Catalonia? Can the brake be put on the continuing accumulation of amenities and services, bureaucratic activities, health and education provision, science and art in Barcelona? When Spain enters the European Community, will not Barcelona's role and opportunities be reinforced? At the autonomy level, delays in delegating powers to the Generalitat make it clear that old attitudes and policies in Madrid die hard—as they must, since personnel do not change overnight. Will finance be forthcoming to allow regional and sub-regional devolution to function?

At the social level it is difficult to be optimistic about the future of a conurbation like Barcelona, in which people have ceased to be individuals and have become mere ciphers manipulated by planners and developers. Man is no longer the measure of the city but often its victim. And yet, although Barcelona exhibits most of the problems (congestion, pollution, overburdened services and infrastructures, high cost but low quality housing) which some would see as putting limits to metropolitan growth, and a scarcity of those elements which are supposed to constitute major attractions to urban immigrants, such as education and medical provision, there is no evidence of growth coming to a halt. The metropolis continues to expand, first of all, by organically planning and scheming to cope with the problems which beset it, before they reach a critical level; and secondly, because immigrants are prepared to contend with these problems. They believe their present personal difficulties to be only temporary and that they can overcome them; they perceive their lot to have improved; they expect fresh opportunities around the corner—if not for themselves, then for their children; they do not wish to lose face by returning to their home towns and villages; and they cannot contemplate a return to agricultural work. The very few rural immigrants who state that they would like to go back to the countryside stipulate a decent-sized farm, with good soils—that is, the very conditions whose absence drove them to the city; and the very small number who do, in fact, express any desire to go back permanently to their areas of origin says a lot about the quality of life in those areas. Faced with these facts, it seems specious to suggest that many immigrants would have been glad not to have had to move, and to have found employment in their own area, had there been a regional policy to promote this, rather than having to confront the daily aggravation of life in Barcelona.

References

Alio, M.A. (1977) 'La evolución de un núcleo suburbano barcelonés: Sant Boi de Llobregat', *Revista de Geografía, 11(1-2)*, 69-87

Banco Urquijo, Servicio de Estudios en Barcelona, (1972) *Génesis y Problemática del Area Metropolitana de Barcelona*, Editorial Moneda y Crédito, Madrid

Bariatua San Sebastián, J.M. (1977) *Las Asociaciones de Vecinos*, Instituto de Estudios de Administración Local, Madrid

Bohigas, O. (1973) *Barcelona entre el Plan Cerdà y el Barraquisme*, Ediciones 62, Barcelona

Borja, Lleixa, Sola-Morales and Verrie (1971) 'El habitat en Barcelona', *Construcción, Arquitectura y Urbanismo, No. 10*, Barcelona

Borja, J. (1973) 'Planeamiento y crecimiento urbanos de Barcelona, 1939-58', *Construcción, Arquitectura y Urbanismo, No. 22*, Barcelona

Busquets Grau, J. (1976) *Las Urbanizaciones Marginales de Barcelona*, ETSAB, Barcelona

Carreño Piera, L. (1976) 'Proceso de suburbialización en la comarca de Barcelona', *Ciudad y Territorio, 1/76*, Madrid

Casassas i Simó, L. (1977) *Barcelona i l'Espai Català*, Curial, Barcelona

Círculo de Economía, (1973) *¿Gestión o Caos? —El Area Metropolitana de*

Barcelona, Ariel, Barcelona

Colegio de Ingenieros de Caminos, Canales y Puertos, (1976) *Ildefonso Cerdá (1815-1876), Catálogo de la Exposición Commemorativa del Centenario de su Muerte*, Barcelona

Duran i Sanpere, A. (1972) *Barcelona i la seva Historia*, Curial, Barcelona

Esteva Fabregat, C. (1973) 'Aculturación y urbanización de inmigrados en Barcelona. ¿Cuestión de etnia o cuestión de clase?', *Ethnica, No. 5*, Barcelona

—— (1974) 'Aculturación lingüística de inmigrados en Barcelona', *Ethnica, No. 8*, Barcelona

Figuerola, L. de (1968) *Estadística de Barcelona en 1849*, Instituto de Estudios Fiscales, Madrid

Galera, M., F. Roca, and S. Tarrago (1972) *Atlas de Barcelona*, Colegio Oficial de Arquitectos de Cataluña y Baleares, Barcelona

Madariaga, M. (1972) 'La planificación parcial en la comarca de Barcelona', *Cuadernos de Arquitectura y Urbanismo, No. 87*, Barcelona

Marti, F., and E. Morena (1974) *Barcelona ¿A Donde Vas?*, Editorial Dirosa, Barcelona

Martorell, V., and A. Florensa (1970) *Historia del Urbanismo en Barcelona*, Editorial Labor, Barcelona

Medhurst, K.N. (1973) 'The central-local axis in Spain', *Iberian Studies, II(2)*, 81-7

—— (1973) *Government in Spain*, Pergamon, Oxford

Miró, J., E. Sena and F. Miralles (1974) *La Catalunya Pobra*, Editorial Nova Terra, Barcelona

Naylon, J. (1981) 'Iberia', in H.D. Clout (ed.) *Regional Development in Western Europe*, 2nd ed., Wiley, Chichester

Olive, M.J. (1974) 'Crecimiento urbano y conflictualidad en la aglomeración barcelonesa. El caso de Santa Coloma de Gramanet', *Revista de Geografía, 8(1-2)*, 99-127

—— (1975) 'Los efectos sociales y urbanos del crecimiento en Santa Coloma de Gramanet', in Servicio de Estudios en Barcelona, Banco Urquijo, *Localización Económica y Desarrollo Regional*, Tomo II, Editorial Moneda y Crédito, Barcelona

Rodríguez, A. and R. d'Alòs-Moner (1978) *Economía y Territorio en Catalunya. Los Centros de Gravedad de Población, Industria y Renta*, Banco Mas Sardà, Servicio de Estudios/Ediciones Alba, SA, Barcelona

Sabater Cheliz, J. (1977) 'Proceso de urbanización en Barcelona y su traspais', *Ciudad y Territorio, 3/77*, Madrid

Serratosa, A. (1977) 'Del Plan Comarcal de Barcelona al Plan Director de Cataluña', *Ciudad y Territorio, 2/77*, Madrid

Sola-Morales, M. (1972) 'Las propuestas del Plan Director', *Cuadernos de Arquitectura y Urbanismo, No. 87*, Barcelona

——, T. Busquets, M. Domingo, A. Font and J.L. Gómez Ordóñez (1974) *Barcelona*, Editorial Gustavo Gili, SA, Barcelona

Tarrago, M. (1971) 'Els Tres Turons', *Cuadernos de Arquitectura y Urbanismo, No. 86*, Barcelona

—— L. Brau and C. Teixidor (1973) 'Planificación y crecimiento de Barcelona y su área, 1958-71', *Construcción, Arquitectura y Urbanismo, No. 22*, Barcelona

Terán, F. de (1977) 'Notas para la historia del planeamiento de Barcelona. La era de Franco', *Ciudad y Territorio, 2/77*, Madrid

Various, (1971) 'Los espacios libres en Barcelona', Vols. I, II, *Cuadernos de Arquitectura y Urbanismo, Nos. 83 & 86*

Various, (1972) 'Barcelona como modelo de ciudad capitalista', *2C Construcción de la Ciudad, No. 10*, Barcelona

Vidal Bendito, T. (1976) *La Despoblación del Campo en Cataluña*, Resumen de
  Tesis, Universidad de Barcelona, Secretariado de Publicaciones, Intercambio
  Científico y Extensión Universitario, Ediciones de la Universidad de Barcelona,
  Barcelona
Vilà Valentí, J. (1960) 'El origen de la industria catalana moderna', *Estudios
  Geográficos, Año 21, No. 78*, 5-40
Vilaseró, M. *et al.* (1977) *Las Asociaciones de Vecinos en la Encrucijada: El
  Movimiento Ciudadano en 1976-77*, Barcelona
Wynn, M.G. (1978) *San Cosme*, OECD Plan Implementation Case Study Series,
  Department of Town and Country Planning, Trent Polytechnic, Nottingham
____ (1979) 'Barcelona – planning and change 1860-1976', *Town Planning Review*,
  April
____ (1979) 'Peripheral urban growth in Barcelona in the Franco period', *Iberian
  Studies, 8(1)*, 3-13

7 WARSAW

Keith Grime and Grzegorz Węcławowicz

This chapter is divided into five sections. A brief résumé is provided of the historical development of Warsaw which concludes with the establishment of the Socialist Republic in 1945. We have resisted the temptation to deal with the restoration of historical buildings and, in particular, with the rebuilding of the old (Stare Miasto) and new (Nowe Miasto) towns because we feel this is adequately covered elsewhere (Ciborowski 1969; Jankowski and Ciborowski 1978) and we wish to concentrate on post-war developments and problems. Accordingly, we have dwelt at some length on post-war housing construction which leads on to a consideration of population distribution. Successive post-war plans for Warsaw are discussed in the framework of national planning objectives and finally we present the current proposals for the city in the context of the latest national plan.

Historical Development

To understand Warsaw it is essential to be familiar with its history and the role the city has played in the development of Poland. The origin of the city dates back some 700 years but its future importance was assured in 1596 when the royal court was moved from Krakow. In that year Warsaw became the capital of Poland and began to expand. By the end of the eighteenth century the population had reached 120,000 but with the partition of Poland between the three powers of Austria, Russia and Prussia, which was completed in 1794, many people deserted the city and its population was halved.

Even though the national state ceased to exist, Warsaw continued to fulfil the role of capital for the Polish people. Economic stagnation in the first half of the nineteenth century can be directly attributed, however, to this loss of status. Indeed, economic development did not really get underway until 1864 when the peasants were emancipated as a result of the January Insurrection against Tsarist Russia which led, as Figure 7.1 clearly shows, to more rapid population increase and the start of a trend which continued unabated to 1939. In addition the first railway to connect Warsaw with the Upper Silesian coalfield had

Figure 7.1: Population Change in Warsaw, 1800-1977

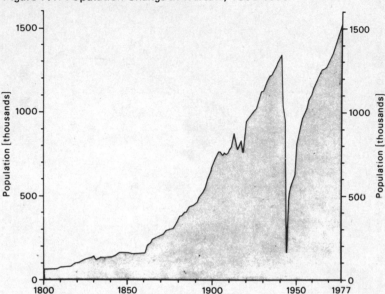

been opened in 1848, which strongly affected industrial development. This railway had a powerful effect on urban spatial structure leading to the decline of the existing industrial area situated along the Vistula valley dependent on river transport, and promoting the growth of the western industrial district in Wola. Development on the east bank (Praga), however, had to await the construction of the first permanent road bridge in 1863 and the opening of three railway lines leading to the east between 1862 and 1877 in which year the east and west bank systems were connected by the Gdanski bridge. The development of Warsaw in the second half of the nineteenth century can best be illustrated by comparing its growth with other European cities. Between 1850 and 1914 it moved from the seventeenth to the eighth largest city in Europe. This dynamic growth was all the more remarkable if we take into account the fact that Warsaw was the 'capital' of a 'non-existing state'.

The spatial development of the city was restricted by the nineteenth century fortifications and the high density of population in a relatively small area (Figure 7.2a) was partly attributable to this constraint. During World War I the city boundary was extended, as it has been several times since. However, in spite of this increase in area, the development of Warsaw was halted during the period 1914-18 because

Figure 7.2a: Density of Population in 1897 by kilometre grid square   b: Density of Population in 1931 by kilometre grid square

B

Nowy Dwór Maz

Radzymin

Wołomin

Otwock

Pruszków

Bronie

Grodzisk Maz

Góra Kalwaria

DENSITY PER KM² 1931

< 300   300-599   600-1199   1200-2399   >2399

A

Nowy Dwór Maz

R. Narew

Radzymin

Kobyłka

Warszawa

R. Wisła

Bronie

Góra Kalwaria

DENSITY PER KM² 1897

< 300   300-599   600-1199   1200-2399   >2399

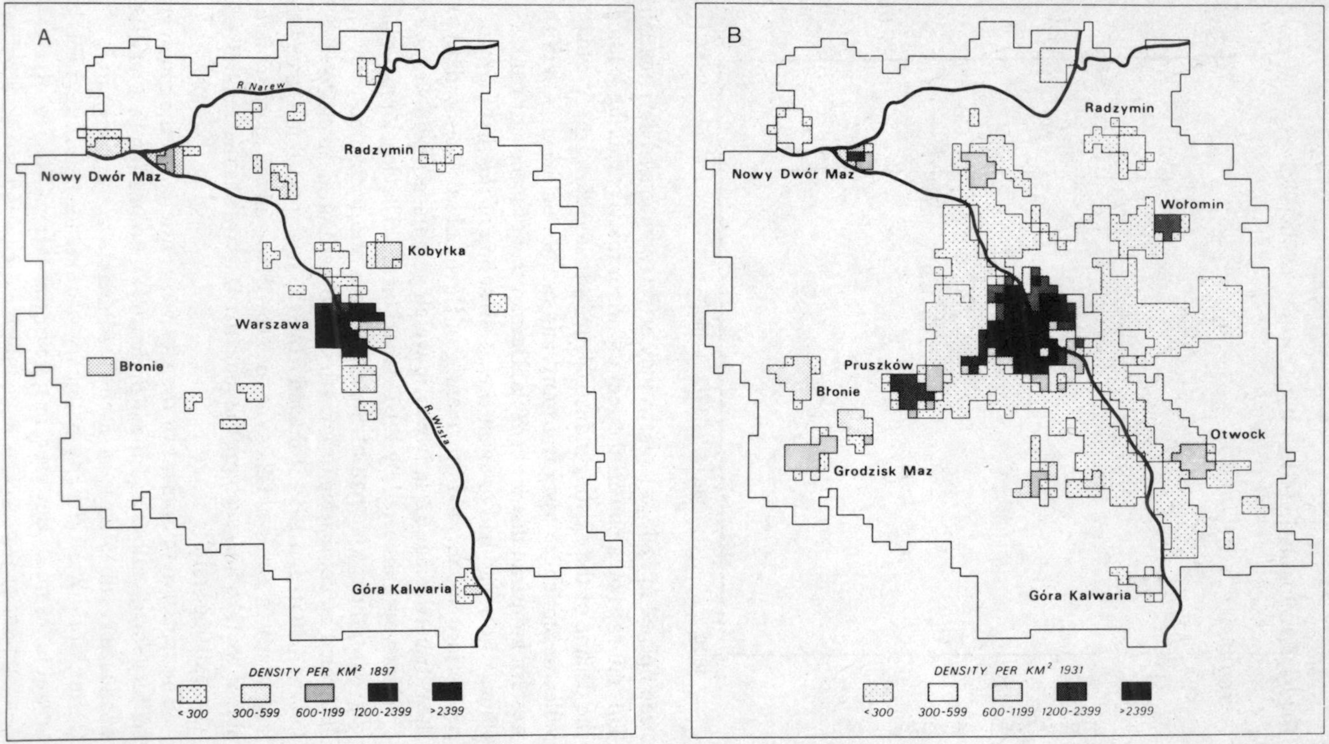

industrial plants were transferred from Warsaw into what were regarded by the Russians as strategically safer locations further east and substantial numbers of people were evacuated (Figure 7.1). In 1918 Poland gained its independence and Warsaw once again became the state capital. This increased the rate of development of cultural, scientific, political and economic functions. The high level of migration to the city after 1918, coupled with the poor infrastructure and housing, intensified the problems which already existed. Not all the migrants could be accommodated within the city because of the shortage of housing and while the city increased by 25.8 per cent the outer zone population rose by 80 per cent in the period 1921-31. During this period the development of the Warsaw agglomeration gained impetus.

This expansion was facilitated by improvements in railway transport which had taken place between 1896 and 1914. New suburban stations were constructed on existing routes and three narrow gauge lines were built. Along these routes some new development occurred which was originally intended for recreation while other settlements were transformed from rural to urban places. Many of the recreational houses soon became permanent homes especially in the west of the city but in the east the recreational function was, in many cases, maintained.

In 1931 (Figure 7.2b) we can see for the first time the general shape of the developing Warsaw agglomeration. The main directions were in the west to Grodzisk, in the east to Wołomin, and south to Otwock. Linear suburban development was the settlement pattern which resulted from the construction of an electrified railway from Warsaw to Pruszków and Grodzisk, opened in part in 1927, and it was emphasised still more by the electrification of the existing lines to Grodzisk and Wołomin in 1936.

The development of the Warsaw agglomeration in the 1920s and 1930s was to a large extent uncontrolled. Transport improvements led to speculative development in housing. There were two opposite processes in operation: high income groups were moving out from the overcrowded city centre searching for more space, larger houses and a better physical environment, while low income groups from rural areas who were unable to gain access to the city also settled in the periphery usually along roads which led into the city providing the essential link with workplaces. This chaotic development led to segregation of social groups in the periphery and on occasions to the mixing of functions so that housing services and industry developed in the same zone. Frequently, however, the speculation resulted in a dispersed settlement pattern making it impossible to provide infrastructure such as water, gas, electricity and, in many cases, surfaced roads.

The development of the city and agglomeration of Warsaw until 1939 was shaped, therefore, by several factors: firstly, continuous industrialisation; secondly, uncontrolled population growth; thirdly, the rebirth of Polish Statehood and the recovery by Warsaw of its capital functions; and fourthly the low level of economic development of the whole country.

The first attempt at physical planning was in 1916 when the Circle of Architects (Koło Architektów) guided by Tolwinski, Jawornicki and Jankowski made proposals for the modernisation of the city. They suggested many innovations including the cross-city railway line under one of the city centre's major east-west thoroughfares, Aleje Jerozolimskie, two new bridges across the Vistula and two river ports in addition to many new road improvements. This 1916 work provided a basis for subsequent plans in 1920, 1923 and 1928 but the first plan to receive ministerial approval (Ministerstwo Robot Publicznych) was introduced in 1931. It proposed definite zones within the city centre for commerce, banking and offices and suggested plot ratios and building heights for 10 zones throughout the whole city. The plan as a whole had little chance of success because the city owned only 20 per cent of the land and there were continuous disagreements between the local and central authorities.

The main principle underlying each successive plan followed a general trend for the formation of the town which was connected with economic development, for example Śródmieście (the central part of the city) was slowly by natural process and planning converted into a Central Business District. Węcławowicz (1979) has shown that between 1921 and 1938 the population decline in the central area gathered momentum. Certain housing developments, especially those in Żoliborz, and private areas of Mokotow and Saska Kępa represented new spatial departures from the east-west trend which had been imposed on the city by the alignment of the railway in the nineteenth century. The development in Saska Kępa was made possible by the building of the new Poniatowski bridge which Ciborowski (1969) claims drew the 'well to do' away from the overcrowded centre and provided individual houses in relatively low density development on the east bank of the Vistula. Other schemes from the 1930s which are worthy of mention but which, unfortunately, were not implemented were those to construct a new city centre on the area known as Mokotów Field, a large area just to the south of the existing centre which had become available for development when the city's airport was moved to Okęcie in 1932, and the proposals to provide an underground railway, which is still not built, but which appears in future proposals. A major piece of new investment, however, was the cross-town railway line which was placed in a tunnel beneath the Aleje Jerozolimskie and continued across the Vistula on a new bridge.

Perhaps the most innovative pre-war housing project was completed by the Warsaw Housing Co-operative (WSM) on land owned by the city. The co-operative planned on a large scale and attempted to provide the best possible facilities for its members. As a result, the WSM design offices and building sites became experimental workshops where the latest ideas in town planning were tested and put into practice (Ciborowski 1969). The significance of the WSM project in Żoliborz was that it provided the development with its own shops, laundry, central heating plant, schools, kindergarten and children's playgrounds; acted as a model for other estates in Warsaw, Łódz and Gdynia; and guided the planners of urban development in the post war reconstruction.

Many European cities suffered war-time devastation and many have been subsequently redeveloped, but none on such a scale as Warsaw. On the eve of World War II, Warsaw housed 1,300,000 people which increased to around 1,800,000 by the end of 1940. This growth was made up partly of Poles who had been evicted from towns and villages in the west of Poland, and partly of Jews who were brought to live in the ghetto. During the war Warsaw faced a specific type of town planning. The Germans intended to replace the Polish city with a new town which would house 100,000 Germans on the west and 80,000 Polish slaves on the east bank of the Vistula (Pabst Plan 1940). In 1942 they actually started rehousing the indigenous population from the area of Aleje Ujazdowskie and Plac Unii Lubelskie (south of the city centre) to create the first German district and in 1943 they started to demolish the area of the ghetto (to the north of the city centre in Muranów) during the uprising. Systematically they proceeded to destroy the city, intensifying their efforts during the Warsaw uprising of 1944 and continuing until liberation. Losses incurred through bombing, street fighting and planned extermination left only 162,000 people in 1945. The physical structure of the city was also destroyed; some 72 per cent of dwelling units along with 90 per cent of industrial buildings were damaged beyond repair.

Post-war Housing Construction and Policy

The wholesale destruction of the housing stock caused a major problem. The spontaneous return of the Warsaw population demanded immediate action. An Act fixing rents at the 1939 level was one of the first pieces of legislation to be introduced in an attempt to stop speculation. The principle that housing should be available irrespective of income and the allocation process based on need was adopted as the means of attaining social justice.

In addition to rent control city councils were empowered to direct families without accommodation to live in privately owned houses which were under-occupied. The housing commission in each city was therefore able to redistribute the housing stock on a more equitable basis, but the actual houses remained in private hands. This indicates that immediately after the war the main characteristic of housing policy was concerned with making full use of the existing stock rather than concentrating on new building. Initially, reconstruction and rehabilitation was financed spontaneously by both private and public capital. Soon, however, this spontaneous investment was replaced by organised planning action.

The first three-year national plan of reconstruction of the economy covering the years 1947-9 concentrated almost exclusively on industry, transport and agriculture. Only in Upper Silesia and Warsaw was there any substantial public investment in new housing. In 1947 standards were laid down for new housing construction and in the following year investment was centralised by the creation of the Institute of Workers' Housing Estates (Zaklad Osiedli Robotniczych). By 1949 private and co-operative investment was strongly discouraged by the negative attitude of the government and in the period 1949-55 new housing was provided and financed mainly by the state. The role of co-operatives was limited to the administration and maintenance of the stock they owned.

The six-year plan of heavy industrialisation (1950-6) coincided with the period of reduced expenditure on housing, indeed it goes a long way towards explaining it. The development of housing policy became subordinated to national industrial development and new housing was provided mainly in association with new industrial enterprises. The most striking aspect of this period was that demand for housing outstripped supply for there were high rates of both natural increase and household formation linked with rapid urbanisation and industrialisation.

In Warsaw, as far as co-operative housing is concerned, the period

1945-9 saw the continuation of trends already begun in the 1930s. The Warsaw Housing Co-operative's Estate at Żoliborz was extended and a start was made on reconstructing war damaged buildings. In the Kolo district of the city Helena and Szymon Syrkus designed an estate which used pre-fabricated units which were later adopted in state and co-operative housing in Mokotów and Muranow.

Major changes in architectural style were introduced into Warsaw from the Soviet Union almost as soon as peace had been declared in 1945. The new doctrine, known as 'Socialist Realism',[1] was founded on, among other things, the principle of protecting Polish architecture and town planning against the influences of cosmopolitan, Western architecture (Chrościcki and Rottermund 1978). The MDM (Marszalkowska Housing District) and the Palace of Culture and Science are perhaps the best examples in the city centre, although housing estates such as Praga II should also be mentioned. The MDM, which has as its centre piece the Plac Konstytucji, is a classic example of town planning from this period. Situated just to the south of the city, the colonnades, the heavy stonework and the wide streets are features which distinguish the style from all others. In Praga II the flats are built around courtyards with the focus of the development, Plac Juliana Lenskiego, being centrally placed. In the Plac are shops, a restaurant, bus station and landscaped gardens. The flats, although small, are well built and compare favourably with later multi-storey blocks in design and facilities.

The leadership of the Communist Party (Polish United Workers Party, PZPR) changed in 1956 and a new attitude towards investment priorities emerged. Less emphasis was placed on heavy industrial development which enabled an increase to be made in the proportion of total investment devoted to housing. In the period 1956-60 the average yearly figure increased to 19.4 per cent. In Warsaw marginally lower rates of natural increase together with reduced in-migration slightly eased the pressure on housing and a start could be made on remedying the acute shortages. In 1958 a new national housing policy was introduced. Housing co-operatives which had their origins in pre-war days were now given official encouragement, thereby drawing private funds into the house building programme to help increase the total annual output. The co-operatives have commanded an increasing share of new construction ever since. Many people joined them for they were seen as a real alternative to the state system and afforded an opportunity for people to have some control over their future housing provision. Also loans, at low interest rates, were provided by the state for private house building. The new housing policy was linked with rent increases, for previously rent levels had been so low that maintenance costs were not even covered and the stock was rapidly deteriorating.

Throughout the whole of the post-war period the distribution of flats has been closely related to employment policy. Nationally, this has meant that where new industrial enterprises have been established, housing has, in theory, been provided. Within Warsaw, for example, workers at the steelworks have in many cases been provided with flats in Żoliborz. The link between housing and workplace was particularly strong in the period 1950-6, when public housing was practically the only source of supply. One of the elements of new housing policy formulated in 1958 and modified after 1960 was that municipal housing was mainly available to those in greatest housing need because of low income or bad housing. The drastic limitation after 1965 in the state sector resulted in most of the economically weaker households having to find their flats in the more expensive co-operative sector. Co-operatives were called upon to fulfil a social function and also to cover the needs of employment policy. These two factors changed the character of the housing co-operatives and the state assumed much greater control over them. This situation remains true to the present day.

In spite of the rapid increase in the co-operative building sector the state continued to be the dominant provider until 1965. Generally in the period 1960-5 decreasing investment in housing to an average of 16.1 per cent per annum was caused by the difficult economic situation. Not only did investment fall but the quality of housing was reduced in both sectors. Between 1966 and 1970 the demand for housing increased because the age group born in the immediate post-war period was now marrying and forming new households. The proportion of total investment devoted to housing once again fell in this period, however, to 14 per cent. Supply was unable to match demand because of under investment in the building supply industry.

As a result of another change in leadership, the political attitude to the housing problem changed sharply yet again in 1970. Housing became a key issue in the economic and social development programme of the Polish United Workers Party (PZPR). In 1971 the party proposed a long term programme designed to increase the supply of housing and ensure that each family should have a separate flat by the second half of the 1980s. To implement this strategy new prefabricated building techniques were introduced on a massive scale which has led to the design and construction of increasingly large housing areas.

In Warsaw the first larger estates were actually built between 1957 and 1965. Early examples are to be found in Bielany and Batory with later even bigger versions developed at Bródno, Młociny and Stegny. The largest estate in Śródmieście is Za Żelazną Bramą. It is located near the city centre. The area consists mainly of slab blocks of 16 storeys. This type of development was the outcome of the search for the least expensive solutions at the expense of social and structural values (Jankowski and Ciborowski 1978).

As a result of introducing new building techniques from 1970 onwards the scale of development has increased even more. The housing district of Ursynów in the south of the city covers an area as large as the whole of the city centre and is intended to house 150,000 people. This development was planned on an assumption that a metro would serve the area and link it to the city centre but nothing has been built nor has the main spine road been constructed and the transport problem, already large, will be greater in the future.

In the 30 year period from 1945 to 1975 approximately 400,000 apartments have been either rebuilt or erected in the city. The latest flats are equipped with gas and electricity while hot water and central heating are usually provided by district heating schemes. In spite of this tremendous effort 30 per cent of the apartments are officially overcrowded and 25 per cent of families[2] do not have their own flats. As Jankowski and Ciborowski (1978) comment 'Warsaw's housing needs have not yet been completely fulfilled and it will still be some years before there is an individual apartment for every family'. Many of the flats (including some built since the war) have a low provision of basic amenities. Some 30 per cent have no mains water supply, 35 per cent have no WC and 40 per cent are lacking a bathroom.

These figures and comments clearly indicate that future investment in housing must be maintained at a high level, but although demand continues to outstrip supply, it would be gross misrepresentation not to point out some of the improvements which have taken place since 1931. Table 7.1 shows that overcrowding has been reduced—the average number of persons per flat having fallen from 4.70 to 2.89 and persons per room from 2.07 to 1.03. Of course, family size is generally lower now than pre-war and that, in itself, reduces the gross densities. In Srodmiescie for example there are now some 300,000 living in an area which before the war housed 800,000. The city as a whole covers an area three times larger than before the war (Figure 7.2b), and there are now over twice as many flats but the population has increased by only 23.5 per cent. Overall the shortfall of flats is substantial and even official estimates admit that there will still be

Table 7.1: Housing in Warsaw: Selected Indices, 1931-77

	1931	1950	1960	1970	1977
Number of apartments	249,100	193,645	307,480	407,963	530,105
Number of rooms	566,135	404,674	696,034	1,035,585	1,453,118
Average number of rooms in an apartment	2.27	2.09	2.26	2.54	2.74
Average number of people to an apartment	4.70	4.00	3.58	3.14	2.89
Average number of people to a room	2.07	1.92	1.58	1.24	1.03
Population	1,171,900	804,000	1,157,400	1,308,900	1,532,070

Source: Jankowski and Ciborowski (1978); Rocznik Statystyczny Województwa Stołecznego Warszawskiego (1978).

a deficiency in 1990.

One of the most important aspects of post-war housing policy has been the uniformity of space provision. Housing is an area in which the egalitarian principles of socialism have been systematically applied. Both in the standard of housing provision and in the allocation of dwellings the government has attempted to secure equality of opportunity (Blowers 1973). National space standards were laid down in 1951. A figure of 15.5 m² per person was established and, although this level is considered inadequate, attempts to raise it have been constrained by the necessity to produce as many units as possible to go some way to satisfying the continuing demand. Future standards will, it is hoped, be more generous and the latest plan for Warsaw suggests an increase to 19.5 m² per person by 1990.

Table 7.2 shows that, today, the co-operative sector has replaced the state as the principal investor in housing. No less than 89.3 per cent of all socialised housing built in 1977 was co-operative and in three city districts, Ochota, Praga Południe and Żoliborz, co-operatives were responsible for all the investment. In towns outside Warsaw, especially those in which major projects are in progress, the picture is much the same: Pruszków and Wołomin have all their socialised housing built by co-operatives.

Over time, however, the co-operatives themselves have evolved. Although there are 213 in existence in the Warsaw voivodship, most are simply administering an existing stock and actual development is concentrated in the hands of about six enormous enterprises. No longer do

Table 7.2: Distribution of Housing Units Built in 1977, by Town and by District within Warsaw

	Total	Socialised sector	Of which co-op sector	% of socialised sector in co-ops	Private sector
Total	16,500	15,441	13,791	89.3	1,059
Warsaw:	12,850	12,534	11,512	91.8	316
Mokotów	4,964	4,922	4,192	85:2	42
Ochota	1,064	1,007	1,007	100.0	57
Praga Południe	1,946	1,847	1,847	100.0	99
Praga Połnoc	1,788	1,757	1,668	94.9	31
Śródmieście	302	302	191	63.2	0
Wola	1,369	1,289	1,197	92.9	80
Żoliborz	1,417	1,410	1,410	100.0	7
Błonie	58	45	45	100.0	13
Brwinów	47				47
Góra Kawaria	10				10
Grodzisk Maz	38				38
Józefów	28				28
Karczew	1				1
Kobyłka	48				48
Konstancin	5				5
Legionowo	1,677	1,622	1,162	69.3	55
Marki	47				47
Milanówek	23				23
Nowy Dwór	72	60	40	66.7	12
Otwock	341	286	270	94.4	55
Ożarów Maz	16				16
Piaseczno	189	133	103	77.4	56
Piastów	33				33
Podkowa	17				17
Pruszków	404	364	364	100.0	40
Radzymin	11				11
Serock	5				5
Sulejówek	72	40	0	0.0	32
Wesoła	20	8	0	0.0	12
Wołomin	348	295	295	100.0	53
Zakroczym	29	24	0	0.0	5
Ząbki	48				48
Zielonka	63	30	0	0.0	33

Source: Rocniz Statystyczny Wòjewództwa Stołecznego Warszawskiego (1978).

they deal on a small scale for a recognisable group of workers, instead they are implementing state housing policy while deriving some funds from private sources. The co-operatives are directed by the Central Association of Housing Co-operatives (Centralny Zwiazek Spoldzielni Budownictwa Mieszkaniowego). It is possible to be a tenant or an owner in a co-operative. Most people are tenants but owner co-operatives have recently been receiving official encouragement. In some schemes, like Ursynów, the two tenure types are mixed. Tenants can transfer their tenancy to other members of the family provided they are living together and they also have a right to buy their flat. Tenants pay a lower deposit, usually 10-12 per cent of the full price, and take a loan at one per cent interest rate over 60 years. Owners in a co-operative usually pay a deposit of 25 per cent and raise a loan over 30 years. If one joins the co-operative as an owner the waiting time is usually less than for tenants and, once having joined, owners have a number of privileges. They may sell their membership and their flat on an 'open' market and in addition they get more space for the extra money they are paying. A special discount representing 30 per cent of the purchase price is available to those who complete their transaction in the first five years. Initial access to a tenant co-operative is based on present housing conditions, family size and type of job. This latter criterion is particularly important since a large proportion of flats built are distributed through the work place. Owners enter the co-operative mainly on the ability to pay and they usually benefit by obtaining a flat of a slightly larger than average size.

The private sector is still important. It continues to grow by the purchase of flats from both co-operatives and the state and by the construction of new single family houses especially in the area outside the city. In the Warsaw voivodship the private sector accounted for 6.4 per cent of all urban house building in 1977. The space provision is superior to that achieved in the socialised sector. While only 2.5 per cent of all housing completions in Warsaw city were private, it will be seen from Table 7.2 that in many of the smaller towns in the region private housing was the only type built, while in the rural areas almost all (87.1 per cent) new building was in this sector (Table 7.3). The significant difference in size between the socialised and private sectors is shown in Table 7.4. The average size of a new socialised urban housing unit in 1977 was 52.5 m^2 whereas a new private unit measured 92.1 m^2. The same variation applies also in the rural areas. Further inspection

Table 7.3: Distribution of Housing Units built in 1977 in Rural Areas

	Total	Socialised sector	Private sector	Private sector as % of total
Total	1,264	163	1,101	87.1
Błonie	114	69	45	39.5
Brwinów	47		47	100.0
Celestynów	28		28	100.0
Czosnów	25		25	100.0
Góra Kalwaria	56	10	46	82.1
Grodzisk Maz	20		20	100.0
Halinów	32		32	100.0
Jabłonna	15		15	100.0
Kampinos	25		25	100.0
Karczew	24		24	100.0
Konstancin	19		19	100.0
Leoncin	19		19	100.0
Leszno	30	6	24	80.0
Lesznowola	63	12	51	81.0
Łomianki	83		83	100.0
Michałowice	46		46	100.0
Nadarzyn	21	2	19	90.5
Nieporęt	37		37	100.0
Ożarów Maz	53	20	33	62.3
Piaseczno	67		67	100.0
Pomiechówek	29		29	100.0
Prażmów	32		32	100.0
Radzymin	28		28	100.0
Raszyn	94	24	70	74.5
Serock	27		27	100.0
Skrzeszew	5	2	3	60.0
Stare Babice	36		36	100.0
Tarczyn	77	18	59	76.6
Tułowice	11		11	100.0
Wiązowna	45		45	100.0
Wołomin	48		48	100.0
Zakroczym	8		8	100.0

Source: Rocznik Statystyczny Województwa Stołecznego Warszawskiego (1978).

Table 7.4: Comparison of Socialised and Private Sector Housing Units Built in the Warsaw Region, 1975-77

Socialised Sector

Housing units built			Average size in m^2	
	Towns	Villages	Towns	Villages
1975	23,034	345	49.8	52.8
1976	19,447	342	52.2	45.6
1977	15,441	163	52.5	48.5

Private Sector

Housing units built			Average size in m^2	
	Towns	Villages	Towns	Villages
1975	880	900	93.2	85.5
1976	996	1,013	93.0	87.7
1977	1,059	1,101	92.1	84.9

Source: Rocznik Statystyczny Województwa Stołecznego Warszawskiego (1978)

of Table 7.4 displays what might be a disturbing downward trend in housing completions in the region. In 1975 23,034 units were completed in the socialised sector, but in 1977 only 15,441. Most of the decline presumably occurred in Warsaw, for there most of the investment is concentrated. It is little consolation to note that there was a slight increase in the small private sector. The most likely explanation for the decline is that the Polish economy has been over-stretched and less investment has been allocated to housing again.

Over 76 per cent of all new housing in 1977 was geographically concentrated in Warsaw city, and within the boundary Mokotów (which includes Ursynów) had the largest share with 38.6 per cent. Apart from Śródmieście, which is almost completely built up, the other city districts had roughly equal shares of the remainder. The importance of Legionowo as a focus of new housing development is emphasised for more units were constructed there than in four of the Warsaw districts. Other out-of-town centres being developed are Otwock, Pruszków and Wołomin (Table 7.2).

Population Distribution

The Warsaw Voivodship (Figure 7.3) whose boundaries were re-defined

Figure 7.3: Warsaw Voivodship: Administrative Divisions

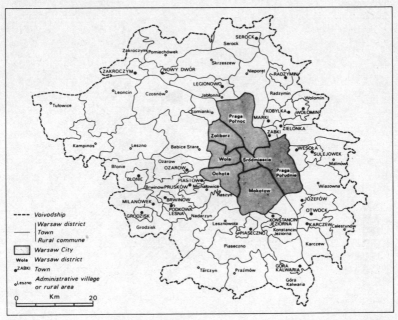

in 1975 had a population of just under one million in 1946; this had risen to 2,225,900 by 1977.

A general picture of population density for the whole voivodship is presented in Figure 7.4. It is based on information for 65 administrative divisions. It reveals a 'core' area of five districts all with population densities in excess of 3,000 persons per square kilometre. These five are all in the western part of the city which has traditionally been the area of industrial and commercial activity. Of the next three with densities between 2,000 and 2,999 people per square kilometre two are contiguous but one is an outlier in the north. This outlier is Legionowo which is currently being intensively developed. Included in the third group with over 1,500 persons per square kilometre are Praga Północ and Praga Południe with the adjacent town of Ząbki. Overall densities in the eastern bank tend to be lower than elsewhere in the city because firstly there is land zoned for housing but not yet developed and secondly substantial areas are devoted to industry. Net residential densities therefore are very much higher than the gross density presented in Figure 7.4.

Figure 7.4: Warsaw: Density of Population in 1977, by Administrative Divisions

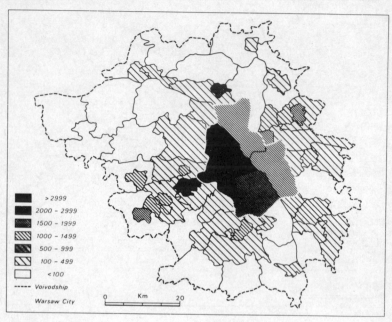

The other two towns are at either end of the south-west – north-east axis which has dominated development since the advent of the railway. The fourth group consisting of four towns located to the west of the main city and one to the south are all on commuter lines. The fifth group of eight small towns are mainly in the south-east and east of the voivodship. Otwock is already developing and others such as Nowy Dwór are earmarked for expansion. The remaining seven towns and thirty-two villages are unlikely to be developed – indeed they contain large areas of land of high value for recreation, especially the group located to the north-west of the city whose area is largely covered by the Kampinos National Park, a superb unspoilt leisure area within 30 minutes of the town centre.

The distribution of population and economic activity allowed us, for analytical purposes, to divide the Warsaw agglomeration[3] into 11 sectors (Figure 7.5 and Table 7.5). We distinguished three zones within the whole agglomeration; the central city (Śródmieście), the remaining

Figure 7.5: Warsaw Agglomeration: Zones and Sectors used to Analyse
Population Change

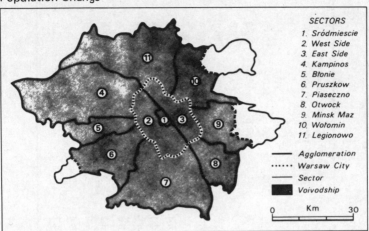

six districts of the city (inner ring) and the outer ring. The inner ring
we divided into two units separated by the Vistula while in the outer
ring we identified eight sectors. Differential growth of population
between the sectors might be the result of natural processes, planned
action, or a combination of both. In the immediate post-war period
Śródmieście had its highest rate of growth. This rate gradually slowed
until in the period 1970-6 it actually showed a decrease. Its share of
the population of the whole agglomeration has fallen by 2.3 per cent
between 1960 and 1976. The west bank experienced continuous population growth but, again over time, the rate has decreased. However,
its share of total population has steadily increased from 22.5 per cent
in 1946 to 36.1 per cent in 1976. The east bank witnessed its largest
increase in the immediate post-war period but the increase slowed down
until 1970 in which year the rate accelerated again. The left bank and
Śródmieście initially had the fastest growth because together they were
the first to be rebuilt. The right bank was, at the end of the war, relatively
undamaged and it housed almost 25 per cent of the total population. The
percentage share gradually fell in the period to 1970 in spite of the
intended policy to make each side of the city more equal in size. Since
1970 the trend has changed although the rate of growth is still lower
than on the left bank.

The Kampinos sector is extremely important for recreation and
development is strictly controlled. The small increase which did occur
during the period 1950-70 was located only in the area adjacent to the

Table 7.5: Population Change in the Warsaw Agglomeration, 1946-76

Sectors	Rate of increase in selected time periods				% share of total population					% of total area
	1946-50 1946=100	1950-60 1950=100	1960-70 1960=100	1970-76 1970=100	1946	1950	1960	1970	1976	
Whole agglomeration	128	136	113	112	100	100	100	100	100	100
Warsaw	137	138	115	111	57.6	61.6	62.6	63.0	63.3	10.5
Śródmieście	140	136	122	94	10.2	11.1	11.1	9.9	8.8	0.4
West Side	156	157	128	115	22.5	27.5	31.7	35.0	36.1	5.1
East Side	119	117	104	113	24.9	23.0	19.8	18.1	18.4	5.0
Outer ring	116	133	110	113	42.4	38.4	37.4	37.0	36.7	89.5
Kampinos	99	123	112	99	4.1	3.2	2.9	2.8	2.5	18.4
Błonie	106	134	112	102	2.1	1.7	1.7	1.6	1.5	3.7
Pruszków	114	130	115	116	12.0	10.8	10.2	10.0	10.7	9.7
Piaseczno	109	123	117	105	6.6	5.6	5.1	5.0	4.9	15.6
Otwock	150	134	109	104	3.2	3.8	3.7	3.5	3.4	5.5
Mińsk Maz	116	139	116	105	4.3	3.9	4.0	4.0	3.9	9.9
Wołomin	128	146	121	109	5.4	5.4	5.8	6.0	5.9	12.1
Legionowo	109	135	120	103	4.7	4.0	4.0	4.1	3.9	14.6

Source: Various National Census Returns.

city boundary. Its share of population fell from 4.1 per cent to 2.5 per cent. Development in the Błonie sector has been restricted because of the high quality of the land for agriculture. The Pruszków sector has been traditionally the most urbanised part of the outer ring and in spite of several attempts to restrict growth, slow but continuous development has taken place and its share of population has remained constant at around 10 per cent. An explanation for this is that there is relatively good infrastructure and certainly good access by rail and road to the city centre.

The predominantly agricultural character of the Piaseczno sector has resulted in a slow increase in population and a declining proportion of the share. A similar pattern of change is found in the Otwock sector although it does have a more recreational character. The large increase up to 1950 is explained by the fact that in this sector there were many large villas which could be crowded with homeless families who were suffering from the shortage of accommodation in Warsaw city. The three remaining sectors of Mińsk, Legionowo and Wołomin had their highest rate of increase in the 1950s. Wołomin, in contrast to the other two, has held its relatively high share of total population although it will be the northern (Legionowo) sector which will be developed most intensively in the future.

Taking the agglomeration as a whole the fastest rate of growth occurred in the immediate post-war period. This trend applied to all but three of the sectors. It is only since 1970 that the outer zone has developed more quickly than the city itself, which is partially explained by the deglomeration policies of the late 1960s and partly by the simple fact that building land in Warsaw is now a scarce resource. Indeed, the search for building land has resulted in the city area being extended three times since the war, the last being in 1977. Generally, however, the proportionate share of the various sectors has remained relatively constant throughout the post-war period.

National Planning Framework and Post-war Plans

The Spatial Planning Act of 1946 provides the legal framework for both physical (spatial) and economic planning. The Act, which was revised in 1961, set up three time-horizons for which the plans should be prepared. They are:

(1)   Five-year plans for the development of the national economy.

(2)   Perspective plans (looking forward 20 years).
(3)   Even longer term plans than the perspectives which have no fixed time period.

The post-war development of Poland can be divided into the stages covered by successive medium-term economic plans. Stage one was the three year plan of reconstruction (1947-9), followed by the six-year plan of building the foundations of a socialist economy (1950-5) and five consecutive five year plans covering the period 1956-80. Since 1957 the long term (20 year) programmes for the socio-economic development of the country have provided the basis for the medium term plans. These plans are elaborated for sectors and branches (i.e. for various industries, agriculture and transport etc.). The leading planning authority is the Planning Commission directly responsible to the Council of Ministers. Parallel to the economic plans there are spatial plans prepared on three levels; for the entire country, for voivodships (regional plans) and for towns and districts.

Although it was always intended that physical and economic plans would be developed in tandem this did not occur in the early post-war years. The slow process of integration started only after the passing of the 1961 Spatial Planning Act (Jachniak-Ganguly 1978). Malisz (1974) suggests that, even with a tidy structure, supported by the national-isation of the means of production, there are too many independent variables which influence the processes of development, thus destroying the structure of the programme. He continues 'the Polish experience has shown that, even for a twenty year period it is not feasible to establish an economic plan in the true sense of the term. It is strongly felt now that long term plans should be replaced by prognostic pro-cedures'. Broniewski (1974) considers that the local plan should be concerned with the development of any particular settlement unit and the distribution in space of such a programme. Further, he suggests that the development, extension or reconstruction of the settlement unit must be viewed as one big investment. Spatial plans tend to concentrate on allocating land to particular users. Economic planning decides what to develop and when to develop it, while spatial planning guides the location of the developments.

To facilitate both planning and reconstruction the National Council (Krajowa Rada Naradowa) established an office for the reconstruction of Warsaw (Biuro Odbudowy Stolicy) and a Ministry for Reconstruction (Ministerstwo Odbudowy) was created to co-ordinate and plan the re-construction programme. Post-war planning has had a much greater chance of success than in the inter-war period because in October 1945 all land within the 1939 city boundary was taken into public ownership. The planners were restricted, therefore, only by the economic and technical problems which were often acute in a city which had suffered so much damage. The liquidation of private land ownership was a matter for much political debate, but the act was clearly vital for future development. Only land was nationalised, dwelling units were left in private ownership.

In addition certain long range political and economic goals were immediately established. Firstly, it was decided that Warsaw, as the capital city, should play an important part in the political, cultural and economic life of the nation. Secondly, its occupational structure ought to be modified to ensure that industrial workers formed a large enough group to take a lead in building the new political system, and thirdly, the new society had to develop without social classes and all had to have equal access to the best living conditions.

Chmielewski and Syrkus had been the first to conceive a plan for the development of Warsaw in relation to its surrounding region. They produced their scheme in 1934 and called it 'Warszawa Funkcynalna'. Further work continued during the war which meant that a physical plan was ready almost as soon as hostilities ceased. This plan, although influenced by the concepts of Chmielewski and Syrkus, related mainly to the reconstruction of the city itself and concentrated on the rebuilding of the central part (Śródmieście) including the reconstruction of the Old Town. It was decided to have mixed functions of administration, services and housing in the central area. In the western part of the city, adjacent to the central area, two high density housing developments in Muranów, on the area of the ghetto, and in Mokotow were planned. These were to be separated from the industrial area of Wola by a green zone running north to south. Four other housing areas, built at lower densities, were planned on the periphery of the city. Much less development was initially planned on the east bank. One high density housing development and three lower density developments were suggested, and also the rebuilding of the Targówek industrial area. The spatial arrangements are shown in Figure 7.6.

This plan was modified in 1948 by eliminating the green zone separating the central areas from Wola, and generally a decision was taken to increase housing densities, particularly in the outer areas. These changes were based on an economic principle that areas with existing infrastructure (much of it pre-war and relatively undamaged) should be used intensively. Housing areas were built up at very high

Figure 7.6: The First Post-war Plan for Warsaw, 1945

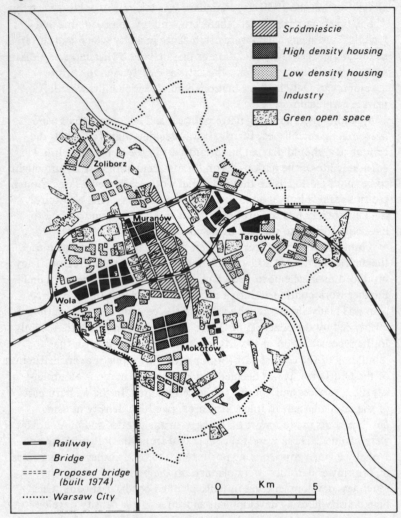

densities but in spite of these changes the new city showed considerable improvements over the pre-war provision. The new housing estates actually had lower densities than pre-war and they were planned with basic services and open space.

Since the war there have been many revisions of future population targets. In 1946 the Office for the Redevelopment of Warsaw initially suggested a figure of 800,000 by 1960 but this estimate was made in an atmosphere of uncertainty for discussions continued amongst planners concerning the future location of the capital, with Łódz and Poznań, both of which suffered less war damage than Warsaw, often mentioned as suitable alternatives. By the end of the year, however, a firm decision was taken in favour of Warsaw and the estimate of future population was adjusted to 1,200,000.

In the next plan (1949) it was envisaged that the city would reach 2.3 millions by 1980, but in the early 1950s the figure was revised downwards to 2 million and in 1954 reduced still further to 1.6 million. In this year the first legal restrictions on migration to Warsaw were introduced and from then on the planners had much more control over future development. The outcome of this control was that in 1965 another 200,000 was deducted from the 1980 target.

In the period 1965-70 a policy involving the deconcentration of economic activity was implemented ('deglomeracja Warszawj') but in 1971 the restrictive policies regarding both population movement and cultural, scientific and economic activities were eased. Naturally, the restrictions had had the direct effect of causing dynamic population growth in the outer zone but throughout the period 1945-70 Warsaw city actually grew faster than the outer zone (Table 7.5). The adjustments in population forecasts were closely related to the manufacturing role assigned to Warsaw in successive national economic plans.

The policy of heavy industrialisation in Warsaw, which the 1945 plan did not envisage, created great pressure on land which either had, or could be provided with, infrastructure. New industrial districts were created at Żeran in Praga Północ and at Służewiec in Mokotów. In 1951 work began on the construction of a new car factory in Żeran and other factories, many associated with vehicle manufacture, were also sited there. In 1952 an even bigger transformation to the industrial structure was initiated for work began on the construction of the Warsaw steelworks at Bielany in the northern part of Żoliborz. This heavy industrialisation combined with the developing administrative functions, increased migration in-flow and consequently increased pressure on the already highly inadequate housing stock. This led to increased commuting from the suburban zones and around Warsaw substandard and unplanned private housing areas lacking proper levels of infrastructure were developed. The 'Warszawa Funkcynalna' ideas had no direct influence whatsoever on shaping the development of the suburban zone.

The physical plan for the city has been modified periodically to cope with changing population targets and alterations to the industrial structure but in the late 1960s, largely because of the worsening housing situation in both the city and the surrounding region, the concept of 'deglomeration' was conceived as we have already observed. This notion formed the basis of the plan, approved in 1968, which was prepared for the whole Warsaw region. For the first time the whole agglomeration (Warszawskiego Zespolu Miejskiego—WZM) was covered by one plan. On the basis of the guidelines provided by the national and regional plans it was anticipated that the agglomeration would house some 2,350,000 inhabitants by 1985, of which around 1,600,000 would be in the city itself. It is clearly stated in the plan that 'the adopted principle of counteracting excessive growth of population has a bearing on all elements in the programme'.

According to the plan future housing would be constructed along four main growth corridors. There was to be infilling of sites in the two traditional directions—east to Wołomin and west towards Grodzisk, because there existing infrastructure could be utilised. Departures from the existing pattern were proposed, however. In the north Nowy Dwór and Modlin were to house 400,000 people and in the south Góra Kalwaria was planned to expand to 500,000 by 1990 (Warsaw Master Plan 1968).

The general plan consists of three basic parts: firstly, a long range plan covering a period of 30 to 40 years which establishes goals; secondly, a perspective plan prepared for 20 years which sets objectives; and thirdly, a stage plan, operationalising the objectives covering the current five year period. Planning is assumed to be a continuous process and therefore every five years, simultaneously with the preparation of the economic plan, the perspective plan is revised and adjustments made to the stage plan.

The Future Development

The future development of Warsaw, then, must be viewed in both a regional (Voivodship) and a national context. The former essentially concerns the location of new development; the latter is linked to the role Warsaw will play in the national urban strategy and between 1972 and 1975 the Planning Commission at the Council of Ministers prepared a new National Spatial Development Plan in which Warsaw figures very prominently. This plan necessitated a substantial revision of the 1968 WZM proposals.

The national plan itself is perspective in nature and covers the period to 1990. It identifies 25 urban agglomerations in which it is anticipated growth will be concentrated. The agglomerations themselves are presently in various stages of development. Twelve, including Warsaw, are already well developed, a further seven are classed as developing,· while the remaining six are, at the moment, towns with development potential (Jędraszko 1977). The forecasts indicate that these agglomerations will, in total, increase their populations by some 44 per cent by 1990, rising from 12.8 to 18.5 millions. At the same time, the number of workplaces they contain is expected to increase from 6.5 to 10.5 million. If these forecasts prove correct then 50 per cent of the nation will be living in the agglomerations at the end of the plan period compared to 39 per cent in 1970.

Growth on this scale may arise from three sources: firstly, by administrative boundary changes; secondly, by natural increase; and thirdly, by migration. The first can be eliminated for the boundaries have been drawn to include all the territory into which development may spread. The second is likely to be relatively unimportant for the trend in Poland now is towards smaller families and a reduction in birth rate which leaves the third possibility, namely migration.

Migration is thought likely to account for 70 per cent of the increase in general and for 97 per cent of the growth in Warsaw in particular. To encourage migration on this scale represents something of a departure from existing practice, especially with respect to Warsaw, for which residential permits have been necessary since 1954. The strategy seems to imply a major attempt to transform Polish society from rural to urban.

Most urban areas in Poland have, in the post-war years, expanded substantially by receiving migrants from the adjacent rural areas, but Jędraszko (1977) suggests that rural urban migration is likely to be substantially reduced in the period 1981-90, unless there are fundamental changes in the agricultural structure, which seems unlikely. Therefore, the migrants will originate from smaller urban centres which seems to indicate a reversal of the policy of encouraging the general development of such places. To fulfil the plan, the agglomerations must increase their populations by receiving an in-migration of some 3.5 to 4 million people, which represents a movement of over 10 per cent of the population. On accommodation grounds, such massive migration appears unrealistic for, even if people are willing to move, housing shortages will become even more acute.

This new national strategy was incompatible with the thinking behind the physical planning of Warsaw as it existed in 1973. The following five main principles were then guiding development:

1. Curbing the number of new jobs so that the population would
   not grow too quickly;
2. Increasing the level of services for all inhabitants;
3. Abolishing the variation in standards between the towns in the
   Voivodship and between the different districts of Warsaw;
4. Increasing the amount of leisure time;
5. Providing suitable ecological and climatic conditions.

In response to the National Spatial Strategy, the People's Council of
Warsaw announced a competition for schemes which would indicate
the future spatial development of the Warsaw agglomeration. They
received four submissions which were used to assist in the preparation
of the latest plans which were approved for the agglomeration in 1978
and for the city in 1979.

These plans forecast that population will increase in the whole
agglomeration from 2,155,000 in 1975 to 2,600,000 by 1990 and in
the city from 1,455,000 to 1,650,000 in the same period. The city
figure is based on the amount of housing which can be provided as
space is limited. Increases will occur in Mokotów, Praga Północ and
Południe, while decreases are envisaged in Ochota, Wola, Żoliborz and
Śródmieście. Forecasts for employment indicate an increase in the
number of jobs for the whole agglomeration from 1,170,000 to
1,400,000 and in the city from 870,000 to 980,000. If the percentage
of economically active population remains constant then a further
40,000 commuters will have to travel if these estimates prove correct.

Current employment figures for Warsaw are difficult to obtain on a
disaggregated basis but some indication of available jobs per 100 population for 1977 is presented in Table 7.6. The higher the ratio, the
greater the number of local employment opportunities in the socialised
sectors. The highest concentration is in the city centre (Śródmieście)
where there are 119.2 jobs for every 100 people (of all ages). Clearly
this indicates a substantial daily commuting flow of the type well known
in all Western European cities for the total number of jobs is 226,518.
The next highest ratio is found in the relatively small town of Ożarów
to the west of the city (65.8), followed by Piaseczno, which is to the
south (57.1). They are both industrial towns but although their ratio
is high, the total number of jobs is low — 4,574 in Ożarów and 13,317
in Piaseczno. Of much greater significance are the city districts of Wola,
Praga Południe and Ochota with 123,413, 116,479 and 101,065 jobs
respectively and ratios of 55.8, 53.6 and 53.3. Most of the city is a net
importer of labour (although, of course, cross-town flows complicate

the pattern). The one exception is Żoliborz, which is mainly a residential zone, even though it contains the Warsaw steel works at Żeran which employs around 10,000 workers. Many of the settlements in the hinterland, such as Brwinów, Józefów, Sulejówek and Ząbki are 'dormitory' towns for the city.

It is expected that 100,000 housing units will be built in the city in the period 1975-80 with a further 85,000 between 1981 and 1985, and 25,000 in the last five years of the plan period. The intention is to increase the size of new flats from an average of 50 m^2 in the first period to 56 m^2 in the second and finally to 64 m^2 in the final quinquennium. By 1990 all families should have a separate flat and 80 per cent of one person households should also be separately housed. Some planned losses will occur as a result of demolishing 36,000 smaller units to give a smaller number of larger flats. The total housing resources of the city by 1990 should amount to 31,500,000 m^2, consisting of 640,000 flats of which 120,000 will be one person with an average size of 22 m^2, and 520,000 family flats each having an average area of 55.4 m^2. In addition it is intended to build a further 200,000 flats in the area outside the city boundary, particularly in the northern Legionowo sector.

The general development of the region is shown in Figure 7.7. The present urbanised area extends in a star-like fashion which is to be reinforced especially in the south-west, south, and south-east by development in the next ten years. Development will also take place in the north but it is this zone which is earmarked for investment in the period beyond 1990. The map also shows the large areas of open space which are adjacent to the built-up areas.

The current plan (Figure 7.8), then, re-emphasises with modifications the general lines of development first proposed in its 1968 predecessor. The northern corridor, on the right bank of the Vistula, will be partly developed before 1990, especially in Legionowo and Nowy Dwór, but it is envisaged that this will be the area of growth after 1990 when it is possible that a new international airport will be built at Modlin and a new large-scale urban centre developed which will offer an alternative to the present city centre. Such proposals it must be emphasised are very long term and extremely speculative.

A second corridor is being developed to the south of the existing city. It includes Ursynów, Natolin and terminates at Piaseczno. The proposals substantially to enlarge Góra Kalwaria appear to have been shelved or abandoned. The eastern corridor through Ząbki to Wołomin and the western through Ursus (now incorporated in the city boundary) to Pruszków will accommodate an increased population but it is also

Table 7.6: Population and Employment by Towns in Warsaw Voivodship, 1977

	Population	Employment	Jobs per 100 people
Total	1,966,727	964,476	49.0
Warsaw:	1,532,070	829,933	54.2
Mokotów	292,515	120,356	41.2
Ochota	189,621	101,065	53.3
Praga Południe	222,928	91,963	41.3
Praga Północ	217,133	116,479	53.6
Śródmieście	190,058	226,518	119.2
Wola	221,184	123,413	55.8
Żoliborz	198,631	50,139	25.2
Błonie	12,915	6,373	49.4
Brwinów	11,067	1,046	9.5
Góra Kalwaria	10,058	5,583	55.5
Grodzisk Maz	23,137	8,661	37.4
Józefów	14,662	1,163	7.9
Kobyłka	11,939	2,661	22.3
Konstancin	16,670	5,710	34.3
Legionowo	27,027	6,642	24.6
Marki	15,999	4,592	28.7
Milanówek	14,978	3,767	25.2
Nowy Dwór	21,169	7,482	35.3
Otwock (with Karczew)	50,471	16,713	33.1
Ożarów	6,950	4,574	65.8
Piaseczno	23,314	13,317	57.1
Piastów	19,677	4,318	21.9
Podkowa Leśna	3,308	282	8.5
Pruszków	47,864	21,106	44.1
Radzymin	8,054	1,974	24.5
Serock	2,730	668	24.5
Sulejówek	16,608	890	5.4
Wesoła	9,100	437	4.8
Wołomin	29,353	11,541	39.3
Zakroczym	3,644	423	11.5
Ząbki	18,951	1,368	7.2
Zielonka	14,992	3,252	21.7

Source: Rocznik Statystyczny Województwa Stołecznego Warszawskiego (1978).

Figure 7.7: Warsaw Voivodship: Existing and Planned Urbanised Areas

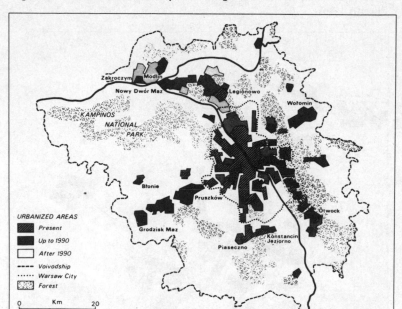

anticipated that there will be substantial urban renewal in both directions.

Services are being provided on an hierarchical basis. At the first level are service centres to which the walking distance should not exceed 500 metres. Each should serve between 5,000 and 10,000 people and be for frequent shopping needs. Second level facilities will be (and in some cases have been) provided to serve a radius of 800 metres catering for residential districts of between 20,000 and 50,000 population. The third grade will contain special service facilities such as hospitals, sports facilities, administrative buildings and more specialist shops. They will be accessible to 200,000 people by public and private transport. The fourth and highest level is the city centre.

To enable such an hierarchical system to function efficiently effective transport links have to be provided. At present car ownership is low but rising fairly quickly. In 1970 there were only 55 cars per 1,000 population, consequently most people depend on public transport for both work and

Figure 7.8: Warsaw City plus Adjacent Areas— the Current Physical Plan to 1990

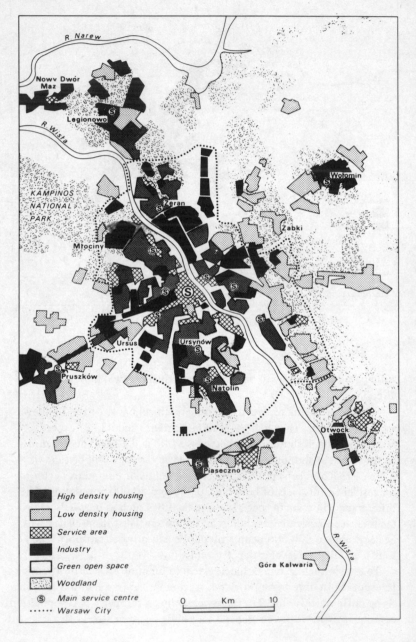

Figure 7.9: Transport Proposals for 1990

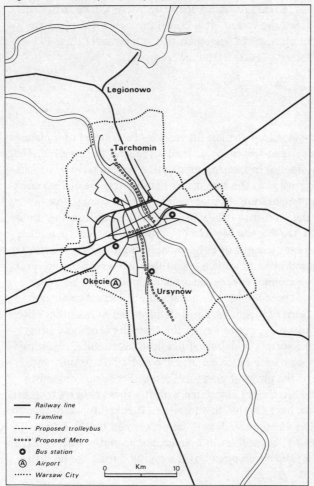

leisure trips. Although it is anticipated that the figure will rise to 200 by 1985, priority in the plans has been given to public transport.

The future public transport system will be based on buses, trams and, it is hoped, an underground railway. An underground has been discussed since 1928 and many seem very sceptical as to whether it will ever be built. This has not stopped major developments like Ursynów being constructed on the assumption that it will eventually be implemented. The public transport pattern for 1990 certainly includes a north-south line linking Tarchomin (in Praga Pótnoc) with the residential area of

Ursynów in the south by a route which crosses the city centre and the river (Figure 7.9). Eventually it is hoped that there will be sufficient resources to extend the system. It is hoped that when the plans are implemented no place in the agglomeration will be more than 45 minutes from the city centre by public transport.

Conclusion

Warsaw has developed for the last 35 years in the context of a planned society, but in spite of this many difficulties remain to be solved. The major problem lies not in the plan preparation, which is often imaginative and innovative as in the case of the housing scheme at Ursynów, but in plan implementation. Resources have always been scarce in Poland and at the moment (1980) there seems little chance that funds for schemes like the Warsaw Metro will be found. To a considerable extent, the current demands of Polish society are linked to the shortages which have caused plans to remain unfulfilled. We recognise, however, that the rapid economic redevelopment and rebuilding of post-war Warsaw could not possibly have been carried out in a rational way without some form of planning. The difficulties we have outlined are not caused by planning, but rather by the changing needs and rising expectations of a society which itself has been restructured. Political upheavals in Poland have twice led, in 1956 and 1970, to substantial modifications of the physical plan for Warsaw. Economic objectives, which in Poland are closely associated with the views held by members of the Politburo, have also led to alterations. It is highly likely therefore that changes in leadership, such as those occasioned by the Polish workers' strike of 1980, will set in train economic and political changes which will affect the development of the capital during the next five-year plan period.

Notes

1. Socialist Realism is a style of architecture first developed in the USSR in the 1930s. It was introduced throughout Eastern Europe in the period 1950-6, particularly in new housing estates and public buildings.
2. Family is defined as 'an independent economic unit'.
3. For this analysis we take the Warsaw agglomeration to be the Voivodship plus the neighbouring administrative units of Zyrardow and Jaktorow in the west, Tluszcz and Klembow in the north-east, and Minsk Maz and Debe Wielkie in the east.

References

Blowers, A. (1973) *The City in the Socialist World*, Notes to accompany Course DT 201 Urban Development, Open University

Broniewski, S. (1974) 'The Local Plan and Its Relations to the Regional Plan', in K. Secomski (ed.) *Spatial Planning and Policy – Theoretical Foundations*, Polish Academy of Sciences, Polish Scientific Publishers, Warsaw

Chroscicki, J.A. and A. Rottermund (1978) *Atlas of Warsaw's Architecture*, Arkady Publishers, Warsaw

Ciborowski, A. (1969) *Warsaw: A City Destroyed and Rebuilt*, Interpress Publishers, Warsaw

Jachniak-Ganguly, D. (1978) *Administration and Spatial Planning as Tools of Land Management in Poland*, Occasional Paper 4, Centre for Environmental Studies, London

Jankowski, J. and A. Ciborowski (1978) *Warsaw 1945, Today and Tomorrow*, Interpress Publishers, Warsaw

Jędraszko, A. (1977) 'The Migration of Population and Its Influence on the Planning of Urban Agglomerations in Poland', in A. Kuklinski (ed.) *Regional Studies in Poland*, a special issue of a Bulletin published by the Polish Academy of Sciences, Warsaw

Malisz, B. (1974) 'Spatial Planning on the National Level' in K. Secomski (ed.) *Spatial Planning and Policy – Theoretical Foundations*

Pabst Plan, (1940) Prepared in Wurzburg by Pabst for the annihilation of Warsaw

Węcławowicz, G. (1979) 'Socio-economic Space in Warsaw' in R.A. French and F.E.I. Hamilton (eds.) *The Socialist City*, Wiley, London

8 LENINGRAD

Denis J.B. Shaw

Few of the world's great cities have experienced such fluctuations in fortune as Leningrad in the present century. On the eve of World War I St Petersburg, as the city was then known, was a flourishing port and industrial centre, capital of the Russian Empire, a city of over two million people. The war, the two revolutions of March and November 1917, the ensuing Civil War, and the loss of the city's capital status in 1918 had a catastrophic effect. By 1921, the population had fallen to 830,000. It was not to regain its pre-war population until the early 1930s. In the late 1920s, however, with the launching of Stalin's campaign of industrialisation, Leningrad's economy revived and expanded, and migration into the city resumed its pre-revolutionary vigour. By 1939, Leningrad's population stood at over three million people. Disaster struck once more during World War II when the city withstood a 900-day siege and the population fell to a fraction of its former level — a level it was not to reach again until the 1960s. Since the war Leningrad has experienced first a gradual revival from wartime ruin, and then renewed progress in its development as a socialist city. That progress has brought many problems to the fore, not a few of which derive from the uneven nature of Leningrad's development during the twentieth century.

Although no longer capital of the country, or even a capital of one of the Soviet Union's 15 constituent republics, Leningrad is still the USSR's second city in size and importance. This fact is reflected in the political power of the city's government (consisting of the city soviet and its executive committee, together with the city committee of the Communist Party) and thus in the city's ability to control its own future. Within the highly centralised political and economic system of the USSR this factor of local political power is very important, especially with regard to the effectiveness of city planning. The organ primarily responsible for city planning in Leningrad, the Main Architecture-Planning Administration (GlavAPU) is very powerful and highly organised, possessing both research sections and sub-branches at district (*rayon*) level. Though a department of the city soviet's executive committee, GlavAPU, like analogous bodies in other cities, is closely supervised by national organisations such as the State Construction Committee (Gosstroy) and the State Committee for Civil Construction

292

and Architecture (Gosgrazhdanstroy). In planning the city, GlavAPU liaises with other administrations of the city executive committee, such as those for construction and housing. However city planning is complicated by the sectoral nature of the USSR's economic planning system, and powerful industrial ministries are able to frustrate city planning goals in various ways.

During the Stalin era, city planning was a neglected procedure in Leningrad, certainly by comparison with Moscow where the prestigious 1935 General Plan laid down criteria for the socialist development of the capital. Nevertheless, both pre-war and post-war plans for Leningrad did provide certain guidelines for the city's development. With the revival of Soviet interest in urban planning in the late 1950s, work on city plans began in earnest. Leningrad's present development is guided by the General Plan for the city which was drawn up in the early 1960s and finally approved by the USSR Council of Ministers in July 1966. The General Plan is meant to be effective until approximately 1990. In view of the national importance of this plan, the role of major organisations such as Gosgrazhdanstroy in its composition and implementation is particularly significant. Leningrad's Architecture-Planning Administration is also aided in the implementation and reworking of the General Plan by other local bodies, such as the Leningrad Research and Design Institute for City Planning (LenNIIP *gradostroitel'stva*). This is a research body of national significance, part of the system of Gosgrazhdanstroy. In this way it is probably true to say that Leningrad's General Plan receives far more expert attention than do the general plans of lesser cities.

The provisions of Leningrad's 1966 General Plan have been examined elsewhere (Shaw 1978). This chapter is particularly concerned with those problems in the planning of the city which have become most apparent since the General Plan was drawn up.

The Growing and Expanding City

During the Stalin period the Soviet authorities' first priorities were industrialisation and economic growth. The leadership was little inclined to devote much consideration to the question of urban development, but soon found that it could not afford to ignore this matter entirely. Rural to urban migration in the wake of the launching of the first Five Year Plan at the end of the 1920s and the collectivisation of agriculture threatened to produce unmanageable problems in the largest cities such as Leningrad and Moscow. These cities were already suffering an acute housing shortage and their services were under severe strain. Moreover, it was believed that uncontrolled expansion of the largest cities in the west of the country would have strategic disadvantages in a country in international isolation and undermine the regime's policy of eastern development. Thus in 1931 it was decreed that all new industrial expansion was to take place outside Leningrad and Moscow. Henceforth, industrial development in these cities was to proceed along intensive rather than extensive lines. The following year the internal passport regime was introduced and migration into Leningrad and Moscow was controlled by the need to obtain special permission before a migrant could take up residence. Since the 1930s the doctrine of controlling urban expansion in the case of the largest cities has become deeply enshrined in Soviet policy-making and applied to many more cities. It is regarded as a major means whereby the economic and social costs of metropolitan growth can be minimised, of bridging rural-urban differences in living standards, and of ensuring that economic growth in one region does not proceed to the detriment of the development of other regions. The Soviet state's monopoly of industry and of land, and its high degree of control over labour migration into large cities, are the major buttresses to this policy.

The policy of controlling urban growth, however, has not met with the success expected of it. In the case of Leningrad, for example, the General Plan envisaged the city proper having a population of 3.4-3.5 millions by the late 1980s, or 4 millions including its subsidiary settlements. In fact this level was reached in 1970. Although World War II had a retarding effect on population growth, Leningrad's recent demographic expansion has been quite rapid, as Table 8.1 indicates:

Table 8.1: Leningrad's Population Growth (in millions), 1939-79

	Greater Leningrad	Leningrad proper
1939	3.401	3.119
1959	3.367	3.003
1970	4.027	3.550
1975	4.311	3.853
1979	4.588	4.073

The 36 per cent increase in Leningrad's population between 1959 and 1979 certainly exceeds previous expectations. In common with other large cities in the Soviet Union, Leningrad's birth rate is low compared with the national average (13.7 per thousand in 1978, compared with a USSR average of 18.2 and an average for the Russian Federation or RSFSR in 1977 of 15.8). The natural growth rate in 1978 was 2.7 per thousand. The low birth and natural growth rates reflect comparatively low marriage and high divorce rates, a propensity for small families and an ageing demographic structure. Between 1959 and 1974, for example, the proportion of the city's population of working age (20-59 years) fell from 64.9 to 60.6 per cent while in the same period the proportion of old people (60 years and over) increased from 8.7 to 15.6 per cent. Of much greater importance as a contributor to urban growth is in-migration which in 1973 exceeded out-migration by 48,800. In 1977 in-migration contributed 89 per cent to the total population growth.

It is a continuing labour shortage in the city of Leningrad that has contributed to the pressure for in-migration. Some idea of the employment trends in different sectors of the city's economy can be derived from Table 8.2.

Table 8.2: Employment Trends in Leningrad by Sector, 1965-76

	1965[a]	1970	1976
Total employment	100	107.8	117.2
Industry	100	101.0	102.1
Transport	100	107.6	126.4
Communications (post etc.)	100	106.3	127.2
Construction	100	111.2	125.7
Trade	100	115.2	125.4
General services	100	113.8	124.7
Health services	100	118.9	130.2
Education and culture	100	107.4	121.3
Science and research	100	116.6	136.9

Note: a. 1965=100
Source: *Narkhoz Leningrada za 60.*

As Table 8.2 indicates, the industrial sector has been remarkably successful in keeping its employment needs to a minimum (over a period in which industrial output, measured at constant prices, increased by 87 per cent). Other sectors of the economy, particularly those serving the population and those which have expanded in line with the growing

technical needs of the economy, have experienced significant employment increases. Clearly when they were making their population
projections the planners failed to anticipate fully the employment
demands that would be generated as the standard of living rose and
technical needs developed.

It must not be concluded from Table 8.2, however, that industry
has been blameless as a contributor to Leningrad's growing labour
needs. In fact, quite the contrary is true. The General Plan envisaged
that the further intensification of industrial development would actually
release labour which could then be employed in other sectors. Clearly
this has not happened. Industry has in actuality failed to conserve
labour to the extent expected of it and has even expanded its activities
in various ways contrary to the General Plan. A favourite device is to
hide expansion under the guise of reconstruction. It is the cost and
associated advantages of a location in Leningrad which prompt
industrial ministries thus to evade the planning rules. The literature is
frequently critical of such evasions and of the failure of ministries to
keep the city authorities informed of proposed developments (Filonov
1974; Usanov 1979).

Illegal migration into Leningrad is but one of several means whereby
people evade the residence laws. Ministries in need of labour put
pressure on the local authorities to make exceptions to the rules, and in
the face of the fact that some of the USSR's most advanced industry
is located in the city, the authorities are aware that a too rigid application
of the laws might harm the Soviet economy as a whole. Another means
whereby the labour shortage is combated is through commuting.
Opportunities for migrants to obtain housing are far better in the
peripheral settlements than they are in the city proper. Indeed this
mode of living often appeals to migrants from the countryside since
housing in the commuter settlements is often low-rise with an associated
garden plot. At the present time a total of 370 million commuter
journeys per year are made into the city, 84 per cent of which are by
rail (Zhukovskiy 1979).

Commensurate with Leningrad's population growth and increasing
labour needs has been the expansion of its built-up area. At the present
time the city occupies almost 400 square kilometres which is nearly
three times its area in 1917 (Alymov 1978). The spatial expansion of
the city was particularly marked after the mid-1950s when Khrushchev's
housing programme led to the rapid development of new residential
areas, especially to the north and south of the city. This in turn
produced a redistribution of the city's population with the central parts

of the city losing one-third of their population between 1959 and 1970 (Litovka 1976) and peripheral areas gaining commensurately (Shaw 1978). This policy, which was further reinforced by the provisions of the General Plan, has come under increasing criticism in view of the high infrastructural costs associated with such spatial expansion. There is also serious concern at the ensuing pressure on the green belt and the detrimental consequences for agriculture. Criticism particularly focuses on the low density of development envisaged in the General Plan. The latter made provision for an average residential development of 3,800 square metres of 'useful' space[1] per hectare of land in buildings of 7.5 storeys on average. Present policy favours an increase in these figures to 5,500-6,000 square metres and 10 storeys (Usanov 1979). Schemes are also in hand to make use of land which was previously considered unsuitable for building because of engineering difficulties. Examples include land on the western periphery of the city currently liable to flooding (Nazarov 1979).

Figure 8.1: The Leningrad City Region

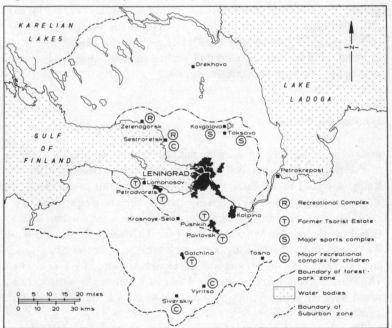

Leningrad is now surrounded by a ring of smaller settlements (Figure 8.1) which, together with the central city, are generally recognised as forming a single agglomeration (Lappo 1978). The rise of commuting has meant that the growth of these peripheral communities has been considerable and this growth has been furthered by their development as industrial, scientific and tourist centres. At the present time almost half a million people live within 70 kilometres of the Leningrad city boundary. One estimate envisages that by the end of the century 6.2 million people will live in Greater Leningrad with 5.5 million in the central city and its immediate environs (Makhrovskaya and Semenov 1974). Such prospects are discouraging for the future of the green belt, and there has been some discussion about the possibility of channelling urban growth into fingers of development or of providing alternative development nodes away from the central city (Makhrovskaya and Semenov 1974; Panov 1975).

The failure to control the growth and expansion of Leningrad is a serious problem for its development if the provisions of the General Plan are to be observed. Some Soviet scholars, however, regard such growth as the natural result of the economies of scale achieved by large cities and deprecate the attempt to constrain them too rigidly (Kochetkov 1975; Pivovarov 1972). For such people planning restrictions must take full account of economic realities and are unlikely to succeed as long as the labour shortage continues.

Housing the Workers

For the great majority of working people the pre-revolutionary city of St Petersburg was a wretched place in which to live. Housing was frequently poor in the extreme and sanitary conditions were among the worst in Europe (Bater 1976). After the Revolution, despite sanitary improvements, the housing situation deteriorated even further. The Civil War, the rural-urban migration of the 1920s and 1930s, and World War II all had their effect. By 1951 each apartment in the city housed an average of 3.3 families and many lacked baths and hygienic kitchens. The average living space[2] was only 3.5 square metres per person compared with the 9 square metres minimum sanitary norm accepted in the 1920s (Cattell 1968).

The situation in Leningrad was not untypical of Soviet cities during the Stalin era. For Stalin's successors the housing question has thus become a central issue. By his housing decree of 1957 Khrushchev committed the regime to solving the housing problem over the next 10 to 12 years (DiMaio 1974). While this rate of housing construction proved unrealistic in the event, the progress was nevertheless unprecedented. This achievement was the product of large-scale financing, reform of the construction industry and the adoption of prefabricated building techniques. The effects of the housing drive in the case of Leningrad are shown in the following table:

Table 8.3: Leningrad's Housing Fund, 1913-76

(Millions of square metres of 'useful' space)	
1913	21.8
1940	25.7
1965	39.1
1970	48.0
1975	58.0
1976	59.9

Source: *Narkhoz Leningrada za 60.*

The result has been a major improvement in the housing situation of Leningraders. Between 1965 and 1973, for example, 393,000 apartments were completed, equivalent to 19 million square metres of 'useful' space (Buldakov 1974). In total between 1966 and 1978 over 700,000 families or over 2 million people improved their housing conditions, most of whom moved into new flats in new blocks (Usanov 1979). The amount of 'useful' housing space in the city was raised from 11.7 square metres per capita in 1968 to 15.3 in 1978 (Lavrov 1979). It is also worth noting that Leningrad's housing space average is well above the USSR average for all cities (12.7). However, much progress remains to be made for many people in the city still share apartments or live in hostels (Shaw 1978). V.P. Usanov (1979), the head of GlavAPU, has recently stressed the need to raise the average housing space per capita to 20-21 square metres, doubling the total housing space which existed in 1966.

The progress in housing construction has been contingent upon the acceptance of apartment-style living as the norm and the adoption of industrialised house building methods. This in turn has necessitated the reorganisation of the construction industry which under Stalin had been split between various ministries and consisted of a multitude of small firms and organisations. Under Khrushchev one central construction administration came into being in Leningrad, known as Glavleningradstroy. Glavleningradstroy supervises the work of several house-building combines, the first of which came into being in 1959, and which combine into one organisation the construction work previously undertaken by disparate concerns. The house-building combines currently build 80 per cent of the city's housing mainly through industrialised techniques. The rest of the city's housing largely consists of specially designed buildings built of brick or other special materials and constructed by small trusts and combines often in con- servation areas (Usanov 1979). In 1975, in line with tendencies towards amalgamation in industry, two large construction 'associations' were formed in the city to group the house-building combines together. The associations include design and repair facilities and are responsible for the construction of entire districts, including the infrastructure, services, open space and other features (Kazanskiy 1979). One of the associations would appear to specialise in large-panel construction methods and it is envisaged that it will eventually incorporate the actual manufacture of the panels themselves (Bochkov *et al.* 1979).

Leningrad has been a pioneer not only in the reorganisation of the construction industry but also in certain aspects of industrialised house building. Industrialised house building in the city dates from the late 1950s when the first housing, generally five-storeyed and without lifts, was constructed utilising large panels. From the mid-1960s new national house-building norms were adopted and a nine-storey average was accepted for housing. Then, from the early 1970s, the so-called 'block- section' method was generally introduced (Krivov 1978). Whereas previous methods had relied upon 'typical' building designs and gave rise to monotonous suburban areas, the block-section method allows architects much greater flexibility in designing buildings using standard- ised elements manufactured on the basis of a uniform catalogue (Matusevich *et al.* 1979). In this way maximum creativity is permitted within the constraints imposed by economy and nationally approved norms.

In spite of the genuine advances that have been made in industrialised house building in Leningrad during the past quarter of a century, this is still an area which attracts much criticism in the press and architectural journals. One problem concerns the design of the housing. Leningrad's architects feel themselves to be too constrained by nationally approved norms and strict considerations of economy imposed because of the sheer scale of the housing programme. The block-section method of building is still felt to be insufficiently flexible to be able to produce the rich variety which an urban environment demands. Too little attention is also paid, in the opinion of some, to adjustment to demographic variables so that minority groups such as single people and childless couples suffer (Uspenskiy and Berezin 1979; Merzhanov 1978; Karaletyan and Sarkisyan 1979). One author notes that the problems associated with high-rise development in other countries have also been experienced in Leningrad with the ground floor and the upper floors of buildings being regarded as particularly undesirable for residence (Lavrov 1979). This writer advocates a stricter attention to zonation of buildings by floor with the block-section method being used to provide extra facilities to residents of upper floors who might include young people and childless couples. Some writers have also argued that such policies could be used to counteract the isolation of the modern city by inducing different social groups, such as old people and young families, to live in closer proximity than is the case at present (Ruzhzhe 1979). This would help alleviate the loneliness of many old people by bringing them into the family circle. Moreover, it might encourage more mothers to work, leaving their children in the care of aged relatives.

In addition to the design question, Soviet writers are also frequently critical of the construction industry itself. This industry has always been something of a problem in the Soviet economy and Leningrad's construction industry is no exception. Complaints especially focus on the low quality of building work (Tret'emu godu 1978; Remizov 1978). A survey of the work of Glavleningradstroy undertaken by the State Architecture Control in 1978 was able to classify only 20 per cent of the work as 'good' and 80 per cent as merely 'satisfactory'. The problem of building quality is thus said to be 'severe' (Kalinkina 1979) and results from difficulties with building materials, 'storming' by the workers (i.e. hurrying to complete the work by the end of the plan period) and problems with costings, accounting and documentation. Another failing of this industry is the continuing problem of co-ordination in suburban development whereby new residents are often left for months without essential services (Merzhanov 1978; Usanov 1979). There are also many difficulties with repair and maintenance, in spite of the centralisation of such work in Leningrad in 1965. At present only about one-third of the desired degree of maintenance work is being done (Usanov 1979; Ivanov 1979). No doubt worsened by such inadequate maintenance, the problem of replacing outworn housing is now assuming great significance. Such housing is said to include some of the five-storeyed housing completed under Khrushchev, although rising expectations in terms of space and facilities also play a part here (Romanov 1979).

At the present time only about 3 per cent of the housing in Leningrad belongs to the private sector—usually low-rise housing. Of the 'socialised' sector, 70 per cent is controlled by the city soviet, and much of the rest by various ministries and organisations (Chikovskiy and Movchan 1978). The 1971 decree on city soviets envisaged the transfer of most ministerial housing to the soviets in view of the scale economies that would be achieved in maintenance and repair. However, bureaucratic resistance to such a transfer has been considerable, though Leningrad's city soviet does control a higher proportion of the city's housing than is the case in many other cities. The ministerial sector in the city is now expected to stabilise. Co-operative house building by citizens and co-operatives using state credits forms a small but important contribution to the housing programme.

Suburbanisation and the Journey to Work

Leningrad's housing programme over the past quarter of a century has considerably worsened the journey-to-work problem. Thus a series of studies at one of the large industrial enterprises in Lenin district close to the city centre revealed that over a ten year period between the early 1960s and the early 1970s the average journey to work had increased from 34.2 minutes to 38.9 minutes or by 14 per cent (Belinskiy 1975). A substantial portion of this increase derives directly from the growing distance between work and home. The average passenger journey on the city's transport system increased from 4.5 to 5.2 kilometres over the eight year period 1971-9 (Zhukovskiy 1979). The speed of transport does not compensate for the increased distance between work and home, and indeed in view of a 60 per cent increase in passenger car journeys since 1970, traffic jams are now a commonplace. The average journey to work currently takes 48 minutes, but many journeys exceed 1.5 hours.

The 1966 General Plan provided for a considerable suburban expansion for Leningrad, but made little provision for relocation in employment or industry. Much of Leningrad's employment in the service and office sectors is located in the centre of the city, and the greater part of the industry is concentrated in a ring of older suburbs surrounding the urban core (Shaw 1978). During the 1970s the basic shortcomings of the General Plan policy, which would have placed an increasing strain on the city's transportation system, became ever more apparent. In the case of the newly developing north-western suburb, for example, the

Figure 8.2: Leningrad: Urban Districts and New Residential Expansion

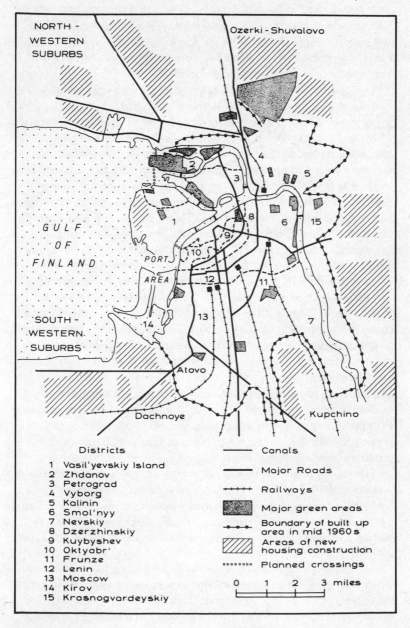

Districts

1 Vasil'yevskiy Island
2 Zhdanov
3 Petrograd
4 Vyborg
5 Kalinin
6 Smol'nyy
7 Nevskiy
8 Dzerzhinskiy
9 Kuybyshev
10 Oktyabr'
11 Frunze
12 Lenin
13 Moscow
14 Kirov
15 Krasnogvardeyskiy

——— Canals

—— Major Roads

++++ Railways

Major green areas

•-•-• Boundary of built up area in mid 1960s

///// Areas of new housing construction

°°°°°°°° Planned crossings

0   1   2   3 miles

General Plan policy would have necessitated the construction of three
new underground railway (metro) lines—including extensions to two
lines already in existence—one new railway line, five new highways,
and several bridges (Nazarov 1979). The expense of thus augmenting
the transportation system is rendered especially expensive in view of
Leningrad's river delta location (Figure 8.2).

The new policy thus seeks to ease the journey-to-work problem by
moving places of work closer to home. Thus industrial estates are now
being planned for the Frunze district, including the suburb of Kupchino
whose construction began in 1964 (Mondonen 1979). The policy is
also being applied to the three new large suburban zones which are
currently arising in the western part of the city close to the coast. These
suburbs are mainly being built on reclaimed land or on land liable to
flooding, thus necessitating expensive engineering works, in accordance
with the new land-conserving policy. Their construction is in line with
one of the principal aims of the General Plan—that of securing
Leningrad's 'outlet to the sea', or its transformation into a coastal city.
The first of these suburbs, the north-western suburb located on the
Lakhtinskiy Plain, is planned to house 800,000 people over the next
20 years, 80 per cent of whom will work locally (Buldakov 1979b).
Part of this expansion is the Shuvalovo-Ozerki district, currently under
construction north of the city at densities of 5,200-5,500 square metres
of housing space per hectare. Various means are being devised to save
on open space without allowing a deterioration in environmental
standards. Eventually Shuvalovo-Ozerki will house 100,000 people,
and industry, educational and research institutes are being developed
in close proximity (Svirskiy 1979) By thus providing local employment,
the north-western suburb will now only require two major highways to
connect it with the city centre, in place of the much larger extra
provision detailed above. *required of 6 was in the city centre,*

The second major western development is the new suburb on the
western end of Vasil'yevskiy Island, whose construction began in the
late 1960s. Here again building densities have been raised, to 4,500 to
5,000 square metres of housing space per hectare. Several 22-storey
buildings are being built on the sea coast. The district will house about
100,000 people (Sokolov 1979).

The south-western suburb is the third major suburban development
which will grow out along the southern shore of the Gulf of Finland,
south-west of the port of Leningrad. This district will house 310,000
people by 1995 at a housing density of 5,500 to 6,000 square metres
per hectare as against the 3,750 square metres envisaged in the General

Plan. Once again industry and employment opportunities are to be developed in close proximity so as to ensure an average 10 to 15 minute journey to work. By the 1990s 94 per cent of the population should work locally (Dmitriyev 1979).

The provision of employment, including industrial employment, close to residential areas represents a major departure from the zonation principles enshrined in the General Plan and approved by Gosstroy. However, this new policy is in recognition of the social disadvantages of a lengthy journey to work, the inevitable product of the housing policy pursued since the late 1950s, and of the serious implications of this fact for Leningrad's already overburdened transportation system.

Urban Transport

Like other cities in the Soviet Union Leningrad is heavily dependent on the public sector for passenger transportation. The sector now carries over 3,000 million passengers per year. The system is a multi-modal one, with metro (subway), bus, trolleybus and tramway systems. Their changing relative importance is indicated in Table 8.4:

Table 8.4: Numbers of Passengers Carried by Leningrad City Transport, 1950-78 (millions)

Mode	1950	1960	1970	1976	1978
Tram	860	909	783	863	895
Trolleybus	112	238	332	453	492
Bus	182	565	810	1047	—
Metro	—	106	418	613	666

Sources: *Narkhoz Leningrada za 60*; *Vestnik statistiki* no. 11 (1979).

The popularity of the public transportation system in Soviet cities has been assured not merely by the scarcity of the private car but also by the uniform low-fare policy. Leningrad's General Plan envisaged the continued expansion of all forms of transportation as the major solution to the city's public transport needs. Thus the metro currently has 60 kilometres of route length (with 37 stations) compared with only 41 kilometres in 1970, and 24 kilometres in 1965. The length of trolleybus lines (calculated on a single track basis) grew from 213 kilometres in 1965 to 525 kilometres in 1976, while that for trams (measured on a

similar basis) grew from 484 kilometres to 608 kilometres over the same
period. By 1979 the total route length had reached 275 kilometres for
trams, 270 kilometres for trolleybuses and 700 kilometres for buses
(Zhukovskiy 1979). Considerable investment has also gone into rolling
stock, as Table 8.5 indicates, though only on the subway system has
this investment significantly reduced passenger pressures over the last
decade.

Table 8.5: Rolling Stock on Leningrad's Electrically-powered Passenger
Transport System, 1965-76

	1965	1970	1976
Tramcar units	1,706	1,702	1,877
Trolleybus units	503	730	1,006
Metro car units	218	460	800

Source: *Narkhoz Leningrada za 60.*

Current policy continues to favour the guidelines as laid down in the
General Plan. The provisions of that plan were further reinforced by
the Complex Plan for the Development of Transport in Leningrad to
1990, approved by the Council of Ministers of the RSFSR in 1975
(Zhukovskiy 1979). According to this plan, the metro system will have
130 kilometres of route length by 1990, eventually expanding to 240
kilometres, new diameters will be added and a new circular line constructed (Figure 8.3). The plan also provides for a programme of express
highway construction, a semi-circular railway line passing round the
eastern side of the city, a new passenger rail terminal to serve the eastern
suburbs (*Segodnya i zavtra* 1979) and a series of express radial tramways.
After a period in which the tram fell into disfavour, its future now seems
to be assured (Gumnitskiy 1979).

Despite the considerable progress that has been made in augmenting
Leningrad's passenger transportation network, it is generally agreed
among commentators that this progress has not been rapid enough.
Particular problems include difficulties with the rate of output of new
vehicles, with servicing, spares and maintenance, and a tendency for
the system as a whole to run into deficit. The lag in progress means that
in the newer suburbs there is now an average of 6 to 8 passengers per
square metre of passenger vehicle (Zhukovskiy 1979). A priority of
the Complex Plan is to increase the average speed attained on particular
transport modes from the present 26.5 kilometres per hour on the metro

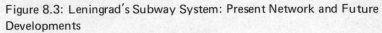

Figure 8.3: Leningrad's Subway System: Present Network and Future Developments

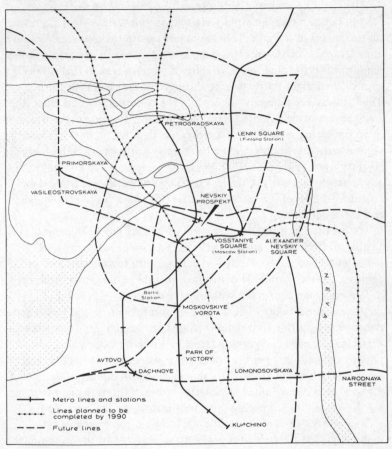

(inclusive of time taken to get to the trains, change trains, etc.), 17.5 kph by tram, 17 kph by trolleybus and 19.6 kph by bus. Under a future scheme of hierarchical provision it is envisaged that intra-district transport (tram, bus, trolleybus) would average 18 kph, inter-district transport (express tram, bus) 27 kph, all-city transport (metro) 40 kph and city region transport (railway, express bus) 60 kph. Of the 4,000 million passengers expected to use the system in 1990, it is envisaged that the metro will carry 27 per cent (34 per cent in the longer perspective), the bus 25 per cent, trams 22 per cent, trolleybuses 13 per cent, intra-urban railways 6 per cent and automobiles 7 per cent (17 per cent in the longer perspective).

The highway construction programme proposed by the Complex Plan is a response to the rapidly growing problem of vehicular pressure on the streets of the city. The number of cars in the city increases by an annual average of 10 per cent, there is a 6 to 7 per cent increase in the amount of traffic, and the geography of the city is such that 40 per cent of the freight traffic passing through the city is transit traffic. The highway programme will result in the completion of an inner ring road, part of which should be finished in 1982, the eventual construction of an outer ring road utilising a protective dam to the west of the city, various cross-city routes, and an increase in route length of highways in the city from 1,900 to 2,700 kilometres, including 200 kilometres of express highway. Many of the new highways will follow existing railway routes by means of tunnels or raised sections in order to save on land and avoid demolition.

At the present time there is a total of 25 cars per 1,000 people in Leningrad (Belinskiy and Sobol 1979). This modest figure, however, is expected to rise quite quickly—to perhaps 200 towards the end of the century. Although only 24 per cent of private passenger car journeys in Leningrad are connected with the journey to work, the rapid increase in the number of cars and their use for leisure and associated purposes are putting considerable strains on the city's infrastructure. Servicing, garaging and parking facilities are quite inadequate, and at present only about 4 per cent of cars are properly kept in multi-storey garages (Zhukovskiy 1979). The almost random building of individual garages often runs counter to planning considerations, while the growing use of cars for leisure is adding to pressures on the green belt.

The infancy of the automobile age in Leningrad may give the impression that the transport problems of the city are as yet minimal compared with those of many cities in the West. However, statistics about the frequency, reliability and low cost to the passenger of public transport in this and other Soviet cities often hide the discomfort of the passengers travelling on seriously overcrowded vehicles. The ambitious investment programme of the Complex Plan is designed to alleviate this discomfort.

Raising Living Standards

Leningrad's housing programme is but one facet of a much broader policy to raise the standards of living of its citizens. Under Stalin and afterwards the inhabitants of the city had to tolerate not only a minimal level of housing but also many shortages in foodstuffs and consumer goods, and all manner of inconveniences in services in general. It was Khrushchev who changed official priorities by emphasising the necessity of catching up with and overtaking the United States in living standards. In Leningrad the 1966 General Plan proposed to tackle the consumer and service problem by investing heavily in this sphere (Shaw 1978). In this city, as in many others, the consumer and service spheres suffered from two problems. One was that services in general were heavily oversubscribed. Another was that available services were mainly concentrated in the city centre. As the suburbs expanded, the problem of access to these services was exacerbated. The General Plan, therefore, envisaged the establishment of service and retail centres throughout the built-up area following a hierarchical principle, from the level of the neighbourhood unit (*mikrorayon*) at the lowest level up to major service and retail centres serving entire sectors of the city.

The suburbanisation of services was an inevitable concomitant of the housing programme. Since the General Plan was compiled, however, planners in Leningrad and in other cities have become critical of an inflexible application of the hierarchical principle utilising norms of population and distance laid down by Gosstroy. In particular, it is felt that an inflexible approach does scant justice to the reality of social life and mobility in the city. The provision of a basic level of shops and services in the centre of a neighbourhood unit, for example, is found to cause considerable inconvenience to workers who are more likely to require shops and services close to bus or metro stops or near to places of work. A more flexible approach to service provision has therefore now been adopted. In the General Plan, for example, major suburban centres were to stand in the centre of large planning regions containing 250,000 to 300,000 people. A rather more dispersed pattern has now been accepted incorporating nodes of service of city-wide significance at strategic points (Rassokhina 1979). The new perspective, together with the policy of saving on land, have also led to a re-evaluation of the functional importance of the city centre (Kaganov 1979). As well as providing a symbolic and functional focus for the city, the centre still contains 40 per cent of Leningrad's housing stock (Kraynyaya 1976). The movement of people out to the suburbs is allowing careful renovation of housing in the centre, involving the revamping of apartments, reconstruction of the highway network in residential districts, and the incorporation of services and shops into the ground floors of apartment blocks (Vlanina 1972; Makhrovskaya 1976). In 1970 the principle was adopted of modernising the central housing stock on a grouped or neighbourhood basis, incorporating the advantages of economy and overall aesthetic considerations (Sharlygina 1976). The residential and service role of the city centre will thus be assured and protected/

Unlike many other cities Leningrad has managed to centralise the administration of retail trade and most of the provisions and consumer goods are now sold through the city's own trade network. However, industrial ministries and other organisations do retain a handful of retail outlets (Tsirtsin 1978). This centralisation has made it easier to expand the retail trade system and also to take full advantage of economies of scale and of modernised sales methods. An indication of the expansion of the system is given in Table 8.6.

Table 8.6: Development of Retail Trade in Leningrad, 1940-76

	1940	1965	1970	1976
No. of shops	3,622	3,644	3,560	3,487
Trading area of shops (thousands of sq. metres)	–	494	560	633
Trading area per shop (sq. metres)	–	136	159	182
No. of catering establishments	3,048	3,654	4,069	4,432
No. of seats in catering establishments (thousands)	173	243	315	385
Average of seats per establishment	57	73	83	91
Provision per 10,000 people:				
Shops	21	14	15	15
Trading area in shops (sq. metres)	–	1,337	1,386	1,431
Catering establishments	9.0	9.6	10.1	10
Seats in catering establishments	514	642	780	870

Source: *Narkhoz Leningrada za 60.*

/ In real terms the purchase by Leningraders of foodstuffs between 1940 and 1976 increased by 84 per cent and of consumer goods by 312 per cent (a total increase of purchases of 162 per cent). There has thus been a real increase in living standards. There are still, however, real problems in the range and standard of goods on offer and in the abilities of retail outlets to cope with the pressure of demand./

Leningrad has also experienced real improvements in other areas of welfare. Some indicators of this progress are given in Table 8.7. However, the progress in fulfilling some of the targets laid down in the General Plan has been slower than originally anticipated.

Table 8.7: Selected Indicators of Consumption, 1940-78

	1940	1965	1970	1976/8[a]	USSR average 1976/8[a]
Average income (roubles)	—	107.3	132.4	157.1	—
Purchase of foodstuffs as % of all purchases	67.9	60.4	55.1	54.7	—
Hospital beds per 10,000 people	101	117	119	118[a]	122[a]
Doctors per 10,000 people	33	68	71	77[a]	35[a]
Annual number of cinema visits per person	—	21	21	16	—
Theatre seats per 1,000	—	—	—	3.3[a]	2.2[ab]

Notes: a. 1978 figures
b. Urban population only.
Sources: *Narkhoz Leningrada za 60*; *Vestnik statistiki* No. 11 (1979).

Details of the geography of services within the city of Leningrad are not easy to obtain, but clearly there are problems. Thus whereas the consumption of services in the city exceeds the RSFSR average by 33 per cent, the distribution of services within the city is very uneven (Shargey 1979). In terms of personnel employed in services, 15 out of the 21 districts of the city come below the norms set by Gosstroy. Leningrad as a whole achieves 60 per cent of the norm. City centre districts, however, frequently exceed the norm—for example Lenin (131 per cent), Kuybyshev (125 per cent), Smol'nyy (111 per cent)—while more peripheral districts fall well behind—for example Zhdanov (29 per cent), Kolpino (31 per cent). In Kuybyshev district shoe repairers greatly exceed the norm (201 per cent) but Krasnoye Selo on the periphery only achieves 26 per cent of the norm. The same uneven situation is characteristic of public baths, repair services and many other facilities. Shargey (1979) says that part of the responsibility for this situation lies with the enterprises, organisations and ministries which control many services but fail to augment them in the way expected by the planners. In the 1971-5 Five Year Plan GlavAPU planned the establishment of ten servicing points in ten of the city's districts. In the event, only one appeared.

While real progress has thus been made in raising the living standards of Leningrad's citizens, a significant gap still remains between some of the aspirations of the General Plan and the official norms and achievements to date.

Planning the Environment

Ever since the 1920s, when Soviet planners and theoreticians debated the relative merits of different settlement forms, a significant majority have expressed concern for conserving and planning the urban environment. Thinkers in the 1920s were united in their distaste for the large industrial cities produced by capitalism. There was a widespread desire to avoid the squalor and disease associated with many of the larger cities of the day and to achieve a harmonious relationship between the built environment on the one hand and nature on the other. Some of these principles subsequently entered into Soviet planning practice.

For the newer suburbs of Leningrad the General Plan envisaged not only that these would provide for much more spacious and convenient accommodation than most people had known hitherto, but also that great attention would be paid to aesthetic considerations, to architecture and to the planning of the landscape. In actuality, however, some of these objectives have been neglected in the rush to provide housing. Mention has already been made of the dissatisfaction of some at the architectural standards of many suburban districts, and of the problem of monotony. There is also evidence that the provision of open space is not getting the priority it deserves according to the General Plan. B.P. Usanov (1979), for example, notes the necessity of increasing the amount of open space per person to 27 square metres, four times the present level. The policy on saving land, now leading to denser residential development in many suburbs, is having detrimental consequences for open space provision in some districts. Indeed according to A.N. Alymov (1978) the whole exercise of landscape architecture is a neglected procedure in Leningrad by comparison with other cities. According to this writer, only 70 hectares of the 450 hectares of newly built-up area which appear each year in the city are fully landscaped, and the city spends only a third or less of Moscow's outlay and less than one-fifth of that of Vilnyus in Lithuania on landscape architecture. He pleads that industrialised methods, first pioneered in Leningrad and now adopted with greater zeal elsewhere, be applied to this problem. Leningrad does, on the other hand, have a good record when it comes to the care and maintenance of its historic parks with a special administration responsible for this task. It is a record not always emulated in other Soviet cities (*CDSP, 29*, No. 19).

The central area of Leningrad is of major architectural and historical significance, a product of the city's former role as the nation's capital. The General Plan made provision for the careful conservation of the city's core, and for the strict observance of conservationist principles where reconstruction was undertaken. Though much has been achieved in the field of conservation and reconstruction, especially in the restoration of war-damaged buildings, the expense is such that by no means the whole of the inner areas can receive the necessary attention. In 1969 the city soviet proclaimed the establishment of conservation zones for the city, including a zone of strict conservation and one of regulated construction. Together with outlying zones around individual architectural features, these zones now embrace a total of 5,000 hectares (Buldakov 1979).

Although conservation practice has made considerable progress in recent years, Leningrad's architects have expressed some disquiet at the achievements in the city centre. At a round table discussion of architects in 1979, reported in the city's official architectural journal, concern was expressed at the lack of a single co-ordinating authority responsible for conservation and restoration matters in the city (Priobreteniya 1979). According to this discussion, the administration of Architecture-Planning (GlavAPU) is mainly concerned with the outer suburbs. The task of reconstruction in the city centre is left largely to Lenzhilproyekt (a subdivision of the Housing Administration concerned with design but apparently not fully equipped for the task of restoration) and to an array of other organisations of both local and national significance. The architects were also worried that the adoption of a broader-scale perspective on conservation and reconstruction, which has advantages in terms of economy and the goal of overall architectural harmony, might lead to the acceptance of a standardised approach.

One of the central principles of the General Plan was that the city should be planned together with its surrounding region. The plan thus encircled the city with a series of green zones (Shaw 1978), a principle which goes back to 1932 when the first green belt was set up, embracing 94,800 hectares (Karpov *et al.* 1979). In addition to aesthetic and general environmental purposes, a major function of the entire suburban zone is that of recreation. With rising living standards and shorter working hours the pressure of visitors upon the green belt has grown considerably in recent years. This fact is now a source of concern for the planners. According to Khromov (1979a), for example, despite the considerable amount of research undertaken by the Leningrad Research and Design Institute of City Planning (LenNIIP *gradostroitel'stva*) and other institutes, the General Plan's provisions for the green belt have still to be translated into agreed practical policy. In the face of a lack of unified policy, pressures on the green belt threaten to undermine the goals of the General Plan. For example there is a severe shortage of public accommodation and 70 per cent of that which is available is designed for children only (230,000 beds). The pressure of demand for overnight accommodation leads to random camping, to the development of recreational facilities by ministries, enterprises and other organisations, sometimes contrary to the General Plan, and to the spontaneous development or renting of dachas (second homes, chalets). Whereas in 1960, 350,000 people rented or used dachas in the Leningrad region, by the mid-1970s that figure had reached one million with a further half a million people using cabins on collective garden plots (Khromov 1979b). Pressures on the green belt are liable to grow through the increased use of the motor car, and have reached critical levels in some popular places such as the historic Tsarist estates (Khromov 1979a).

The General Plan paid considerable attention to the green belt and contained provisions for major investment in the recreational infrastructure (Shaw 1978, 1979). Leningrad's planners have since spent much time and effort in devising further plans on the basis of the General Plan. That their efforts have not met with greater success is testimony to the comparatively low priority yet given to this question.

New Frontiers in Planning

The 1966 General Plan for Leningrad was adopted towards the end of two decades of post-war experimentation with long-range physical planning in Soviet cities. By the early 1960s, the revival of interest in urban planning questions associated with Khrushchev had led to a reorganisation and systematisation of urban planning agencies at both national and local level. A decade later most Soviet cities had long-range plans. But by the early 1970s some of the essential weaknesses of the then Soviet approach to physical planning had become apparent. It had long been the Soviet contention that control by the state of all the means of production, including the land, and the centralised allocation of resources would permit the planned and harmonious development of society along desired lines. It was also believed that this would enable society to avoid the errors and contradictions characteristic of capitalism. In the case of Soviet cities, however, many of these goals seemed difficult to realise in practice. By the early 1970s the root of the problem appeared to be the difficulty of reconciling physical and economic planning. For one thing the time-scale over which the two types of planning operate is different. Physical planning, as already noted, operates with a perspective of up to 25 years or more. Economic planning, on the other hand, operates over five year periods only and even the five year plans are rarely fulfilled in practice. Soviet planners have of course always been aware of this difference in perspective and have assumed that the general plans of cities would be reworked and modified to take care of discrepancies. By the late 1960s and early 1970s, however, it was becoming clear that in many cases the discrepancies were so serious that the effectiveness of general plans was being called into question (Mezhevich 1977).

Perhaps more serious and fundamental than the perspective difference between the two types of planning are the organisational and functional differences. Physical planning, as already noted, is the responsibility of the State Construction Committee (Gosstroy) and its many agencies. Gosstroy is typically responsible, among other things, for the drawing up of physical plans for cities and city regions, for the co-ordination of such plans with those for the neighbouring regions, and for intra-urban plans. Economic planning, on the other hand, is the responsibility of the State Planning Committee (Gosplan). In Leningrad the task of co-ordinating the economic plan for the city is performed by the city's planning commission, a sub-branch of Gosplan. Part of this economic plan is the two-year construction plan, approved by the city soviet and the instrument whereby the General Plan and other physical plans are realised. In practice, however, it is not always easy to reconcile the construction plan with the long-range physical plans, and in any case the city authorities find difficulty in getting access to the plans and intentions of many enterprises on their territories, especially those administered by powerful industrial ministries. There are numerous problems of communication and conflicts in aims. Mezhevich (1977) thus comes to the conclusion that, in spite of all the planning that goes on in the Soviet city, the city in effect develops in an unplanned and unco-ordinated manner.

Some of the problems of the physical planning process in the Soviet

city have recently been examined by Uspenskiy and Berezin (1979).
These writers maintain that physical planning has traditionally been
undertaken in the absence of the long-term social and economic
prognoses which are essential to its success. Such prognoses, they argue,
are beyond the capabilities of the architecture-planning bodies who
have in effect been called upon to tackle problems beyond their skills.
Because of this, the general plans remain inadequate documents in many
important respects and their inadequacy is reinforced by their uncertain
legal status. In the absence of the necessary long-term social and
economic prognoses, continue these writers, architect-planners have
been forced to rely on fairly inflexible norms approved nationally by
Gosstroy which are insufficiently adjusted to local conditions and often
too economical to form the basis of long-term planning. The call, then,
is for more information and research and for a more flexible and
realistic approach to planning.

In the late 1960s Leningrad was one of the first Soviet cities to
pioneer a more comprehensive approach to urban planning. At first
this took the form of an attempt to combine the economic plans for
individual enterprises with their social needs in such matters as labour
resources, housing, services, health and educational facilities, and the
cultural and political life of their workers. By the time of the ninth
five-year plan, beginning in 1971, this comprehensive approach was
being applied to districts both of Leningrad itself and of the Leningrad
region. Then, in 1975, the five-year Complex Plan for the Economic
and Social Development of Leningrad and its Region was formally
accepted (Uspenskiy and Berezin 1979). This complex plan is intended
to integrate the planning of the city's economic base with its demographic structure, the living standards, education, culture and
socio-political life of the populace, and the development of the city's
administrative system. This comprehensive approach involves the
broader use of complex mathematical models.

Complex planning also involves research into long-term economic
and social forecasting and modelling. In Leningrad such work is being
pioneered by bodies such as the Institute for Socio-Economic Problems
of the Soviet Academy of Sciences, and by institutes of Gosplan. At
present work on the city's complex plans for the 1980s is far advanced.
Preparatory work on long-term prognoses up to the year 2000 is also
underway and should provide the basis for the next General Plan. In
the meantime the present General Plan is being further developed, in
the light of this comprehensive approach, in three directions (Usanov
1979)—firstly, through large-scale development plans for individual

districts; secondly, through new branch plans dealing with particular
aspects of the city's life (for example, the engineering infrastructure,
the transport system); and thirdly, through the drawing up of new two-
year, five-year and fifteen-year construction plans.

Conclusion

The modern development of Leningrad, as one of the major cities of
the USSR, reflects the development of the Soviet Union as a whole. That
development has clearly produced numerous problems for the city and
the major lesson which the Soviets have learned in the past two decades
is that the central planning system needs modification to cope with
such problems. In the late 1950s and the 1960s that modification took
the form of the development of a co-ordinated physical planning system
which would set national standards and provide a unified approach. In
the 1970s and 1980s there has been a move towards a more comprehensive local planning system, one that would embrace both economic
and physical planning, and short-term and long-term perspectives. It is
as yet too early to say whether such modifications will provide satisfactory
solutions to the complex problems of urban development, though it is
to the credit of Soviet planners that they are prepared to learn from past
errors. What can be said is that the current attempt by Soviet planners to
view and plan the city as a complex whole over many different time scales
is a pioneering venture in the planning field and one which, if successful,
could provide important lessons for foreign planners. At the present
time Leningrad is a centre for these pioneering developments.

Notes

1. Useful space measures the entire area of apartments, including utility rooms,
corridors, etc.
2. Living space, sometimes described as housing space, does not include
kitchens, bathrooms, utility rooms, corridors etc.

I should like to thank Mrs Jean Dowling, of the Department of Geography,
University of Birmingham, who drew the maps.

References

Alymov, A.N. (1978) 'Arkhitekture zemli – industrial'nuyu bazu', *Stroitel'stvo i arkhitektura Leningrada*, No. 12, 18-21
Bater, James H. (1976) *St. Petersburg: Industrialization and Change*, Edward Arnold, London
Belinskiy, A.Yu. (1975) 'Poyezdki na rabotu – kak sokratit' ikh prodolzhitel "nost"?' *Stroitel'stvo i arkhitektura Leningrada*, No. 6, 24-6
——and I.A. Sobol (1979) 'Avtolyubitel' na lone prirody', *Stroitel'stvo i arkhitektura Leningrada*, No. 8, 27-9
Bochkov, V.I., G.F. Levina, and S.S. Savkin (1979) 'Na osnove yedinogo kataloga', *Stroitel'stvo i arkhitektura Leningrada*, No. 7, 8-10
Buldakov, G.N. (1974) 'Arkhitekturnyye ansambli novogo Leningrada', *Stroitel'stvo i arkhitektura Leningrada*, No. 9, 2-5
—— (1979a) 'Sokhranim nepovtorimyye cherty', *Stroitel'stvo i arkhitektura Leningrada*, No. 5, 3-4
—— (1979b) 'Vykhodit gorod k moryu', *Stroitel'stvo i arkhitektura Leningrada*, No. 1, 3-7
Cattell, David T. (1968) *Leningrad: A Case Study of Soviet Urban Development*, Praeger, New York
Chikovskiy, N.I. and B.S. Movchan (1978) 'Sovremennyy etap zhilishchnoy programmy', *Stroitel'stvo i arkhitektura Leningrada*, No. 3, 12-13
Current Digest of the Soviet Press (*CDSP*), (1949-) Vol. 1 and continuing, Joint Committee on Slavic Studies, Washington
DiMaio, A.J. (1974) *Soviet Urban Housing: Problems and Policies*, Praeger, New York
Dmitriyev, L.B. (1979) 'Yugo-zapad. Zhilyye kvartaly sredi sadov i parkov', *Stroitel'stvo i arkhitektura Leningrada*, No. 1, 12-15
Filonov, M.D. (1974) 'Ustremlennost' v budushcheye', *Stroitel'stvo i arkhitektura Leningrada*, No. 6, 2-4
Gumnitskiy, L.B. (1979) 'Iz biografii tramvaya', *Stroitel'stvo i arkhitektura Leningrada*, No. 8, 33
Ivanov, N.V. (1979) 'Chtoby v kvartirakh stalo uyutno', *Stroitel'stvo i arkhitektura Leningrada*, No. 6, 30-1
Kaganov, G.Z. (1979) 'Chem privlekayet tsentr', *Stroitel'stvo i arkhitektura Leningrada*, No. 6, 6-7
Kalinkina, Ts.S. (1979) 'Pochemu stroyka na "troyku"?' *Stroitel'stvo i arkhitektura Leningrada*, No. 6, 20-2
Karaletyan, S. and E. Sarkisyan (1979) 'Proyektirovaniye i zastroyka zhilykh mikrorayonov s uchetom demograficheskikh izmeneniy v vremeni', *Arkhitektura SSSR*, No. 1, 34-5
Karpov, L.N., M.M. Ignatenko, and G.M. Gavrilov (1979) 'Zabota o zelenom druge', *Stroitel'stvo i arkhitektura Leningrada*, No. 2, 26-8
Kazanskiy, Yu. N. (1979) 'Stroitel'nyye ob'yedineniya: opyt, problemy, perspektivy', *Stroitel'stvo i arkhitektura Leningrada*, No. 2, 9-11
Khromov, Yu. B. (1979a) 'Dlya tekh, kto otdykhayet', *Stroitel'stvo i arkhitektura Leningrada*, No. 10, 28-31
—— (1979b) 'Formirovaniye sistem zagorodnogo otdykha v Leningradskoy oblasti', *Arkhitektura SSSR*, No. 4, 45-8
Kochetkov, A. (1975) 'Sotsial'no-ekonomicheskiye aspekty gradostroitel'stva', *Voprosy ekonomiki*, No. 19, 23-34
Kraynyaya, N.P. (1976) 'Obnovleniye i sokhraneniye zdaniy i zhilykh rayonov v slozhivshikhsya gorodakh', Unpublished paper, Leningrad

Krivov, A.S. (1978) 'Arkhitektura i tekhnologiya', *Stroitel'stvo i arkhitektura Leningrada*, No. 12, 29-32

Lappo, G.M. (1978) *Razvitiye gorodskikh aglomeratsiy v SSSR*, Moscow

Lavrov, L.P. (1979) 'Mnogoetazhnaya zastroyka: uroki i perspektivy', *Stroitel'stvo i arkhitektura Leningrada*, No. 2, 21-23

Litovka, O.P. (1976) *Problemy prostranstvennogo razvitiya urbanizatsii*, Nauka, Leningrad

Makhrovskaya, A.V. (1976) 'Rekonstruktsiya istoricheski slozhivshikhsya zhilykh rayonov tsentral'noy chasti Leningrada', Unpublished paper, Leningrad

—— and S.P. Semonov (1974) 'Kontury bol'shogo Leningrada', *Stroitel'stvo i arkhitektura Leningrada*, No. 6, 12-14

Matusevich, N., A. Tovbin and A. Ermant (1979) 'Gradostroitel'nyye tseli i metodicheskiye sredstva', *Stroitel'stvo i arkhitektura Leningrada*, No. 1, 18-22

Merzhanov, B.M. (1978) 'Slagayemyye zhiloy sredy', *Stroitel'stvo i arkhitektura Leningrada*, No. 1, 40-4

Mezhevich, M.N. (1977) 'Upravleniye razvitiyem gorodov: potrebnosti i real'nosti', *Chelovek i obshchestvo, 16*, 50-61

Mondonen, A.I. (1979) 'V rayone gde vse – novosely', *Stroitel'stvo i arkhitektura Leningrada*, No. 6, 6-9

Narodnye khozyaystvo Leningrada i Leningradskoy oblasti za 60 let, (1977) Lenizdat, Leningrad

Nazarov, V.F. (1979) 'Severo-zapad: v interesakh cheloveka, v soglasii s prirodoy', *Stroitel'stvo i arkhitektura Leningrada*, No. 1, 8-11

Panov, L.K. (1975) 'Bol'shoy Leningrad: Puti yego razvitiya', *Stroitel'stvo i arkhitektura Leningrada*, No. 6, 22-3

Pivovarov, L. Yu. (1972) 'Sovremennaya urbanizatsiya: sushchnost', faktory i osobennosti izucheniya', in L. Yu. Pivovarov (ed.) *Problemy sovremennoy urbanizatsii*, Statistika, Moscow, pp. 9-32

Priobreteniya i poteri, (1979) *Stroitel'stvo i arkhitektura Leningrada*, No. 5, 15-21

Rassokhina, G.N. (1979) 'Organizatsiya tsentrov planirovochnykh rayonov', *Stroitel'stvo i arkhitektura Leningrada*, No. 6, 23-5

Remizov, A.B. (1978) 'S vysokoy vzyskatel'most'ya', *Stroitel'stvo i arkhitektura Leningrada*, No. 4, 33-6

Romanov, K.V. (1979) 'Ispytaniye vremenem', *Stroitel'stvo i arkhitektura Leningrada*, No. 7, 15-16

Ruzhzhe, V.L. (1979) 'I vroz' i vmeste', *Stroitel'stvo i arkhitektura Leningrada*, No. 2, 13-15

Segodnya i zavtra vokzalov Leningrada, (1979) *Stroitel'stvo i arkhitektura Leningrada*, No. 8, 22-5

Shargey, D.M. (1979) 'Geografiya uslug', *Stroitel'stvo i arkhitektura Leningrada*, No. 2, 18-19

Sharlygina, K.A. (1976) 'Modernizatsiya starogo zhilogo fonda', Unpublished paper, Leningrad

Shaw, Denis J.B. (1978) 'Planning Leningrad', *Geographical Review, 68(2)*, 183-200

—— (1979) 'Recreation and the Soviet City', in R.A. French and F.E. Ian Hamilton (eds.) *The Socialist City*, Wiley, Chichester, pp. 119-43

Sokolov, V.N. (1979) 'Vasil'yevskiy ostrov. Tsentral'noye zveno primorskoy panoramy', *Stroitel'stvo i arkhitektura Leningrada*, No. 1, 16-19

Svirskiy, A.Ya. (1979) 'U severnykh granits goroda', *Stroitel'stvo i arkhitektura Leningrada*, No. 2, 14-18

Tret'yemu godu pyatiletki – udarnyy start, (1978) *Stroitel'stvo i arkhitektura*

Leningrada, No. 2, 2-6

Tsirtsin, P.G. (1978) *Organizatsiya upravleniya ekonomikoy gorodskogo rayona*, Ekonomika, Moscow

Usanov, B.P. (1979) 'Prochnyy fundament genplana Leningrada', *Stroitel'stvo i arkhitektura Leningrada*, No. 2, 6-10

Uspenskiy, S.V. and M.P. Berezin (1979) 'Razvitiye goroda: proyekt i plan', *Stroitel'stvo i arkhitektura Leningrada*, No. 2, 11-12

Vlanina, M.M. (1972) 'Osobennosti organizatsii sistemy obsluzhivaniya starykh zhilykh rayonov Leningrada', in *Planirovka i zastroyka zhilykh rayonov i mikrorayonov*, Budivel'nik, Kiev

Zhukovskiy, A.P. (1979) 'V osnove – kompleksnaya akhema', *Stroitel'stvo i arkhitektura Leningrada*, No. 8, 8-11

NOTES ON CONTRIBUTORS

Professor G.W. Carey, Department of Urban Studies, Rutgers University, USA.

Professor T.J.D. Fair, Institute for Social and Economic Research, University of Durban-Westville, South Africa.

Dr E.K. Grime, Department of Geography, University of Salford, England.

Professor R.J. Johnston, Department of Geography, University of Sheffield, England.

Professor J.G. Muller, Department of Town and Regional Planning, Witwatersrand University, Johannesburg, South Africa.

Dr J. Naylon, Department of Geography, University of Keele, England.

Dr P.W. Newton, CSIRO, Melbourne, Australia.

Dr M. Pacione, Department of Geography, University of Strathclyde, Glasgow, Scotland.

Dr D.J.B. Shaw, Department of Geography, University of Birmingham, England.

Dr G. Węcławowicz, Institute of Geography, Polish Academy of Sciences, Warsaw.

Dr M.E. Witherick, Department of Geography, University of Southampton, England.

INDEX